D0141767

ANCIENT CONCEPTS OF PHILOSOPHY

ISSUES IN ANCIENT PHILOSOPHY
General Editor; Malcolm Schofield

GOD AND GREEK PHILOSOPHY
L. P. Gerson

ANCIENT CONCEPTS OF PHILOSOPHY
R. W. Jordan

forthcoming
LANGUAGE, THOUGHT, AND FALSEHOOD IN ANCIENT GREEK PHILOSOPHY
N. Denyer

ANCIENT CONCEPTS OF PHILOSOPHY

William Jordan

London and New York

First published 1990
by Routledge
11 New Fetter Lane, London EC4P 4EE

Simultaneously published in the USA and Canada
by Routledge
a division of Routledge, Chapman and Hall, Inc.
29 West 35th Street, New York, NY 10001

Phototypeset in Linotron Garamond by
Input Typesetting Ltd, London
Printed and bound in Great Britain by
Mackays of Chatham PLC, Chatham, Kent

British Library Cataloguing in Publication Data
Jordan, William
Ancient concepts of philosophy. –(Issues in Ancient Philosophy)
1. Classical philosophy
Title
180.938

ISBN 0–415–04834–6

Library of Congress Cataloging in Publication Data
Jordan, Robert William
Ancient concepts of philosophy / William Jordan.
p. cm.—(Issues in ancient philosophy)
Includes bibliographical references.
ISBN 0–415–04834–6
1. Phliosophy, Ancient. 2. Methodology—History. I. Title.
II. Series.
B178.J67 1990
180—dc20
90–31959
CIP

CONTENTS

PREFACE

I hope that this book will prove accessible to anyone interested in this subject, from the general reader to the professional philosopher. But I have particularly borne in mind the needs of a second- or third- year undergraduate student taking a degree in philosophy or in classics. This preface provides some basic historical and geographical information.

Greek philosophy is generally reckoned to have begun in Miletus, a Greek colony in Asia Minor, in the sixth century BC with three figures, Thales, Anaximander and Anaximenes, about whom we know little. Thales is said to have been the oldest of the three and to have predicted an eclipse of the sun – this is reckoned to have been the eclipse that occurred in 585 BC. Heraclitus, the next major philosopher, hailed from Ephesus; his philosophical activity is dated to around 480 BC (by KRS, 1983: 182). The Eleatic school, which included Parmenides and Zeno, lived in Elea in southern Italy. Parmenides is thought to have been a contemporary of Heraclitus. Plato tells us that Zeno was Parmenides' pupil and lover. Anaxagoras formed part of the circle around Pericles in Athens but was prosecuted for impiety and left Athens before his death. KRS place his philosophical impact before 450 BC; he may have left Athens in 433. Leucippus and Democritus, the Atomists, lived in Abdera in the late fifth century BC.

At about the same time, Socrates was asking questions about the virtues in Athens, where he was prosecuted for impiety and executed in 399 BC. Plato, who lived from 427–347 BC (in the view of Guthrie, 1975: 10), mostly in Athens, was one of Socrates' pupils. He set up the first philosophical school, the Academy, perhaps soon after 387 BC (Guthrie, 1975: 18). He also, famously, paid one or more visits to Syracuse, in an unsuccessful attempt to persuade the tyrant there, Dionysius II, to become a philosopher-tyrant. Aristotle, a pupil of Plato's, lived some of his life in Athens, where he founded his own philosophical school, the Lyceum. He also spent some time in Macedonia, tutoring the youthful Alexander the Great.

In Hellenistic times, Athens remained the world centre for philosophy, though not many of the important philosophers were native Athenians. The Epicureans set up shop in a co-operative community in a so-called 'Garden'. Zeno of Citium set up the Stoic school; one of the following famous heads of the school was Chrysippus; later Stoics included the Roman Emperor, Marcus Aurelius. Sceptics came in two varieties, Academics and Pyrrhonists. Academics peopled Plato's Academy, and held that one could not reach the truth in philosophy; they are mostly notable for their champion Carneades, who combated Stoicism very effectively in the second century BC. Pyrrhonists – on whom I concentrate in Chapter 5 – were followers of Pyrrho, a figure about whom not much is known. They held that they were simply enquiring into each question without being able to reach any judgements. The main source for their views is Sextus Empiricus, a doctor who wrote in the second century AD.

ACKNOWLEDGEMENTS

My greatest debt is to Malcolm Schofield, the editor of this series, who originally suggested that I write this book, and who has offered firm support at all stages of its gestation. With great generosity, Malcolm has read and commented on two complete drafts of the book. I have found his many creative suggestions concerning the content of Chapter 3, and his forthright criticisms of early drafts of Chapters 1 and 4, of particular value. I have also been greatly helped by discussion with Melanie Johnson, which has enabled me to clarify my thinking and my writing throughout, but most notably in the introduction, the conclusion, and in my account of the Milesians. I would like to thank Galen Strawson for many subtle and perceptive comments on Chapters 1–3, and Margaret Atkins for helpful comments on the style of the first three sections of the book.

LIST OF ABBREVIATIONS

DK	Diels and Kranz
KRS	Kirk, Raven and Schofield
NE	*Nichomachean Ethics*
EE	*Eudemian Ethics*
MM	*Magna Moralia*
Fin	*de Finibus*
PH	*Outlines of Pyrrhonism*

REFERENCES TO ANCIENT TEXTS

The fragments of the Presocratic philosophers are cited from Diels and Kranz (1960). Diels and Kranz divide the fragments into an A-series, which they think are not direct quotations from the Presocratics, and a B-series, which are. I quote almost exclusively B fragments. Quotations from Heraclitus follow Kahn's numeration and translation (Kahn 1981). Translation into English and commentary on most significant fragments is provided Kirk, Raven and Schofield (1983).

The texts of Plato are referred to by the page numbers of the edition of Stephanus. The texts of Aristotle are referred to by the page numbers of the edition of Bekker.

For the Hellenistic period, I have cited fragments from *The Hellenistic Philosophers*, translation of the principal sources with philosopical commentary by Long and Sedley (1987).

INTRODUCTION: PHILOSOPHY ANCIENT AND MODERN

This book constitutes an examination of the many different answers offered by ancient philosophers to the questions 'what is philosophy?' and 'why should we study philosophy?'. The different notions of the nature and purpose of philosophy advanced in ancient Greece are all of great intrinsic interest; we may hope, by studying them, to clarify our own conception of such notions. But philosophy as it was practised in ancient Greece differs in a significant number of respects from philosophy as it is studied in universities today; and ancient views about the nature and purpose of philosophy differ accordingly from modern ones. In this introduction, I propose to examine a number of contrasts that we might want to draw between ancient and modern philosophy, and to look briefly at the nature of contemporary analytic philosophy.

Three main differences between ancient Greek philosophy and contemporary analytic philosophy stand out. First, philosophy as practised in ancient Greece is conceived as a discipline with practical implications for the conduct of life, whereas few philosophers today hope to affect the lives of their students. Second, philosophy in ancient Greece would seem to constitute a far wider field of study than does contemporary analytic philosophy. Third, there is a difference in the practical organisation of philosophy. Philosophers in ancient Greece organised themselves into rival, and competing schools, each one claiming a monopoly on the truth; philosophers today, by contrast, are mostly employed by universities, and tend to regard the study of philosophy as a co-operative endeavour. Let us now examine these three differences between ancient and modern philosophy more closely.

An extreme contrast can be drawn between the views of Socrates and Wittgenstein concerning the relevance of the study of philosophy to the conduct of everyday life. Socrates thought that the study of philosophy was nothing less than the study of how to live, and that the unexamined life was not worth living. Wittgenstein thinks we are better off if we never feel the need to philosophise; that the aim in philosophy is 'to show the fly the way out of the fly-bottle' (Wittgenstein, 1953: §309) and that 'philosophy leaves everything as it is' (Wittgenstein, 1953: §124).[1] We might well feel that Wittgenstein is by no means a typical modern philosopher, and that Socrates is not a typical ancient philosopher. But ancient philosophers generally agree that the practice of philosophy can alter our lives, for good or ill, whereas philosophy today is often thought to lack practical import.

Is this because ancient philosophers asked different (i.e. more practically oriented) questions than their modern counterparts? Is it that they returned different (i.e. more practically oriented) answers to essentially the same questions? Or is it that, as first epistemology, and later the philosophy of language, have come to seem central to philosophy, so philosophy has come to lose its link with life as it is lived?

Perhaps there is some truth in all these ideas. Certainly it is important what sort of questions we ask in philosophy; and certainly it matters what questions we take to be central. If, in the realm of ethics, for example, we ask, 'should we eat animals?', we can expect to arrive at an answer that bears on the conduct of life. If we ask about the meaning of the term 'good', perhaps our results will be less relevant to our everyday lives. And if we concentrate our attention on questions in epistemology and the philosophy of language, then it can seem that the results of our philosophical enquiries will not have a very direct bearing on our everyday lives. It just does not seem to matter to us, so far as our everyday lives are concerned, whether we can refute scepticism about the external world, for example, or whether colour terms form part of the fabric of the world, or how proper names refer.

But it is easy to overstate the contrast between ancient and modern philosophy in these respects. After all, not all ancient philosophers asked, with Socrates, how we should live. Zeno, for example, argued that motion is impossible – and while his arguments may stimulate reflection about our concepts of space and time, they are unlikely to lead to change in our everyday lives.

And the first philosophical question asked by the Milesians, 'what is there?', is not itself a practical question (although some answers to the question may have practical implications). Furthermore, we should remind ourselves that questions in epistemology, for example, are not necessarily irrelevant to everyday life. Plato's epistemology leads directly to his theory of Forms and to his conception of an ideal state governed by political experts.

In fact, I believe it will become clear that the nature of philosophical questions has not changed much down the ages; ancient philosophers sought, and today we still seek, knowledge and understanding of the nature of reality, of ourselves, of our place in the world and of the right way to live. And we will find that there was, in ancient Greece, a great divergence of opinion as to what questions we should ask first in philosophy – as indeed there is today.[2] Perhaps, then, the main difference between ourselves and the ancients lies not in the questions that we ask or the order in which we ask them, but in the answers that we return (or fail to return) to philosophical questions.

Burnyeat (1984) has advanced the interesting thesis that, in the case of philosophical scepticism, the results of philosophical enquiry are nowadays taken to be 'insulated' from our everyday lives in a manner that was unthinkable (or at least not thought of) in antiquity. In Burnyeat's view, it was not the central importance that Descartes accorded to sceptical doubt, nor yet was it Descartes' new arguments in favour of sceptical doubt, that led philosophical scepticism to become 'insulated' from our everyday lives and beliefs. Rather the 'insulation' of philosophical scepticism from everyday life arose from a particular sort of answer to Descartes' doubt (an answer hinted at by earlier philosophers but most clearly formulated by Kant).

Burnyeat's view is controversial; and it is unclear, in this case, whether the 'insulation' in question is as yet complete, or whether it may yet be reversed. But there is also a less controversial point to be made, which is that we are a good deal less optimistic nowadays about finding the answers to philosophical questions than were the ancient Greeks. It now seems a central feature of philosophy that we do not have, and cannot hope to achieve, simple and definitive answers to the questions we are driven to ask. Philosophers are not able to complete the tasks they have set themselves; perhaps these are impossible to complete. Perhaps we are making no progress in philosophy (see Chapter 4). Of course, there are those (such as Dummett, 1978) who feel that simple and straightforward progress in philosophy may yet be at hand[3]; others (such as Nozick, 1981) feel that in philosophy, we seek understanding as much as truth, and that our understanding has indeed progressed; others again (such as Craig, 1987) feel that we need to modify our conception of philosophy – perhaps the core of philosophy consists in the mere articulation of a worldview (and not, say, in arguments in favour of a worldview).[4] In any event, where guidance concerning the conduct of our lives is concerned, it is hard to rely on a discipline in which progress is notably non-cumulative and definitive results are thin on the ground.

Let us turn now to the second major difference between ancient and modern philosophy, that concerning the scope of philosophy. One common view about the nature of history of philosophy (not found among the Greek philosophers) is that philosophy tends to contract – that as soon as progress is made in any field of enquiry, that field ceases to be treated by philosophers, and becomes, instead, the domain of specialists.[5] This view originated with the logical positivist 'dogma' that there is a clear distinction between analytic questions and synthetic questions. The idea was that one could hope to make progress treating questions of either sort, but not by treating some of the traditional questions of philosophy, which are metaphysical in character, and give rise to claims that are unverifiable. The view that philosophy contracts still lingers on, although the logical positivist ideas on which it was originally based, can now no longer command assent.[6] Thus Cohen, for example, thinks that 'relatively pure examples of philosophical analysis are not easy to find before the present century' (Cohen, 1986: 10). He explains that prior to this, 'some primitive psychology was often mixed with the epistemology, some cosmology with the ontology, some theology with the metaphysics, some economics or anthropology with the political philosophy, and so on' (Cohen, 1986: 10).

In fact, I believe that this view is highly questionable, and that we will find as we survey the realm of ancient philosophy, that ancient philosophers were recognisably philosophers; and further that the domain of philosophy in this period tends to expand, and not to contract. Still, we will also find that Greek philosophy covers a wider domain than its modern counterpart; and that philosophy emerges partly through defining its boundaries with other disciplines.[7]

Finally, let us turn to the question of the difference in the professional organisation of philosophy. Each of the great original philosophers of ancient Greece reckoned that he had, individually, solved all the central problems of philosophy. Some of the great philosophers then founded schools, in which they disseminated their ideas to disciples. In later antiquity, philosophers became adherents of schools and spent their time expounding the views of the founder, and attacking rival institutions; and original philosophy came to be presented in the guise of interpretation. There was no conception that the tasks of philosophy were shared in common between the different schools and should be pursued co-operatively. Nowadays, by contrast, even the greatest of contemporary philosophers are more modest – no philosopher now hopes to solve all the central questions of philosophy single-handed. The home of philosophy is the university, and professional philosophers at least pay lip-service to the idea that they are engaged in a form of co-operative enterprise, to which their philosophical opponents also make valuable contributions.

This difference between ancient and modern philosophy is partly to be accounted for in terms of the mechanics of earning a living. There were no universities in ancient Greece; and so it made sense for philosophers to organise, on a do-it-yourself basis, into schools. Today psychoanalysts are not supported by universities; they have found it natural to form their own institutions, and to organise into schools. They must appeal directly to potential students to enrol. The parallel also raises intriguing questions in so far as there are several schools of analysis today that compete with each other, just as there were several rival and competing schools of philosophy in antiquity. There are rival schools of analysis today partly because of Freud's inclination to define psychoanalysis by reference to a particular set of doctrines (his own); and not with reference to a set of problems, a particular subject matter, or a method of enquiry (or therapy). In Chapter 5, I shall ask whether ancient philosophy was more like modern psychoanalysis in this respect than modern philosophy.[8]

Second, we might want to reflect here on the nature of contemporary analytic philosophy. There is no single agreed view about what philosophers today are up to. But there is at least one theory about the nature of analytic philosophy that would explain at a stroke the contrast between the co-operative ethos of contemporary philosophy and the rival schools of ancient Greece. This is the idea that most analytic philosophers today see philosophy as a co-operative enterprise because, quite simply, they belong to the same philosophical school. Thus Dummett suggests that today we are all working out, and systematising, the legacy of Frege: 'we may characterise analytical philosophy as that which follows Frege in accepting that the philosophy of language is the foundation of the rest of the subject' (Dummett, 1978: 441). In his view there are shared tenets:

> first, that the goal of philosophy is the analysis of the structure of *thought*; secondly, that the study of thought is to be sharply distinguished from the psychological process of *thinking*; and finally, that the only proper method for analysing thought consists in the analysis of *language*.
>
> (Dummett, 1978: 458)

He expresses the hope that we are at long last on the right track in philosophy (he believes that only time will tell if the hope is misplaced), and this is a hope that is, I think, widely shared. This is one possible explanation of the co-operative conception of the philosophical enterprise. Where the hope is not shared – and Dummett points to the later Wittgenstein as a major contemporary philosopher who did not share Frege's conception of the nature of the subject[9] – then co-operation seems less natural, and something approaching a school emerges. Wittgensteinians are a race apart among contemporary Anglo-Saxon philosophers.[10]

Of course, Dummett's is not the only possible view of contemporary analytic philosophy. Another synoptic view of contemporary philosophy has been offered by Craig (1987), who thinks that both analytic and continental schools of philosophy are currently engaged in the articulation of essentially the same worldview. He calls this the 'agency theory' or the 'practice ideal', by contrast with what he calls the 'image of God' worldview that had dominated the philosophy of the previous three centuries. The basic idea is that whereas formerly philosophers saw themselves as trying to reflect the divine order of the world in their own intellects, nowadays we see ourselves as creative agents whose essence is realised in man-made practices (we may note the key position of Nietzsche's view of the death of God).[11] There is certainly some truth in this view: the parallel Craig draws between the work of Sartre and Mackie in ethics is suggestive, for example. But it seems doubtful that this idea holds the key to understanding the contemporary philosophical scene. As Craig himself admits, his view involves attributing a 'lack of self-knowledge, or even self-deceit' to the practitioners of contemporary analytic philosophy (Craig, 1987: 223). And Craig's theory has difficulties in accommodating the work accounted for on Dummett's view (and vice versa). Neither view explains all the main lines of philosophy explored in Britain and America this century.[12]

Perhaps there is no single simple explanation of the nature of contemporary philosophy. This might seem to be the view of Davidson, when he remarks that 'analytic philosophy is not, of course, either a method or a doctrine; it is a tradition and an attitude' (Davidson, 1985:1). But what is it to share a tradition and an attitude rather than a set of tenets or a worldview? Davidson does not say. But we can fill out this idea if we think how most philosophers are introduced to analytic philosophy – that is, by being shown examples of analytic philosophy. This is how Cavell introduces contemporary analytic philosophy in his paper 'Existentialism and Analytical Philosophy' (Cavell, 1964), discussing first Russell's theory of descriptions, then the logical positivist principle of verification, Moore's defence of common sense, and finally the work of Austin and the later Wittgenstein. The picture of analytic philosophy that emerges from such a history of the movement is not so neat and tidy as the the constructions or reconstructions offered by Dummett or Craig. Cavell himself remarks that at least three revolutions have occurred in the analytic philosophy of this period (Cavell, 1964: 206). But this is the common inheritance of contemporary analytic philosophers, who may indeed share a tradition and an attitude.

I propose in the chapters that follow to examine some ancient concepts of philosophy. I shall ask what it is about ancient philosophy that gives it its practical orientation; how philosophers in antiquity decided what questions it was appropriate to study; and what led ancient philosophers to organise into schools. Finally I shall ask what conclusions our survey enables us to draw about the nature of philosophy in antiquity and the nature of philosophy today.

1

THE PRESOCRATIC PHILOSOPHERS: THE FIRST PHILOSOPHICAL ARGUMENTS

THE MILESIANS

Philosophy emerged in the sixth century BC in Miletus, a Greek colony in Asia Minor, with three figures, Thales, Anaximander and Anaximenes, who were interested in two main questions – 'what is the world made of?' and 'how did the world originate?'. These three Milesians were not the first to ask, and answer, such questions; and today, discussion of them is the work of scientists as much as philosophers. None the less, these three Milesians are correctly regarded as the first philosophers, and in this chapter, I want to ask why this should be so. I shall argue that asking philosophical questions is part of the human condition, and that philosophical questioning arises naturally in the context of everyday life. But what marks out a philosopher is not, or is not simply, the questions that he asks, but the nature of his response to those questions. So I shall ask what it is about the thought of Thales, Anaximander and Anaximenes that makes their response to these questions a philosophical response.

Let us ask first what it was about Miletus at the turn of the sixth century BC that led to these developments. Many theories have been advanced to account for the emergence of philosophy in Miletus. Aristotle pointed to an economic factor: man's interest in philosophical questions can only be liberated when all his time is not spent in a struggle for survival (*Metaphysics* 981b17–24). Another idea (mentioned by Lloyd, 1979: 235) is that magical beliefs are superseded by rational beliefs and rational discussion of beliefs, when men realise that they can control the world and are not at its mercy; this suggests that developments in technology are a crucial factor. A third suggestion is that reflection about ethics is forced on a primitive society as its members learn that people behave differently elsewhere, in other communities (see Horton, 1967).

All three theories are attractive. But, as Lloyd has argued, economic prosperity, technological advance and foreign travel were not confined to Greece of the sixth century BC and yet only in that context do we find an emergence of speculative thought (by which we mean, among other things, science and philosophy) (Lloyd, 1979, 234–238). We must ask what other factors may be involved.

Lloyd (1988) points to three such further factors. First there is a link between what Lloyd calls egotism and innovation. In the Greek lyric poets who succeed the oral poetry of Homer, we find a strong authorial ego, along with technical innovation, and poems that have the imprint of the author throughout. Lloyd cannot claim that the Milesian philosophers were egotistical in this sense – we do not have enough evidence to know whether or not they were egotistical. But he can, and does, claim that Heraclitus, their immediate successor, conforms to this pattern (see Lloyd, 1988: 59). Heraclitus claims that he has newly found the truth, and that it is *he* who has done so and no one else (see pp. 19–28 below for comments). It may be then, that Greeks became at this period newly conscious of themselves as individuals, with a distinctive contribution to make to the world, and that with some individuals, this contribution took the form of philosophical thinking.

A second further factor is the development of alphabetic writing, and the spread of literacy through alphabetic texts (Lloyd, 1988: 70ff.; Lloyd, 1979: 239–40). These texts permit leisured critical scrutiny of their contents. And their existence makes it more likely that innovations will be recognised and will be cumulative. (And in philosophy, written texts may help in the survival of philosophical theories, and may thus foster competition between rival philosophical theories.) Furthermore, it may be that different forms of writing can themselves stimulate interest in different forms of question. (Thus the making of lists may stimulate an interest in questions of classification.)

But the advent of literacy cannot fully explain what happened in Miletus. For literacy often transforms primitive societies without giving rise to philosophical speculation. What is unique to speculative thought in ancient Greece, says Lloyd, is the development of the concept of proof as demonstration by deductive argument.[1] And this, he suggests, may originate from the political turmoil of the period, and the emergence of Greek democracy. It was necessary, both in taking political decisions and in arguing in the lawcourts, to pay due heed to the quality of argument and evidence in favour of a given decision. And attention to argument and evidence is precisely what is necessary for the successful practice of science and philosophy.[2]

Lloyd's argument from the emergence of democracy is undoubtedly powerful. I shall argue, however, that human beings may well have asked philosophical questions long before the emergence of philosophy as a discipline – and certainly before that of deductive argument as a tool of philosophy. In the Greek context, the first philosopher we *know* to have used the method of deductive argument is Parmenides (see pp. 28–36 below). But there is a sense in which it is quite proper to see the Milesians and Heraclitus as philosophers. More generally, we shall discover that there is no *one* method of enquiry that is the philosophical method *par excellence*: Nietzsche is as much a philosopher as Descartes, and Anaxagoras is just as philosophical as Parmenides. We may feel, then, that Lloyd pays undue attention to philosophical method in his characterisation of philosophy, and that his conception of philosophical method is somewhat impoverished.[3] A full account of the nature of philosophy will include a discussion of the nature of philosophical questions and philosophical results.

And yet it may be that we must focus on the nature of philosophical methods if we are to be successful in distinguishing philosophical from non-philosophical responses to philosophical questions. It is helpful here to refer to Horton's comparison of the role of magic in traditional societies with the role of science in modern societies. Horton suggests that both science and magic stand in the same relation to our everyday beliefs, by providing a more sophisticated theory of the world; and both are concerned with explanation, prediction and control of the world (Horton, 1982: 240). Traditional beliefs are conservative, but open to 'gradual adaptive change' (Horton, 1982: 243). There is, however, no competition between rival theories of the world in traditional societies; and wisdom in a traditional society gains authority because it has been handed down by the ancients, and not because, for example, it fits best with experience. Modern societies, by contrast, are characterised by such inter-theoretic competition;

and rival theories are (rationally) assessed in terms of their fit with experience.

Horton's thesis is not designed to account for the emergence of philosophy in ancient Greece. He thinks, in fact, that modern societies began to emerge at AD 1200 or so (Horton 1982: 237). But there is, none the less, a moral we can draw from his work that is relevant to our enquiry. And that is, that what we are concerned with is not primarily the emergence of philosophy (and science), but that of a degree of success in these endeavours, or the emergence of two disciplines with histories. What happened in Miletus at the turn of the sixth century BC, as a result of the coincidence, at that time and place, of the various different factors we have mentioned above, was that there arose the possibility of making some progress in controlling, predicting and understanding the world.[4] The impetus to ask philosophical and scientific questions is to be seen as an intrinsic part of human nature and is common to all societies; it does not stand in need of explanation.

But is the impetus to seek answers to philosophical questions an intrinsic part of human nature? Craig's contention that philosophers typically articulate worldviews that are widely shared (see p. 6 above) would seem to imply this. And the view that in an important sense we are all philosophers has been persuasively defended by Popper (1986) and by Bambrough (1986). Bambrough recalls his war service as a miner, and his experience then of discussing philosophical questions with miners (Bambrough, 1986: 63), and his later experiences, as Dean of St John's, of discussing philosophical questions with rebellious students (Bambrough, 1986: 66). He refers to 'the general conversation of mankind from which philosophy arises and to which it must return' (Bambrough, 1986: 65), and he concludes (though not, of course, solely on this autobiographical basis) that 'even the geniuses among writers and thinkers – Shakespeare and Tolstoy, Plato and Wittgenstein – are doing to a higher power something that we all do and need to do' (Bambrough, 1986: 60). Popper holds that 'all men and all women are philosophers, though some are more so than others' (Popper, 1986: 198). If we do not all have philosophical problems, we have at least philosophical prejudices (Popper, 1986: 204); and professional philosophy is, or should be, the critical examination of widespread and influential theories we take for granted in everyday life (Popper, 1986: 204–5). But 'all men are philosophers, because in one way or another, all take up an attitude towards life and death' (Popper, 1986: 211).

It is sometimes thought, not just that all adult human beings are philosophers, but that so too are all children. Nagel thinks that 'around the age of fourteen . . . many people start to think about philosophical problems on their own' (Nagel, 1987: 3), while Matthews (1980) has detected an interest in philosophical questions among younger children. He tells us, in the Introduction to his book *Philosophy And The Young Child*, how 'It occurred to me that my task as a college philosophy teacher was to reintroduce my students to an activity that they had once enjoyed and found natural, but that they had later been socialized to abandon' (Matthews, 1980: vii). His book opens with a six-year-old child asking the question 'how can we be sure that everything is not a dream?' – a question asked and deemed worthy of discussion by Descartes in his years of maturity.[5]

On this view of philosophy, 'the philosophical raw material comes directly from the world and our relation to it, not from writings of the past' as Nagel puts it (Nagel, 1987: 4). And the questions that, as human beings, we necessarily ask – questions about ethics (how we should live), knowledge (what we can hope to know and how we can hope to know), metaphysics (what there is in the world; our own place in the world) – are questions that are liable to strike us as meaningful and important in everyday life.

On this view of the nature of philosophical questions, it will be easy to understand why philosophy emerged as soon as conditions were favourable. The emergence of philosophy is the emergence of a distinctively philosophical response to philosophical questions; these in turn arise from a natural desire we have as human beings to understand the world and to orient ourselves in relation to the world. (Other views of the nature of philosophical questions will be discussed in later chapters.)

We can now turn to the Milesians, and ask why their treatment of philosophical questions should be seen as philosophical in character.

Aristotle tells us that Thales thought that the *arche*, 'principle' or 'origin', was water, 'perhaps taking this supposition from seeing the nurture of all things to be moist' (*Metaphysics* A3). Aristotle's account seems tentative, and it is hard to interpret. It may be that Thales held that 'everything is water' or it may be that Thales held that 'everything originates from water' (thus KRS 1983: 90). But there is not much doubt that Anaximenes held that 'everything is air'. And of the other Presocratics, Heraclitus maintained that everything is fire (but there is also a cosmic cycle), Anaxagoras held that there is something of everything in everything (everything is a mixture), and the atomists held that everything was composed of atoms and void. We can be confident then that claims such as 'everything is water' were amongst the first philosophical claims – and I propose to proceed on the basis that this particular claim was actually advanced by Thales (although I accept that there is no conclusive evidence that this was Thales' central doctrine). As we are really concerned with asking what sort of a claim this is, and why such claims should be regarded as philosophical in character, it will not matter too much if the claim is incorrectly ascribed to Thales.

Let us first ask what sort of a question a philosopher who claims that 'everything is air' or 'everything is water' is addressing. For Aristotle, it was not difficult to formulate the question to which such views are a response. Aristotle says, in *Metaphysics* Z that 'This is the question to which men have always sought the answer, but which has always perplexed them – what is being?' (1028b2–4). In Greek, the question is *ti to on*?, and Aristotle feels free to gloss the question immediately as *tis he ousia*?, 'what is substance?'. Guthrie comments that 'the question "what is being?" is nothing vague or obscure, but a perfectly natural and sensible one to ask' (Guthrie, 1981: 204). Guthrie thinks that what the question means is 'how are we to set about answering the question "what is it?" when confronted with any object?' (Guthrie, 1981: 208). Aristotle himself thinks that we can answer the question 'what is it?' in many different ways (see pp. 120–1 below). He says, however, in *Metaphysics* A3 that the Milesians were primarily interested in material causation, in the question of what things are composed. A Milesian, on this view, will always answer the question 'what is it?' in the same way. Whatever we point to, he will tell us, for example, that 'it is water'.

It may be, then, that the Milesians were not asking 'what is being?', or 'what is substance?' but 'what is the world made of?'. And about this latter question, Williams contends that

> it is one of the achievements of intellectual progress that [this question] now has no determinate meaning; if a child

> asks it, we do not give him one or many answers to it, but rather lead him to the point where he sees why it should be replaced with a number of different questions. Of course, there is a sense in which modern particle theory is a descendant of enquiries started by the Milesians, but that descent has so modified the questions that it would be wrong to say that there is one unambiguous question to which we give the answer "electrons, protons, etc." and Thales (perhaps) gave the answer "water".
>
> (Williams, 1981: 208)

Similarly, the question 'what is everything made of?' is criticised by Berlin (1950). Berlin sees the propensity of philosophers to ask this question as unfortunate, and remarks that it is really a scientific one. Philosophers give non-empirical answers to the question, but the only meaningful one would be empirical. Their answers cannot be doubted on empirical grounds; but 'a proposition that cannot significantly be denied or doubted can offer us no information' (Berlin, 1950: 76–77). Berlin, of course, is writing in the climate of logical positivism; but thinking along these lines also seems to lie behind Williams' denial that there is a single coherent question here. Not that Williams shares the logical positivist attitude towards metaphysics; but he does, like Berlin, think that a philosophical question is entangled here with a scientific one; and he does, implicitly, agree with Berlin that the discussions we find in the Greek philosophers of the question *ti to on?* are on the wrong track. Berlin implies that they asked a scientific question which they mistook for a philosophical one; Williams implies that they failed to distinguish at least two separate questions.

A different attitude toward such questions, however, was manifest in the early years of the century. To G. E. Moore and Bertrand Russell the question 'what is there?' seemed entirely coherent. G. E. Moore holds that the 'first and most interesting problem of philosophy' is to give 'a general description of the *whole* Universe', or for philosophers 'to express their opinions as to what there is or is not in the Universe' (Moore, 1953: 23). And he thinks that different answers are returned, in this task, by common sense, on the one hand, and by various different philosophers, on the other, some of whom add something to common sense, and some of whom contradict common sense. Russell, in his *Problems Of Philosophy*, drawing on Moore's work, takes the table on which he is writing as an example of an object of common sense, and remarks that for philosophers it is a 'problem full of surprising possibilities'. The philosophers' answers to the question 'what sort of object is it?'

> diverge from the views of ordinary mortals . . . Leibniz tells us it is a community of souls; Berkeley tells us it is an idea in the mind of God; sober science, scarcely less wonderful, tells us it is a vast collection of electric charges in violent motion . . . doubt suggests that perhaps there is no table at all.
>
> (Russell, 1912: 6)

Moore and Russell, then, hold that there is a single question here to which common sense, science and various different philosophers return different, and conflicting answers. Are science and philosophy offering more sophisticated theories about the world than common sense, as Russell seems to suggest in this passage? Or is Williams right to diagnose an absence of conflict here, once the questions have been clarified?

Some considerations seem to favour the view of Williams. Certainly, what answer we will in fact return to the question 'what is there?' will depend on the context in which it was asked. And perhaps the very fact that different answers, or different kinds of answer – scientific and philosophical, philosophical and common sense – can be proffered to this question, is some indication that the question is in fact ambiguous (or that is has no clear meaning). But at the same time, we must acknowledge that philosophers (if not scientists) have often taken themselves to be either contradicting, or adding to, the common sense view of what there is. And certainly, they try hard to contradict and supplement the views of other philosophers. Moreover, these remains a major philosophical problem of how we should relate what Williams has termed the 'absolute' conception of the world to more local and particular representations of it (Williams, 1978).

We shall return to the question of how the results of philosophical reflection or scientific enquiry relate to our common sense view of the world in pp. 54–9 below. Let us here simply accept that scientists, philosophers, and common sense, all, on occasion, ask the question 'what is there?', and examine the Milesians' answers to this question.

It seems clear that in asserting that 'everything is water' or 'everything is air', Thales and Anaximenes were not aiming to formulate the traditional wisdom of Milesian society or to articulate a common sense worldview. Dummett has plausibly suggested that common sense does not offer a 'single, permanent, unified "theory of the world" ' (Dummett, 1981: 18), but that it is 'culturally conditioned and subject to evolution' (Dummett 1981: 20). But it seems clear that at no time or place has it been a common sense view that the world is composed of water or air. Rather, the world is composed of a diversity of inanimate physical objects such as tables and chairs, together with a diversity of animate objects such as human beings.

As adults, we do not reflect very much on what there is, or on what the world is composed of. We take the answers to these questions for granted in everyday life. (Children, of course, do ask questions about what there is as they try to understand the workings of the world – they may wonder whether or not there are magicians, for example.) But we all have some theory about what there is which plays some part in our general understanding of how the world works.[6] Deeper understanding of the world certainly seems both possible and desirable and our common sense views are very much open to scientific or philosophical challenge.

What sort of a challenge is Thales making to the common sense position? Is the claim that 'everything is water' scientific in character? If we asked ourselves nowadays if we could make sense of the idea that everything is water, we might perhaps think that science could reveal this. Certainly, it does not *seem* that everything is water; but scientific discoveries have often revealed that the world is not exactly as it seems (that the world is round, not flat; that the earth travels round the sun, and not vice versa; and so on). Perhaps, then, Thales was formulating the first scientific conjecture, when he claimed that the *arche* is water.[7]

Popper (1959) has argued that science advances through a method of conjecture and refutation. A speculative conjecture about the nature of things is formulated; it is then criticised in the light of experimental evidence; eventually it is refuted; it is then superseded by a more adequate conjecture which is, in its turn, subject to criticism and refutation. Popper has commented directly on the Presocratics in his article 'Back to the Presocratics' (Popper, 1958). There he emphasises not so much the claim of the Presocratics to be the first scientists, as the way in which they established for the first time a tradition of critical discussion. (For all knowledge, he holds, proceeds by way of conjectures and refutations (Popper, 1958: 152).) Popper holds that all the Presocratics try to answer the same questions – questions that he sees as philosophical rather than scientific, in fact[8] – but that each philosopher tries to improve upon the work of his predecessors. Thus one of the merits of Thales is that he gives rise to Anaximander. And one can hardly avoid the thought that this is not simply because he was the sort of person who could tolerate criticism (as Popper suggests, 1958: 150) but also because of the nature of the view he expresses. It is, for Popper, a merit of views like 'everything is water' that they are unlikely to be provoked simply by mere observation of what goes on in the world. It is, in fact, the very boldness of the conjecture that makes the view worth first formulating, and then criticising.

So is it the most significant fact about Thales that he formulates a bold and implausible-looking conjecture, and one that goes far beyond our everyday experience of the world? If we demarcate the domain of science a priori, in the manner of Popper, Thales' claim about water will seem thoroughly scientific: it has, after all, now been falsified as a result of scientific progress. If, however, we characterise science by examining, naturalistically, how scientists actually proceed, in the manner of Kuhn (1962), the Presocratics will not look very much like scientists. For science as we now know now it involves some sort of working practice of discovery, some role for observation and experiment, and most of what the Presocratics offer is indeed, as Berlin suspects, just armchair theorising. So there is, then, some reason for doubting whether we should really see Thales' claim as scientific rather than as philosophical.

As to the nature of a critical tradition more generally, it may be that here too the view of Popper needs some modification. The Presocratics can take some credit for establishing a critical tradition. But, as Barnes has emphasised, the criticism offered by the Presocratics of their predecessors consists, generally, not in close attention to their arguments or experimental refutation of their conclusions, but in the formulation of rival theories, that allegedly offer better explanations of the phenomena (cf. Barnes, 1979a: 51).[9] The Milesians do submit their ideas to critical scrutiny; but that scrutiny does not take precisely the form that Popper anticipates.

Now let us revert to the question 'what is there?', and ask why philosophers have thought this question important. For the Milesians themselves, saying what there is, or what the world is composed of, may simply have constituted an attempt to further and deepen our everyday understanding of the world – in the same way that religions might hope to do the same thing. We may compare Guthrie: 'the apparent chaos of events must conceal an underlying order . . . this order is the product of impersonal forces' (Guthrie, 1962: 26). Or Popper: 'I believe that the Milesians envisaged the world . . . as a kind of house . . . There was no need to ask what it was for. But there was a real need to inquire into its architecture' (Popper, 1958: 141).[10] They may well have altered significantly contemporary understanding of the world. As Guthrie implies, it is important that the world is not, for the Milesians, a mythological stage, but is populated by natural forces. The content of the Milesians' teaching differs in this way from the content of religious teaching; and the nature of their views is such as to stimulate us towards critical reflection.

For us, the significance of the question 'what is there?' is rather different. For saying what there is sets the stage for later problems in philosophy (we should remember that Moore calls this the first problem in philosophy – and it occupies the first chapter of Russell's book). Thus Hume argues first that there are ideas and impressions, and then gives an account of the rest of life in terms of ideas and impressions. Quine holds that there are theories and there are things within theories; and this is the groundwork of Quine's philosophy. And David Lewis defends the doctrine of 'Humean supervenience', that 'all there is to the world is a vast mosaic of local matters of particular fact, just one little thing, and then another' (Lewis, 1986: xi). The question then arises whether these philosophers can give an account of our human experience of the world in terms of their ontology (their account of what there is). We do not know whether or not the Milesians attempted this task. Aristotle thought some later Presocratics did make the attempt but without success. He remarks that

> it is not likely either that fire or earth or any such element should be the reason why things manifest goodness and beauty both in their being and in their coming to be . . . nor again could it be right to entrust so great a matter to spontaneity or to chance.
>
> (*Metaphysics* 984b11–15)

A philosopher's ontology may be perhaps be philosophically adequate to this task, but scientifically incorrect. Thus Lewis comments that 'Really what I uphold is not so much the truth of Humean supervenience as the tenability of it. If physics itself were to teach me that it is false, I wouldn't grieve' (Lewis 1986: xi). It seems unlikely, however, that the Milesians would have shared Lewis's view of this question. If Thales said, 'everything is water', I expect he would have grieved to learn that everything is not water, and would not have been quite happy to say 'well, the thesis was tenable; everything *could* have been water'. The Milesians were working within the domain of science and must have hoped that their views would prove scientifically correct as well as philosophically tenable.

Philosophy did not emerge fully developed in Miletus in the sixth century BC. But Thales, Anaximander and Anaximenes found themselves in propitious circumstances, and in their work, philosophy found its first foothold. These figures wanted to understand the world (as do most human beings) and to that end, they advanced a number of (conflicting) simple unifying explanations of the apparent diversity of the world. But what is important to us is that the Milesians offered a new sort of answer to a traditional question – one that invited rational assessment. Thales' views served as a point of departure for his immediate successors, and helped to inaugurate a critical tradition. And that is why we now see these three Milesians as the first philosophers.

HERACLITUS

The text of Heraclitus is preserved only in fragmentary citations. How it was organised, and whether it formed a coherent whole, we do not know. In the fragments we possess, Heraclitus tells us something about the nature of his philosophical conclusions; but more importantly he helps us find our way towards reaching those conclusions for ourselves. One of Heraclitus' central themes is that insight cannot be passed simply and straightforwardly from his text to the reader. As readers, we must work to gain insight for ourselves. Heraclitus' text accordingly presents us with a series of challenges to active self-examination.

In this section, I will first outline a number of plausible, but very divergent, interpretations of Heraclitus' essential worldview.

I shall then ask how it comes about that plausible interpretations of Heraclitus' central message can diverge in this way. I shall offer an explanation of this phenomenon in terms of Heraclitus' conception of philosophy, and the nature of Heraclitus' text. This will involve, in particular, an examination of the nature of the challenge that the individual sayings of Heraclitus present to the reader.

Heraclitus' general view of the world is, very roughly, that the world is composed of fire, in various transformations; that everything in the world is forever changing; and that throughout the world, we experience the phenomenon of unity of opposites. About the unity of opposites, he says that 'They do not comprehend how a thing agrees at variance with itself; it is an attunement turning back on itself, like that of the bow and lyre' (fr. 88, tr. Kahn). Or again: 'The same . . . . living and dead, and the waking and the sleeping, and young and old. For these transposed are those, and those transposed again are these' (113). About change in the world (the doctrine of flux, as it is called), Heraclitus says that, 'as they step in the same rivers, other and still other waters flow upon them' (50). He may also have said that, 'One cannot step into the same river twice'.[11] As to what there is, Heraclitus' view is that there is a 'Cosmic Cycle': 'The reversals of fire: first sea; but of sea half is earth, half lightning storm' (38). The world as a whole is organised: 'The wise is one, knowing the plan by which it steers all things through all' (54) . It is composed of fire: 'The ordering, the same for all, no god or man has made, but it ever was and is and will be; fire everlasting, kindled inmeasures and in measures going out' (37). And it is pervaded by the unity of opposites. Thus: 'The god: day and night, winter and summer, war and peace, satiety and hunger. It alters, as when mingled with perfumes, it gets named according to the pleasure of each one' (123). Or again: 'Graspings: wholes and not wholes, convergent divergent, consonant dissonant, from all things one and from one thing all' (124). And there is a place in this worldview for the human soul, albeit one that is somewhat obscure: 'out of earth water arises, out of water soul' (102). But, 'dry soul is wisest and best' (114).

It is already clear that there is both continuity and discontinuity between the work of Heraclitus and that of the Milesians. In his account of the cosmic cycle, and in his claim that everything is fire, Heraclitus is following the Milesians, and formulating the best 'general account of nature or the world' (Barnes 1979a: 68) that he can come up with. As such, his work has some interest and his claim that 'everything is fire' may well mark an advance on the views of the Milesians. Heraclitus recognises that everything is not manifestly fire; his claim is really that everything is fire in some shape or form – 'everything is fire or a transformation of fire'. And there is an interpretation of Heraclitus' thought, which may be correct, according to which his central claim in this regard comes out true.[12] Following this interpretation, Heraclitus chooses fire as his principle, because fire is the natural symbol of process; and so his central claim is really that 'all things are processes'; this ties in neatly with the doctrine of flux; and thus formulated, the central claim is now known to be true.

But Heraclitus' reputation as a philosopher does not rest on his contribution to the Milesian tradition; much of his philosophy stands outside the domain of science. The doctrines of flux, and of the unity of opposites cannot be simply confirmed or dismissed in the light of our current scientific knowledge. For Heraclitus, the world needs interpretation, and not simply scientific investigation.[13]

What sort of interpretation of the world is called for? The key doctrine is that of the unity of opposites; but commentators have advanced very different views about its significance. Some, such as KRS, believe that the message is that 'the total plurality of things forms a single, coherent, determinable complex – what Heraclitus calls "unity" ' (KRS, 1983: 191). Others, such as Barnes, see this message as 'small beer' (Barnes, 1979a: 71). Barnes takes it that Heraclitus believed in a world of contradictions (Barnes, 1979a: 69ff.). Vlastos remarks that what distinguishes Heraclitus' sense of the interconnection of things from that of his predecessors is his application of this idea beyond the domain of cosmology. He suggests that the doctrine of the unity of opposites would, if true, undermine all morality (Vlastos, 1955: 428). An important fragment on this view is, 'For god, all things are fair and good and just' (68). For Hussey (1982), it is rather that a cosmic struggle in the world is reflected in the human self. War is the central theme in Heraclitus: 'War is father and king of all' (83).

Burnyeat suggests the moral is that we humans cannot adopt a 'god's eye' view of the world from which all the opposites are somehow reconciled. 'There is no naming except from a particular point of view' (Burnyeat 1982b: 47). So 'in the end . . . the god's-eye point of view . . . is simply the human view made aware of itself as being the *human* view and no more' (Burnyeat, 1982b: 47). Another view would be that Heraclitus recommends a relaxed acceptance of the unity of opposites, of change in the world and of the diversity of the world and of the self. His attitude towards contradiction and apparent contradiction may be that of Whitman:

> Do I contradict myself?
> Very well then I contradict myself,
> (I am large, I contain multitudes)[14]

All these interpretations have their attractions. None can be ruled out as impossible. Clearly, Heraclitus' central message is hard to interpret. There are several reasons for this; and most of these reasons have something to do with Heraclitus' conception of philosophy. Four main factors seem to be involved here. The first is that whatever interpretation we emerge with is partly our own construction. If Heraclitus was right about the method by which we can attain truth about the world, we are each in business on our own account, and we must each make what we can of his philosophy. Second, there is the remarkable absence of argument from the work of Heraclitus. This also makes his position harder to understand. A related point is that we have no idea what questions Heraclitus was asking, or what problems Heraclitus was trying to solve when he formulated his doctrines. He gives us the impression that his insights just arose from the blue (or from self-examination). They may help us to understand the world; they may not. Finally, there is the holistic nature of Heraclitus' world-view. Heraclitus believes that the meaning of the world is embedded in each and every part of it (or at least in rivers, seawater and barley-drinks), but that an overall picture of the world emerges when we contemplate its constituent parts. As interpreters, we must try hard to make everything fit; and as assessors we cannot survey his ideas piecemeal.

Let us now look at some of these ideas in more detail. Aristotle tells us (*Rhetorica* 1407b11) that Heraclitus' book opened as follows:

> Although this account holds forever, men ever fail to comprehend, both before hearing it and once they have heard.

> Although all things come to pass in accordance with this account, men are like the untried when they try such words and works as I set forth, distinguishing each according to its nature and telling how it is. But other men are oblivious of what they do awake, just as they are forgetful of what they do asleep' (1) .

Heraclitus thinks that his message is universally valid and that it is universally available. But it is also universally unrecognised; and indeed it is almost unrecognisable. It is a hard message to teach or to convey: we don't understand it, even when it is first drawn to our attention. We don't learn from experience – 'Most men do not think things in the way they encounter them, nor do they recognize what they experience, but believe their own opinions' (4) – and there is some danger that we will not learn from Heraclitus' teaching either. Heraclitus recognises, then, that we may read or hear his work, and come away none the wiser.

Heraclitus is the first, but not the last, great philosopher who thinks of his doctrines as difficult to convey. Some hold that Plato has 'unwritten doctrines' of this kind in his middle period.[15] And certainly in the *Phaedrus* he cautions us about the limitations of the written word, remarking, for example, that you cannot cross-question a book, and that a book can not choose to address itself to the right readers. The written word can, none the less, be valuable: it can serve as a reminder of the truth (277e). A more recent case is that of the early Wittgenstein, who took the central doctrines expressed in his *Tractatus* to be literally unsayable (along with everything else that is of value in life). But Wittgenstein too believes that his writing (in this case, the *Tractatus*) can be helpful to his readers, even if it does not exemplify the correct method in philosophy (6.53). The reader must transcend the propositions it contains in order to see the world aright. Wittgenstein remarks, following Sextus Empiricus, that 'he must, so to speak, throw away the ladder after he has climbed up it' (6.54). (This image will be discussed further in Chapter 5.)

But what of Heraclitus? What does he hope his writing can do for us, and why does he think of his central thesis as difficult to convey? Is his thinking at all like that of Plato or Wittgenstein?

Hussey (1972) suggests that there may be a close analogy between Heraclitus and the early Wittgenstein. Hussey's view is that the development of alphabetic writing in the case of Heraclitus, and the development of formal logic, in the case of Wittgenstein, encourages the idea that the world can be exactly depicted in language. What Hussey says of the early Wittgenstein is obviously true: discussions of formal logic abound in the *Tractatus*. But it is not clear that his view does equal justice to the case of Heraclitus. Heraclitus says 'Nature loves to hide' (fr. 10), and 'The lord whose oracle lives in Delphi neither declares nor conceals, but gives a sign' (fr. 33), in this being both like Nature and like Heraclitus' writing, as we may surmise. Heraclitus tells us in one fragment how he came to understand the message himself: 'I went in search of myself' (fr. 28). I think we can take it here that others may also go in search of themselves, and find themselves, as Heraclitus did.

It would seem, then, that Heraclitus does indeed think that language can mirror reality, as Hussey claims. If his sayings are obscure, that is because reality, or nature, is obscure, and Heraclitus must draw attention to this obscurity. There is no sign, however, that alphabetic writing has anything to do with this – Heraclitus' sayings could equally well be formulated orally.[16] Nor would there seem to be any parallel in Heraclitus to one of Wittgenstein's central ideas – that there is, as it were, a sayable realm and an unsayable realm. Heraclitus' idea is rather that we are now blind or asleep, and that we will later awaken and see. The enlightenment that awaits us is not a realisation of the limits of the communicable. It is, rather, an understanding of the *logos* which is embedded in the world itself, and is mirrored in Heraclitus' writing.

Does Heraclitus, then, share Plato's reservations about the written word? Clearly not: his book encapsulates the truth about reality as he sees it, and there is no suggestion that he could make things a good deal clearer in an oral presentation, or in a question and answer session. Heraclitus does share one crucial theme with Plato, however, and that is the theme of understanding. It is because philosophy is concerned with understanding that Plato thinks we need to practise dialectic, and not just read and write books. It is, similarly, because we need to understand Heraclitus' message, that it's hard to convey, and just simply hearing it may well not suffice. Knowledge admits of (relatively) easy transmission. Understanding, by contrast, is a process which we must each pass through for ourselves. We might think here of the platitude in aesthetics that we must understand works of art at first hand, for ourselves; or of the paradoxical view that no-one can teach anyone else anything.[17]

How, then, does Heraclitus try to convey such understanding to us? It may be that in the first instance Heraclitus presents us with thoughts such as, 'the way up and the way down is one and the same' (103) and 'the sea is the purest and the foulest water: for fish drinkable and life-sustaining; for men undrinkable and deadly' (70) and possibly, 'one cannot step twice into the same river' (51).

How should we describe such sayings? Hussey (1972: 34) and Guthrie (1962: 413–414) point to the standard comparisons with the pronouncements of oracles or prophets. These sayings certainly present a challenge to our understanding. I want here, however, to compare our response to the fragments of Heraclitus with our response to the use of metaphor.

Richard Rorty (1987) contrasts metaphor with paradox. We distinguish metaphor from paradox, he thinks, by asking 'whether the first utterer of what seems a blatantly false remark can offer arguments for what he says' (Rorty, 1987: 295). 'No-one can harm the good man' counts as a paradox, because Socrates goes on to defend the remark. Yeats' utterance in 'Sailing to Byzantium', about the 'gong-tormented sea', however, is a metaphor – Yeats does not defend the remark.

On this conception of metaphor and paradox, fr. 103, 'the way up and the way down is one and the same' would seem to count as a metaphor (we have to work out for ourselves what Heraclitus means – at least as the text stands). But fr. 70, 'the sea is the purest and the foulest water: for fish drinkable and life-sustaining: for men undrinkable and deadly', counts as a paradox (Heraclitus explains what he means). And this would be a surprising result. Rorty's suggestion, however, must be at least slightly astray, in any case. As Davidson has pointed out, what some metaphors say literally is true – for example 'no man is an island' – and do not stand in need of argumentative support. Heraclitus' remarks that 'the way up and the way down is one and the same' and that 'you cannot step into the same river twice' are like the metaphors that are literally true. They tell us nothing we do not already know and what they say is indisputably true.

For all that such metaphors are literally true, however, they remain challenging. That, indeed, on Davidson's well-known account of the nature of metaphor, is its main function (Davidson,

1978). For Davidson, the only meaning a metaphor has is its literal meaning. There is no second, metaphorical, meaning that accompanies the literal meaning and performs the work of the metaphor. It is, then, through its literal meaning that a metaphor does its work – though how it accomplishes this is ultimately mysterious. (Rorty compares the question 'how do metaphors work?' to 'how do surprises work?' (1987: 291).) What a metaphor does is to alert us to some aspect of the world that we might otherwise not have noticed. Davidson actually cites Heraclitus' fr. 33 (quoted above) in pointing out that what is important about a metaphor is not what it says, but what it intimates (Davidson, 1978). But that, on the other hand, what it intimates might just as well be drawn to our attention by a bump on the head.[18] We don't know how Heraclitus would have regarded bumps on the head as a means of conveying the logos. But his fragments are intended to arrest our attention, and to redirect it. We are not simply to attend to their literal meaning.

At the same time, these fragments do not function exactly like metaphors. We must decide what to make of a metaphor for ourselves. But Heraclitus is a philosopher, with a substantive philosophical worldview to set forth. He does not leave us a single image that speaks for itself, but, in the first instance, offers us many examples of the phenomenon he wants to draw to our attention.[19] And Heraclitus then actually tries to spell out for us what morals we should draw from this array of examples, fairly explicitly, in the fragments that outline the doctrines of flux, the unity of opposites and the cosmic cycle.

None the less it seems that Heraclitus' style, generally, is centrally important both to his effectiveness as a philosopher and to his conception of philosophy. It may be appropriate, then, to reflect here a little about the later work of Wittgenstein, which closely resembles that of Heraclitus in terms of style.[19] Wittgenstein can, on occasion, sound very like Heraclitus. Consider, for example 'If a lion could talk, we could not understand him' (Wittgenstein, 1953: § 223). It is not at all clear what Wittgenstein means, if we take this sentence in isolation from the rest of his text. It can, however, be explicated in terms of central Wittgensteinian doctrines.[20]

According to the later Wittgenstein, 'The work of the philosopher consists in assembling reminders for a particular purpose' (Wittgenstein, 1953: § 127). Reminders should be obviously and unquestionably true; they should serve to jog our memories as required. Heraclitus' fragments are, as we have seen, often obviously and unquestionably true; and should serve to jog our understanding as required. The difference between 'memory' and 'understanding' here is crucial, however. For where Wittgenstein and Heraclitus differ is primarily in their view of the goal in philosophy, and of the role that 'reminders' play in attaining to the goal. Wittgenstein says 'What is your aim in philosophy? – To show the fly out of the fly-bottle' (Wittgenstein, 1953: §309). At least part of Wittgenstein's view of philosophy is that one is drawn to the subject by philosophical problems, and that success in philosophy consists in dissolving those problems without remainder. One should feel free to leave the subject when one pleases. This may or may not be an accurate reflection of Wittgenstein's own practice in philosophy. Commentators in fact have no difficulty in setting out substantive theses they think that the later Wittgenstein believed in.[21] But however the case may be with Wittgenstein, the reminders of Heraclitus prepare us for the eventual presentation of a substantive philosophical world view. Where Wittgenstein aims merely to free us from philosophical misunderstanding, Heraclitus aims to instil positive philosophical understanding of the world.

Heraclitus would seem not to have succeeded in this. As we have seen, there is an enormous diversity of understandings of the world that commentators feel that Heraclitus has instilled into them. None the less, Heraclitus' sayings retain the power to intrigue and provoke the reader, and his substantive philosophical views – however we interpret them – hold some prima facie plausibility. In antiquity later philosophers were to accept them and integrate them into their own philosophical systems. Thus the Stoics believed in much of Heraclitus' physics, and Plato (arguably) followed Heraclitus in holding that the sensible world is in flux.

Heraclitus' most significant contribution to philosophy, however, was his view of life (and of philosophy) as a search for common understanding. This view was to influence both Plato and Aristotle, and the idea that philosophers seek understanding as much as truth is one that remains attractive (see p. 38 below). The Milesians had tried to understand the physical world; but with Heraclitus, the search for understanding becomes central and encompasses more of life. Heraclitus did not, though, tackle the whole range of questions we ask nowadays in philosophy. And argument has yet to emerge. To see a further area of questioning emerge, and argument come into its own, we must now turn to the work of Parmenides.

PARMENIDES

Parmenides is an important figure for historians of ancient philosophy. For Owen, his argument 'cuts free of inherited premisses' and 'starts from an assumption whose denial is peculiarly self-refuting'; Parmenides is simply 'the most radical pioneer known to us among Presocratics' (Owen, 1960: 61). Barnes finds that 'the arguments he adduces, though unsound, are ingenious and admirable; their conclusion, though false, has a strange plausibility and attractiveness. Many eminent philosophers have struck Parmenidean attitudes, and have done so for essentially Parmenidean reasons' (Barnes, 1979a: 172).

Parmenides tells us, in his hexameter poem, how horses carried him through the gates of the path of day and night to see a goddess. The goddess says she will tell him 'both the unshaken heart of well-rounded truth, and the opinions of mortals, in which there is no reliance' (fr. 1 ll. 29–30). The Way of Truth (the first of the two promised revelations, and the one that mostly survives) employs a series of deductive arguments that attempt to demonstrate, starting from the first principle *esti*, 'it is', or '. . . is . . .', that what there is is single, continuous, indivisible, and exists at all times and in all places. The Way of Seeming (the second revelation, mostly lost) seems to offer a more traditional, dualistic, cosmogony and cosmology. Parmenides is the first philosopher we know to have used deductive argument. Significantly, the goddess tells him to 'judge by reason the strife-encompassed refutation spoken by me' (fr. 7 ll. 5–6).

In this section, I shall discuss three main sets of questions – those raised by the nature of the starting-point of the argument, the premiss *esti*; those raised by Parmenides' method; and those raised by the nature of his conclusions.

But let us start our discussion by considering the proem (fr.1: 1–32), in which Parmenides travels to see the goddess. It is not standard practice now, and it was not standard practice in antiquity, for a philosopher to attribute his arguments to a goddess (or even a god).[22] So we are bound to wonder why Parmenides starts his poem like this. The goddess's words frame the Way of Truth and the Way of Seeming, and tells us that the fomer is reliable, but the latter is not. They thus have a structural function within the poem. But perhaps there is a further significance to the proem. It could be that Parmenides' journey should serve as our first indication that there is more to what is coming than mere philosophical argument. A complete transformation of worldview will be called for if we are to accept the conclusions of the argument. It may be significant that Parmenides' route takes him through the gates of the paths of night and day (see fr. 1:11–21); for the crucial mistake we mortals make, according to the goddess, is to accept the existence of two principles, light and night (fr. 8.53–9). Where the goddess is, those two principles do not reign (Furley, 1973).

Let us ask, though, why we should accept the premiss *esti* and reject *ouk esti*. As we have seen, Owen reckons (perhaps correctly) that the denial of the premiss *esti* is self-refuting. But we should note first that Parmenides does not take it to be self-evidently true. He presents an argument in favour of the premiss, which is actually an argument against what he takes to be the only alternative, *ouk esti*. What Parmenides says about the alternative route, *ouk esti*, '. . . is not . . .' is that 'you could not know what is not – that cannot be done – nor indicate it' (fr. 2 ll. 7–8).

This may all seem a bit baffling. If it was ever self-evident what Parmenides meant by *esti*, it is no longer. The Greek verb is used in a number of different senses, and it is not clear which of them, or how many of them, is in question. Furthermore, *esti* seems, as Parmenides uses it, to lack a subject. It is not clear what subject should be supplied, or if a subject needs to be supplied by the reader. Finally, it is still unclear how we should assess his argument in favour of *esti*: we still do not understand, philosophically, how we manage, so succesfully, to speak of nothing (of what does not exist) – in referring to mermaids or to Mr Pickwick.

It may be sufficient for our present purposes, however, to remark that it seems generally agreed now that there is at least an existential component in Parmenides' use of the verb *einai* (we often need to take *esti* as 'it exists'). And where Parmenides argues that *esti* is the only possible route of enquiry and rejects the rival route *ouk esti*, *esti* seems to have existential force. As to the subject of the poem, I shall simply note the attractive view of Owen (1960), that Parmenides is examining the conditions of enquiry, and that we can take whatever we want to enquire into as the subject of the verb. As to the problem of speaking about nothing, that would seem to lie well outside our current remit.[23]

Let us turn, then, to Parmenides' attempt to find a secure foundation for his argument, and to the deductive argument he builds on that foundation. In respect of both these features of his philosophy, Parmenides is breaking important new ground. Deductive argument, as we saw on p. 10 above, is sometimes thought to be the philosophical method *par excellence*. Certainly it is the most powerful form of argument in philosophy; valid deductive arguments based on true premisses are not open to challenge. The attempt to build a philosophical position on the securest possible foundation is also philosophically significant, and will resurface later in the history of philosophy, notably with Descartes.

If we want to challenge Parmenides' conclusions, we must either locate a fallacy in his deductive argument, or challenge the truth of his premiss *esti*. I shall look first at the premiss *esti* and explore a little the parallel between this and Descartes' premiss '*cogito, ergo sum*'.

Descartes seeks an 'Archimedean point' which is firm and immovable, at the start of the second Meditation, after he has applied the method of doubt in the first Meditation, and discovered that all his everyday beliefs are not firm and immovable, but are subject to doubt. Descartes finds what he is looking for in the thought '*cogito, ergo sum*'. *Esti* plays the same role for Parmenides. But, whereas Descartes will later reinstate many of the beliefs that he discards in the first Meditation, as his argument progresses, Parmenides aims (at least if we take him at his word) to completely supplant and destroy the everyday beliefs that he has left behind on his journey to see the goddess.

Descartes' argument cannot advance beyond the *cogito* (and propositions of the form 'it seems to me that p'), unless we accept the argument for the existence of God that he advances in the third Meditation. None the less, the Archimedean point of the *cogito* has also been challenged. Commentators ask whether Descartes has a right to his use of the first person here; but also from where the *cogito* derives its certainty. Let us now ask a parallel question about Parmenides' premiss *esti*: from where does it derive its certainty?

As we have seen, Parmenides thinks it derives its certainty from the fact that we do indicate and we do know. The rival route of enquiry, the route of not being, is an 'altogether indiscernible track' (fr. 2. l.4). Thinking, but not thinking about something that is, is self-defeating, in the same way that thinking, but thinking 'I am not thinking' is self-defeating. In the case of Descartes, the claim '*cogito, ergo sum*' is essentially first-personal: it is *I* who must realise the self-evidence of the cogito. In the case of Parmenides, the claim is third-personal: I can perhaps persuade myself that I am indicating what is not; it is a knowledgeable observer who will realise that I am deceiving myself in such a case.

But this is perhaps not the most important aspect of Parmenides' argument against the route *ouk esti*, '. . . is not . . .'. Let us remind ourselves of fr. 2 ll. 7–8: 'you could not know what is not – that cannot be done – nor could you indicate it'. From the idea that we cannot know or indicate what is not, Parmenides draws conclusions about what there is. It would seem then, that he is intent on exploring the conditions of successful knowing and indicating, in the manner of Kant (the comparison between Parmenides and Kant is drawn by Barnes 1979a: 163). Parmenides may be offering here the first example of a transcendental argument in philosophy (though of course he does not recognise it or categorise it as such).

So a brief word about transcendental arguments may be in order. A transcendental argument is supposed to show us the necessary conditions of experience or knowledge. It tells us the nature of phenomena, not noumena, in Kant's terminology. That is to say, it tell us how the world necessarily seems to us to be, and not how the world actually is, and thus gives rise to a position Kant calls 'transcendental idealism'. When the practice of analysing the metaphysics of experience is separated from the belief in the noumenal realm, and is viewed as a self-subsistent method of philosophical analysis, as it is, notably by P.F. Strawson, it has been termed 'descriptive metaphysics'. The idea of descriptive metaphysics is that we learn more clearly how we actually take the world to be, through laying bare the most general features of our conceptual structure (see Strawson 1959: 9).

The metaphysics of Parmenides is, of course, revisionary and not descriptive. Furthermore, Parmenides is not trying to establish a Kantian transcendental idealism. But he does want to set out the necessary conditions of human knowledge and reference. And he is not, in fact, the only ancient philosopher with such interests.

Plato too, after setting out some criticisms of the theory of Forms in the *Parmenides*, remarks that if there are no Forms, there is nowhere for us to turn our thoughts and that it will destroy our ability to talk to one another (135bc). Forms are, for middle-period Plato, the necessary conditions of human language and thought. Parmenides, though, is first in the field, and it is with Parmenides that we find the first trace of idealism (albeit of a transcendental variety) in philosophy.[24]

Parmenides does not ask the question 'what is there?', but 'what must there be, if we are to know and indicate?'. This second question seems more epistemological than ontological; an answer to it will constitute a truth about our conceptual structure, about how things must seem to us, and not a truth about the world. Kant is prepared to accept, and indeed to maintain, in opposition to sceptics, that there is no way forward to knowledge of things in themselves on the basis of knowledge of how things must seem to us. Descartes, whose '*cogito ergo sum*' seems to express a truth about ourselves, hopes to find his way back to truths about the rest of the world through a proof of the existence of a God who is no deceiver. We might expect that Parmenides, like Descartes, would seek to work back from a truth that he thinks we can know for certain, but a truth about ourselves, to some truths about the external world. But Parmenides, by contrast with Kant and Descartes, seems to have a rather unsophisticated attitude towards this problem. So far as we can tell, he simply believes that when he has told us how the world must be, he has told us the truth about the world, and that he has found a sort of short cut through epistemology to truths about metaphysics. (The problem with his approach, of course, is that maybe we are doomed to think of the world as being a way that in fact it is not.)

Parmenides establishes, then, to his own satisfaction, the secure premiss *esti*.[25] And from this premiss, Parmenides proceeds to derive his conclusions. Hussey summarises the general form of Parmenides' argument as follows:

> whatever is, is F; for suppose not, then something is not-F; but to explain what it is for anything to be not-F involves the introduction of what is not into our account; hence, it is inconceivable that anything is not-F. So whatever is is F.
> (Hussey, 1972: 95)

Thus, for example, Parmenides argues that, 'nor is it more here and less there, which would prevent it from holding together, but it is all full of being' (fr. 8. ll. 23–4).

Hussey notes that not all Parmenides' applications of this form of argument are equally convincing. But the point for us to note is that most, if not all, of Parmenides' conclusions do follow, using this argument form, if only we are prepared to accept the premiss. To put it in a nutshell: if there is no notbeing, there is no temporal notbeing and no spatial notbeing, but just uniform being, at all times and in all places.

We are then faced by our next problem, namely how to intepret the nature of Parmenides' conclusions. There are several related problems here. One concerns the coherence of the argument (is it self-refuting?; does this matter?). A second concerns the nature of the conclusions (did Parmenides intend us to take them at face value?). A third concerns the relation of the Way of Truth to the Way of Seeming.

About the Way of Seeming, KRS say, 'why that elaborate account was included in the poem remains a mystery: the goddess seeks to save the phenomena as far as possible, but she knows and tells us that the project is impossible' (KRS, 1983: 262). Owen suggests that its purpose is 'wholly dialectical' (Owen, 1960: 54). It is a device for buttonholing potential converts, who might initially be interested and impressed by the cosmogony, and who might later become convinced by the arguments of the Way of Truth.[26] Guthrie suggests that Parmenides may think of 'seeming' as 'a phantom or image of reality (Plato would call it an *eikon*)' (Guthrie 1965: 75). A more pessimistic interpretation is advanced by Hussey, who reminds us of Aristotle's words, 'Parmenides, being forced to follow the *phainomena*, supposed that, according to reason, the one existed, but according to sense-perception, many things existed' (and so went on to write the Way of Seeming, *Metaphysics* 986b27–33). Hussey remarks that 'between a statement about that which is and one about the world of ordinary experience there can be no contradiction, because the latter is not false but strictly meaningless' (Hussey, 1972: 99).

Hussey suggests that philosophically, 'the position is perhaps tenable, though exceedingly uncomfortable' (Hussey, 1972: 99). As an interpretation of Parmenides, however, the position seems viable: the Way of Truth tells us how things are in the world; the Way of Seeming tells us how things seem to us – both before and after we have learned the truth. It is certainly not that far-fetched a supposition that we live continuously in error about the world. At least, this supposition has been entertained by other philosophers. We might think once again of Descartes: if there were a malicious demon, we could be universally deceived about the source of our sensory experience. And the idea that we might be continuously in error about some part of life has recently been maintained by Mackie (1977) in regard to ethics. According to Mackie's analysis of the language of morals, whenever we use a word like 'kind' or 'cruel', 'good' or 'bad', we presuppose the objectivity of ethics. But, on Mackie's view, this does not guarantee the objectivity of ethics. Far from it – Mackie's thesis is that ethics is, in fact, a human invention, and ethical properties are not part of the fabric of the world. So it seems at least conceivable that for Parmenides, the Way of Seeming tells us how we ordinarily take the world to be; but the Way of Truth reveals to us the way the world must be (or must seem to us if we enquire into it).

Let us now turn to the problems posed by the content of Parmenides' conclusions. Parmenides' conclusions are, of course, completely at variance with our everyday view of the world. That is not in itself problematic. In fact it may sometimes be a welcome feature of a philosophical argument: it may be that we have learnt something new. On the other hand, we might, perhaps, (with the later Wittgenstein and the pragmatist tradition) be suspicious of anything that seems to undermine our everyday experience. But we do not have to think that we must be right about everything in everyday life to view Parmenides' conclusions with some concern. Having initially promised to show us the consequences of analysing necessary conditions of human knowledge and human indicating, he seems to wind up with conclusions that call into question human language itself. His argument seems, thereby, to be rendered self-defeating, and his conclusions incredible.

Our discussion of these two problems must necessarily be speculative. Parmenides gives us no guidance on how to take his argument or his conclusions. He simply presents us with the Way of Truth, and then moves on to the Way of Seeming. His only comment about language in relation to being is 'Therefore it has been named all the names that mortals have laid down believing them to be true – coming into being and perishing, being and not being, changing place and altering in bright colour' (fr. 8, ll. 38–41). This seems to exhibit a recognition that there is only one thing – the one thing that there is, for all words to refer to. But it does not offer a solution of that problem.

Let us recognise at this point first that it is just conceivable that the problem of the coherence of the argument has been overstated. Scott Austin has recently argued that perhaps Parmenides only disapproves of assertoric negative existentials and negative predications, and that his poem is in fact free from such locutions (Austin, 1986: 30). Another approach to the problem of the argument is that of Owen, who offers to Parmenides the Sextus/Wittgenstein image of the ladder that can be thrown away after use (Owen, 1960: 322; Parmenides, as Owen notes, says at 8.2–3 that he is only presenting *signs* on the way to a conclusion).[27] This is perhaps the best reconciliation we can achieve between Parmenides' argument and his conclusions, if we think there does seem to be a problem of potential self-refutation on hand. (There is, however, this difference between Parmenides and Sextus: that Parmenides seems very keen to convince us through the power of his argument; whereas Sextus is unconcerned about everything except our tranquillity. For further discussion, see Chapter 5.)

Ideas first developed in relation to scepticism can also help us understand the problem of how we should regard the conclusions of the argument. The most perceptive discussion of this issue is by Furth (1968), who outlines three possible interpretations. First, it may have been the case that Parmenides simply believed his results himself, and expected us to believe them too. In that case, as Furth comments, he was surely mad (Furth, 1968: 268).[28] Second, he may have done as Hume who entertained his sceptical doubts only in his study. Thus Hume in the *Enquiry* writes that 'the great subverter of Pyrrhonism or the excessive principles of scepticism is action, and employment and the occupations of common life' (pp.158–9). (Of course, there is this difference between Hume and Parmenides, that it would be difficult to believe Parmenides' results even in the study.) But third, Parmenides may not have believed his conclusions at all. He may have seen them, rather, as a sort of Zenonian challenge to the reader to discover the hidden assumptions on which these arguments rest, and then to discard or modify those assumptions.

We simply do not know how Parmenides himself responded to this problem. There are attractions in all three suggestions advanced by Furth; we do not need to choose between them. As to ourselves, Parmenides' conclusions present us with a problem that for us is notional, rather than real. We are not in fact inclined to accept his conclusions; so we do not have to make up our minds how seriously to take them. The problem for Parmenides was real, rather than notional, however, if he did think the Way of Truth proceeded from a true premiss by way of valid deductive arguments.

Parmenides gives us the first extended treatment of epistemology. He is the first (but not the last) philosopher to present us with conclusions that are well nigh incredible, but that none the less are grounded in powerful argument. Thus it is that for his immediate philosophical successors, Parmenides set the first philosophical problem (as distinct from the first philosophical question). The argument seems very powerful; but how can it possibly be right? His successors will attempt to reconcile his epistemology with the common-sense view of the world, or Parmenides' account of being (of how the world is) with the senses' account of seeming (of how the world seems to us). To that extent, they will become deflected from empirical investigation of the world and from questions bearing on the conduct of everyday life.

Parmenides' attempt to find a secure point of departure for his argument and his attempt to discover truths of metaphysics through examining necessary conditions of linguistic experience and knowledge have exercised a permanent influence on the practice of philosophy: we have seen above how his work compares with that of Descartes and Kant. It may be that this influence has not been altogether benign. Few arguments are ultimately coercive; no-one has yet found an indisputably firm starting-point in epistemology; and there may well be no epistemological short cut to the truth about metaphysics. But Parmenides sets us all an example: he follows the argument where it leads. And Parmenides' development of his argument reminds us that philosophy is not just applied common sense, but a subject that can itself evoke awe and wonder.

ZENO

Zeno has provoked very different reactions among modern commentators: KRS sums him up as 'the Presocratic with most life in him today' (KRS, 1983: 279). Barnes calls him, on the one hand, 'the most celebrated of Presocratic thinkers' (Barnes 1979a: 231), but on the other hand 'no original thinker' (Barnes, 1979a:

294) and 'a prince of philosophers *malgré lui*' (Barnes, 1979a: 295). There are also different views as to his intentions. According to Guthrie, he is 'a single-minded defender of Parmenides' (Guthrie, 1965: 100). For Vlastos, he also argues in good faith for his conclusions; but Vlastos sees other construals of his paradoxes as revealing 'a bluffer and a trickster' (Vlastos, 1959: 180). He feels that we must decide whether Zeno is 'honestly misguided or wilfully misleading' (Vlastos, 1959: 181). Barnes chooses the latter option, and sets him in the company of Gorgias. Zeno provokes these reactions on the basis of the three or four verbatim quotations from his work, and on the basis of the four paradoxes of motion reported in Aristotle's *Physics*.

With Zeno, we come, for the first time, to arguments that are termed 'dialectical' and also [by Plato] 'hypothetical'. There is a clear sense in which Zeno's arguments are hypothetical: he follows up the consequences of the hypothesis 'there are many', a hypothesis to which no-one, perhaps, in the normal course of events, explicitly assents, but to which we all, in everyday life, assent implicitly. (The hypothesis 'there are many' is simply that there are many things in the world, and not, as Parmenides had argued, just one.) And there is also a clear sense in which his arguments are dialectical. They are addressed *ad hominem* and find their grip only with those who do assent to the hypothesis. (Of course, Zeno's arguments are not 'dialectical' in all senses of the word. His arguments are not at all like the dialectical arguments of Socrates, for instance, as Vlastos has emphasised (Vlastos, 1983). There is none of the laying on the line of one's own beliefs that we find is so important for Socrates. And Zeno, unlike Socrates, develops his paradoxes single-handedly, without the aid of an interlocutor.)

In this section, I shall discuss first the role of sceptical paradoxes such as Zeno's in philosophy, and enquire into Zeno's motivation in advancing them. I shall then examine the different sorts of response that can be offered to such paradoxes, and discuss Aristotle's report of two of Zeno's paradoxes of motion, the paradox of the arrow, where Zeno argues that a moving arrow is at rest, and the paradox of Achilles who, Zeno claims, is unable to overtake a tortoise.

There is one general view of the nature of philosophical questions and arguments into which Zeno seems to fit quite neatly, and that might lead us to wonder if he is not, perhaps, in an important sense, the archetypal philosopher. This is the view that philosophers typically ask questions about possibility rather than actuality – that the natural form of the philosophical question is not 'is it the case that p?', but rather 'how is it possible that p?'. I shall focus on Nozick's statement of this view in the Introduction to his book *Philosophical Explanations* (Nozick, 1981) – though I believe it is in fact quite widely held to be true.

Nozick develops here at length his view of philosophy as persuasion, and of past philosophers as largely coming up with what he terms 'apparent excluders' of everyday beliefs. Thus one philosopher – Zeno, for instance, comes up with an apparent excluder of an everyday truth – motion is possible, for instance. Thus he sets his successors – such as Aristotle, in this case, the task of showing how motion is possible, of explaining, or accounting for motion. The task is not to demonstrate that we do move (we all know that already). The point of the philosophical enterprise, on this view, is, rather, that we understand motion (or, perhaps, our everyday or scientific beliefs about motion) better as a result of this process.

Whether all history of philosophy can be fitted into this schema is a moot point. We have already seen some philosophers in action; and Zeno is the first we have encountered who seems to fit the bill at all well. But he is, at least, not alone in so doing among ancient philosophers. For example, Plato asks a question of the canonical form in the *Sophist* – namely 'how is falsehood possible?'. We all know that we can, and do, tell lies. What Plato must do is to explain how this is possible in the face of a powerful apparent 'excluder'.

Setting on one side, for now, the question of how far other philosophers' practice of philosophy fits Nozick's schema, let us ask whether it gives the right account of Zeno. KRS think so. They remark about fr. B3 that it is 'designed to provoke in us philosophical reflection about what makes a thing one and not many' (KRS, 1983: 266); about frs B1 and B2 they say 'a diagnosis requires of one a deep and clear-sighted engagement with the philosophical problems of infinity' (KRS, 1983: 268); and about the arrow and the moving rows that 'both paradoxes expose difficulties in our ordinary unreflective thought about motion' (KRS, 1983: 276).

Whether Zeno *intended* the paradoxes to provoke philosophical reflection of this sort, though, is a moot point. We may recall

Vlastos' view that Zeno argues in good faith for his conclusions and that he is honestly misguided rather than wilfully misleading. Vlastos thus holds the view that Zeno believed his conclusions, and sought to recommend them to his readers (rather than to provoke them to philosophical reflection).

This construal of Zeno's motivation has a long history, going back to what Plato says in *Parmenides* 128–9.[29] Plato's 'Zeno' says there that

> There was no pretence of any great purpose: nor any serious intention of deceiving the world. The truth is that these writings of mine were meant to protect the arguments of Parmenides against those who make fun of him and seek to show the many ridiculous and contradictory results which they suppose to follow from the affirmation of the one. My answer is addressed to the partisans of the many, whose attack I return with interest by retorting upon them their hypothesis of the existence of many, if carried out, appears to be still more ridiculous than the hypothesis of the existence of the one.
>
> (tr. Barnes, 1979a: 232–3)

Plato says, then, that Zeno did intend to defend Parmenides, but that he did so indirectly, by attacking the common sense hypothesis of the existence of the many (i.e. the view that there are many items in the world, and not just one). The idea is that the Eleatic position offers the only logically viable account of reality. We should note, however, that Zeno does not consistently occupy the Eleatic position. As KRS comment about their 316, in some cases, 'common sense and Parmenidean metaphysics can be embarrassed by the same dialectical manoeuvres' (KRS, 1983: 269). And, in any event, the Eleatic position is so intrinsically implausible, that it does not seem to constitute very much of a solution to the puzzles. Here, then, is one problem with accepting Zeno's arguments at face value, as Vlastos recommends. This is not to say that we should adopt the other side of Vlastos' dichotomy and say that Zeno was a bluffer and a trickster; but simply that the notion of good faith here is more complicated than Vlastos gives us to believe.

Plato goes on to report a puzzle to the effect that if there are many, they are both like and unlike – a puzzle which Socrates proceeds to resolve with the aid of the theory of Forms. What is initially puzzling about this paradox, as reported is that, it does not seem very paradoxical. Why shouldn't everything be both like and unlike? Everything is, after all, like some things and unlike others. We should remember, however, that Plato did think that this was puzzling, and that he believes that we need to invoke his theory of Forms at this point, if we are to resolve the apparent contradiction here, and still retain a pluralist ontology. So perhaps Zeno too took this puzzle to present a serious problem for the pluralist.[30] It may be salutary to remind ourselves both that philosophical problems sometimes come to be resolved and therefore no longer appear to be problematic, and also that not all Zeno's paradoxes may be pitched at the same level of difficulty.[31]

The second part of Plato's *Parmenides*, which is explicitly said to follow the Zenonian method (135d), may also help us understand better the work of Zeno. Here the interlocutors examine the consequences of the Eleatic hypothesis 'if the One is', and of the companion hypothesis, 'if the One is not'. (It is hard to interpret these hypotheses, which are clearly ambiguous, and whose ambiguity Plato may well exploit, knowingly or unknowingly.) From both hypotheses, they draw a series of apparently contradictory conclusions, just as Zeno is said to have done from examining the consequences of the hypothesis 'if the many are'.

It is hard to know what conclusions to draw from Plato's Zenonian exercise.[32] But one moral that Plato may be encouraging us to draw is that one and many, and being and notbeing, are not opposed to one another. On this view, his *Parmenides* shows us Plato in transition from his middle period to his late period – and, in particular, from his early attempt to explain the coincidence of such apparent opposites with the aid of the theory of Forms, to his later acceptance of the universal coincidence of these terms in the *Sophist*. From this perspective, it seems that some arguments in the dialogue trade on the early notion that 'being' and 'notbeing' are opposites, while in others they are treated as mere non-identicals. This helps Plato produce seemingly contradictory conclusions from a single, apparently coherent, premiss. But, whether we look at the exercise from the vantage point of the middle or the late period, the fact remains that some of the arguments are not going to seem as convincing as others. Some are transparently fallacious. Some trade on equivocations in the premiss 'if the One is'. Others, as I have just indicated, introduce questionable collateral assumptions. Now let us try to imagine what it would be like if we had only six or seven arguments from the second part of Plato's *Parmenides*. Some would almost certainly seem to be better arguments than others. And some would be arguments that Plato himself believed – but by no means all of them. It would be very hard – perhaps impossible, to draw conclusions concerning Plato's purposes. Even though the whole dialogue has survived, this is still by no means an easy task.

Still, let us move on and ask about replies to sceptical arguments, an area where Lear and Kripke have recently produced ideas of great interest.

Lear has argued persuasively that in responding to a sceptical argument, a philosopher is not necessarily aiming to produce a reply that will argue the sceptic out of his scepticism (Lear, 1980, 1981, 1988). In Aristotle's so-called 'dialectical' defence of the law of contradiction for example ('dialectical' here means *ad hominem*), the opponent in question is, obviously, someone who doesn't hold the law of contradiction to be true. Aristotle asks only that the man say something, or signify something, and then claims to be able to refute him. The point Aristotle is making, as Lear draws it out and reformulates it, is that 'assertions divide up the world' (Lear, 1981: 112). But it is the unprejudiced observer who will appreciate the strength of Aristotle's argument, and not the *ad hominem* opponent, the sceptic about the law of contradiction. For the sceptic holds that the law is both true and false, and so no argument that the law is true is going to embarrass him.

Lear offers a similar account of Aristotle's response to Zeno's paradox of the arrow (discussed below). Zeno is not going to be convinced by the Aristotelian resolution (or indeed by any other resolution that we find in the literature). This is because Aristotle starts by assuming the existence of periods of time as well as the existence of the present; whereas for Zeno there is only the present. But Lear holds the best reply to a sceptical argument such as Zeno's will often be to start from truly held beliefs, and work from there. And indeed Aristotle's philosophy of time is what Lear calls 'rigorously presented' rather than argued for.[33]

In Lear's view, this also explains why you can't keep a good paradox down. There might always turn out to be some error among the truly held beliefs that you started from in responding to the sceptical argument. Those who do not accept Aristotle's philosophy of time, will not accept his response to Zeno's arrow paradox. For such philosophers, the paradox will spring to life again, and require a fresh response.

Lear, then, makes points about how we should start to reply to a sceptical argument, and who we should address ourselves to, when we do so. Another sort of classification of replies to sceptical arguments is also possible, and helpful. This is the distinction drawn originally by Hume, and set out recently by Kripke, between 'sceptical' and 'straight' replies to sceptical arguments.[34]

Kripke calls a 'straight' solution to a sceptical argument one that 'shows on close examination that the scepticism proves unwarranted' (Kripke, 1982: 66). Kripke gives as an example Descartes' solution to the sceptical doubts voiced in the first Meditation. A 'sceptical' solution to a sceptical argument, by contrast, 'begins by conceding that the sceptic's negative conclusions are unanswerable. Nevertheless our ordinary practice or belief is justified because – contrary practice or belief notwithstanding – it need not require the justification the sceptic has shown to be untenable' (Kripke, 1982: 66). Kripke cites as an example Hume, who sees his theory of causation as a sceptical solution to a sceptical problem. Hume holds, as Kripke puts it, extending a discussion of Wittgenstein's 'private language' argument, that there is no 'private causation'. That is to say, that 'causation makes no sense applied to two isolated events, with the rest of the universe removed'. None the less, Hume's regularity theory of causation can vindicate our everyday practices. Similarly, in Kripke's view, with Wittgenstein's private language argument. 'It turns out that the sceptical solution does not allow us to speak of a single individual, considered by himself and in isolation, as ever meaning anything' (Kripke, 1982: 68–9). But: 'others . . . will have justification conditions for attributing correct or incorrect rule-following to the subject' (Kripke, 1982: 89).

We can put this point in terms of the common ground shared, in such cases, between the sceptic and his opponent. A 'straight' resolution of a sceptical paradox fully vindicates common sense. A sceptical resolution of a sceptical paradox has at least as much in common with the sceptical, as with a common sense starting point.

For reasons that should now be clear, there is no single, simple, agreed, answer to Zeno's paradoxes. Some philosophers attempt a sceptical, others a straight resolution of the paradoxes; some attack Zeno's position, others are content with self-defence. And not all would-be rebuttals of Zeno depart from the same point (the same philosophy of time and space). But there are certain moves that we all feel tempted to make, and that will probably enter somewhere into our reply to Zeno; and most of them we owe to Aristotle. So I propose to set out Aristotle's reports of two of the paradoxes of motion, and to offer some comments on the solutions that Aristotle offers to those paradoxes.

Aristotle reports the paradox of the arrow as follows: 'if everything always rests or moves whenever it is against what is equal, and what is travelling is always in the now, the travelling arrow is motionless' (239b5–7). The idea is that if we consider an arrow in flight, on its way to a target (as we would ordinarily think), it always in the now occupies the space it occupies, that is, a space equal to itself. But if something occupies a space equal to itself, it is at rest. So the arrow is both in motion and at rest, according to our common sense beliefs.

Aristotle's response to the argument is given, in brief, at 239b30–33: it is that time is not composed of 'nows'. The 'now' for Aristotle is what we might see these days as a sort of hybrid conception, the 'present instant'. And sometimes commentators take the response to be essentially that time is not composed of instants; sometimes, however, the notion of the present is also thought to have a role to play in Aristotle's thinking.

Let us look first at the question of whether time is composed of instants, or whether it is composed of very small periods of time. A commentator who thinks that clarity on this question is a sufficient response to the paradox, is Guthrie, who remarks that the paradox is 'only effective on the premiss that time consists of indivisible minimal instants' (Guthrie, 1965: 93). Vlastos also thinks along these lines, although he gives Aristotle much less credit for seeing the correct solution of the paradox. In fact he maintains that 'now' is 'an Aristotelian plant', designed to 'make it all the easier to feel the appropriateness of his refutation' (Vlastos, 1966a: 187). He concedes that Aristotle's resolution has some force (Vlastos, 1966a: 191); but thinks it does not fully bring out the point that 'the sense in which the Arrow is not moving in any instant is vastly different from that in which the Rock of Gibraltar is not moving in any day, hour, or second' (Vlastos, 1966a: 191–2). To understand the issues involved in the paradox, thinks Vlastos, Zeno 'would have needed to possess a clear-cut understanding of the instant/interval distinction', but 'he did not even have a term for instant and could only get at this concept indirectly' (Vlastos 1966a:192).

Owen criticises Aristotle's solution on very similar grounds. Aristotle says the arrow is neither moving nor stationary in the now – i.e. at any instant 't'. But 'the possibility of talking about motion at a moment rests on the possibility of talking of motion over a period'; and so 'the two senses of motion are not the same' (Owen, 1957–8: 160): 'the two senses of motion are not identical but yet systematically connected' (Owen, 1957–8: 160–1). Aristotle's solution thus involves 'an unjustified departure from usage' (Owen, 1957–8: 161).

Lear (1981) thinks there are two possible resolutions to the paradox, one of which involves central reference to our view of the present: either we must adopt the Aristotelian view that time is not composed of nows and that the present has no duration. Or, if we accept that the present does have duration, we must hold that motion is to be analysed in terms of being at 't' in one position and 't' at another, and agree that at the instant the arrow is stationary.[35]

It is, of course, not our intention here to resolve the paradox of the arrow; but simply to note how we might go about resolving such a sceptical paradox. In the case of the arrow, we can see that Aristotle's initial response to the paradox has great power – but may still stand in need of supplement and correction. Much the same is true of the paradoxes of the race-course and Achilles.

Aristotle says about the paradox of Achilles that 'it amounts to this, that in a race the quickest runner can never overtake the slower but must always hold a lead. The argument is the same in principle as that which depends on bisection' (i.e. the race-course, 239b18–20). The idea is that to complete a journey, one must first complete half that journey; for Achilles to catch the tortoise (who has a head start), he must first reach the starting point of the tortoise. But this leads to an infinite regress, in both cases.

Aristotle makes two responses to these paradoxes. In *Physics* VI, he points out that time too is divisible (233a21); and in *Physics* VIII, he says that we must distinguish between actual and potential infinity (263a28). There is not much mileage in the first of these remarks. But suitably reformulated, the second would seem to offer a fruitful line of approach. Thus Vlastos thinks the crucial distinction lies between the physical individuation of the agent's movements on the one hand (in terms, for example, of strides), and the mathematics of the infinite series invoked by the paradox on the other (½ + ¼ + . . .). The point is that the mathematically infinite series of tasks is not physically individuated and hence it does 'not pre-empt in any way the physical exertions of the agent' (Vlastos, 1966b: 214). Lear has introduced in this context the notion of a 'staccato' run, where the runner goes in for example thirty seconds to the midpoint of his journey, rests thirty seconds, then goes to the three-quarter point in the next fifteen seconds, and rests fifteen seconds, and so on (Lear, 1988: 70). Lear plausibly suggests that this would count as actualising an infinity of points on the line, and that, in Aristotle's view, the physical exertions of the agent would be pre-empted, and he could not complete the run.

As in the case of the arrow, then, Aristotle's response to the paradox stands in need of reformulation, and possibly in need of supplement and revision. And Aristotle's approach, even as modified by Vlastos and Lear, has, on occasion, been rejected outright. Notably, Barnes (1979a) is dismissive of this line of approach, arguing that either the description 'infinitely many tasks' holds good of the journey or it does not and that if it does, the paradox retains its full force (Barnes, 1979a: 273).[36]

Whatever view of the paradoxes we ultimately endorse, our survey of them has helped us understand how the formulation of apparent excluders of known truths, and attempts to rebut the excluders can be worthwhile in philosophy. Zeno's paradoxes do help us clarify our views about motion, space, time and infinity, and lead us into a deeper understanding of these topics. Whether formulating sceptical paradoxes is the only way to bring about such a result, may be doubted, however. We have already encountered other perfectly viable conceptions of philosophical method. Others still will be surveyed in the chapters that follow.

ANAXAGORAS

Schofield suggests a seemingly rather harsh verdict on Anaxagoras' merits as a philosopher in the Introduction to his *Essay on Anaxagoras*. There he presents a contrast between the actual Anaxagoras and the ideal philosopher in the form of a Pythagorean table of opposites, as follows:

Ideal Philosopher	*Actual Anaxagoras*
argumentative	narrative
enquiring	dogmatic
co-operative	didactic
reason	authority
common sense	special insight
clear	ambiguous
determinate	indeterminate
classical	archaic
fluent literate	early literate
epistemological	metaphysical

(Schofield, 1980: 1)

Questions about this table immediately spring to mind. Is the ideal philosopher really wedded to common sense and to epistemology, rather than to special insight and metaphysics? What is the contrast between determinacy and indeterminacy? Is it really a problem that Anaxagoras tells us his results, and does not invite us to join him on his route of enquiry? 'Archaic' and 'early literate' are qualities that Anaxagoras presumably shares with all the Presocratics. And does he really just tell us stories? As we read the first chapter of Schofield's book, however, an image emerges that draws together and explains the rationale behind several of these contrasts. The central point is that Anaxagoras is not writing in the contemporary analytic tradition, but in the Ionian tradition of cosmological narrative. He needs to compress all his teaching into one short and memorable treatise, which can (a) record his thought for posterity, and (b) serve as a basis for oral presentations and discussions of his views. Many features of his style derive from his circumstances. This image of Anaxagoras is reinforced by the apparently kinder judgement of Hussey, that he was 'a sensitive and subtle mind, fertile, but not analytic' (Hussey, 1972: 141).

As may perhaps already be clear, much of the detailed work of modern commentators on Anaxagoras consists in analytic presentations of his central theses, the main task being to try and make them hold together coherently. Was Anaxagoras just an analytic philosopher *manqué*? Perhaps he was. Certainly he could have benefited from a stronger bent for analysis. What we need to ask, though, is what there is to be said for Anaxagoras' work as it stands. Does Anaxagoras need to be that good at analysis to be a worthwhile philosopher? I shall suggest that his work does have some value as it stands – that it presents us with a philosophical picture rather than a philosophical argument, but that this is not necessarily a bad thing. His central theses interlock successfully, and yield a picture of the world that is coherent, persuasive and hard to undermine.

We know, or we can work out, as we did for the first time with Zeno, the problematic – the need to respond to the Eleatics. Thus KRS claim that the views of Anaxagoras and the Atomists 'are each the outcome as much of the Eleatic paradox as of the inventiveness of their respective authors' (KRS, 1983: 378).[37] This is also the view of Barnes, who lists 'five main lines of contact between the Eleatics and the Neo-Ionians' (Barnes, 1979b: 14–15). We can summarise these points as follows:

(1) There is no absolute generation
(2) Alteration is possible
(3) Locomotion is possible
(4) A 'moving cause' is provided
(5) The methodology of empirical observation is reinstated.

(1) marks the extent to which the Eleatics actually convinced anyone of anything. (2)–(5) mark areas of disagreement between the Eleatics and their successors. Barnes thinks that (5) is vital for the progress of science, and that (3) is the crucial point philosophically.

Let us start by measuring the extent of Anaxagoras' agreement with Parmenides. First, there is his fundamental tenet that what there was in the beginning is what there is now. Thus fr. 6, 'everything is together now just as it was in the beginning'. Barnes speaks in this context of a 'fundamental similarity between world past and world present' (Barnes 1979b: 33).[38] Second, Anaxagoras agrees with Parmenides that nothing comes to be from what it is not (fr. 10 if authentic) and nothing comes to be from what is not (fr. 3: what is cannot not-be).[39]

But unlike the Eleatics, Anaxagoras believes in a plural and changing universe. So he cannot simply say that in the beginning there was what there is now, but must also explain how what there was then has changed into what there is now, and how one thing differs from another.

To this end, Anaxagoras formulated a number of principles, differently named by different commentators. Let us start with (1) the principle of mixture, which is the single most important principle, for Anaxagoras, and which underlies his explanation of both plurality and change. This is that 'in everything there is a share of everything' (fr. 11, fr. 12). This is a difficult principle to interpret. Cornford thought it meant that 'a portion of every opposite is in every substance' (Cornford 1930: 311), but his suggestion has not found much favour. And there is a very good reason for this. As KRS and Hussey point out, the two occurrences of 'everything' should be co-referential (KRS, 1983: 366; Hussey, 1972: 135–6). That still does not make the principle straightforward, however. As Hussey says, Anaxagoras manifestly cannot mean for example that 'there is a portion of this chair in that table'. For this just makes no sense (Hussey, 1972: 135–6). Hussey suggests that he means that 'every stuff contains a portion of every other stuff', whilst remarking, however, that this will require us to count, for Anaxagoras, the hot and the cold as stuffs, and not to count earth, air, fire and mind, which Anaxagoras says don't conform to the principle. It will, however, cover the central cases such as gold, flesh, water, and so on.

The other point to note here is Cornford's reason for favouring a more limited version of the principle: namely, that we do not need to assert that there is a portion of everything in everything, in order to account for the changes in the world that we can actually observe. The theory goes well beyond, and even contradicts, the observational evidence. 'Why assert that acorns contain gold, copper and emerald?' asks Cornford (1930: 280). Aristotle says, as if in response to this question, that 'they saw everything coming into being from everything' (*Physics* 187b2–3). But Cornford has doubts about the evidence of Aristotle. And on this particular question, he comments 'This would be the only possible ground for the doctrine as Aristotle understands it'. But 'Anaxagoras saw nothing of the kind' (Cornford 1930: 308).

Now I think we have to accept that Anaxagoras did see nothing of the kind and that Aristotle's criticism of Anaxagoras for making possible too much generation in the world is accordingly justified. Anaxagoras makes no allowance, either with the principle of mixture, or elsewhere in his system, for the fact that the world changes only in certain regular and organised ways. Aristotle's own account of change is superior to Anaxagoras' in this respect.

But there are also other problems with Anaxagoras' view as we have set it out thus far – and problems that he can hope to resolve by calling on some of the other principles that he holds.

Let us return for a moment to Anaxagoras' conception of the Original Position: 'all things were together, unlimited both in quantity and in smallness' (fr. 1). Guthrie comments that

> in the original static mixture, it would seem most natural (at least, for I must be personal here, it would seem so to me) to suppose that the fusion of everything was thorough and complete so that no one thing prevailed over any other in any part of it.
>
> (Guthrie, 1965: 297)[40]

Now of course we can all observe that whatever may have been the case with relation to the original mixture, at the present moment, the fusion of all things is not thorough and complete. So Anaxagoras needs to introduce a principle to explain how things are when their intermixture is not thorough and complete. This principle is introduced at the end of fr. 12: 'Each thing is most manifestly those of which there are the most in it. (tr. Schofield, 1980: 108). For example, what makes gold gold is that gold predominates in it. Let us call this principle the principle of predominance.

Now this is where interpretation becomes difficult. As Strang points out, the problem here is a problem of regress (Strang 1963). If we say that 'what makes gold gold is that gold predominates in it', we can then ask 'what makes that predominating part gold?' and Anaxagoras cannot reply what makes that part gold is that gold predominates in it, because if he does, he will soon reach a point where he will have to admit that gold didn't predominate in the original piece of gold after all.

Of course, Aristotle noticed this problem – and has come in for a lot of criticism, notably from Cornford and Vlastos, for his acuity. Aristotle says that we would sooner or later reach a pure substance (Strang calls them elemental substances, or E-substances) if we divided an everyday specimen of any substance (Strang calls these common substances, or C-substances). Aristotle talks of division where Strang talks of a regress of explanation. But the regress of explanation arises because Anaxagoras' principle of explanation works by division. If we can divide everyday specimens of gold (C-gold) into a predominating part (E-gold) and a non-predominating part (which is not gold at all), and this is what explains why we call the C-gold 'gold', Anaxagoras faces a problem.

Now Cornford says that Aristotle's objection to Anaxagoras here is fatal to his interpretation of Anaxagoras: surely Anaxagoras could not have overlooked this point (Cornford 1930: 309). Now of course, Anaxagoras could not have overlooked this point. And it seems, given his interest in divisibility and his principle of homoiomereity – which I shall discuss shortly – that he had in fact given it quite some thought. This is not to say, however, that he had altogether solved the problem.

One possible solution to the problem is outlined by Strang and Furley: this is the highly Platonic idea that everyday, or C-substances could be explained by the pure or E-substances that predominate in them. To quote part of Furley's comparison of Anaxagoras with Plato:

> Anaxagoras was concerned simply to show how the things of the perceptible world could reasonably be described as having different characters at different times or in different circumstances without supposing that any 'things that are' (*eonta chremata*) have come to be or perished . . . Both theories explain change in the physical world by introducing entities that are themselves eternally unchanging . . . in both, these entities can be described as 'just what [x] is' . . . the objects of the physical world are called after what they partake in. Thus they both function as explanations of predication . . . In both theories the beings that are 'just what [x] is' are inaccessible to sense-perception . . . in both theories it is held that these beings are accessible to the mind.
>
> (Furley, 1976: 83–86)

Now of course there are also differences between Anaxagoras and Plato (some of them are pointed out by Furley in the passages omitted from my quotation). The important point is that Plato is interested not just in metaphysics but in epistemology. Plato, unlike Anaxagoras, wants to explain how we can know the world, and his pure unmixed unitary Forms are set up as ideal objects of knowledge. For Plato the problem is that we cannot know the sensible world, if it is as it seems to be (i.e. if it is characterised by the universal compresence of opposites – for discussion of Plato's view, see Chapters 3 and 4). Anaxagoras, by contrast, is simply concerned that the world should be as as it seems, on the one hand, and that it complies with Eleatic logic, on the other. None the less, the fact remains that Anaxagoras may have believed that there are E-substances that explain why C-substances are as they are.

An alternative solution would be to say that C-substances are what they are because of their ingredients, where these ingredients are not E-substances, but opposites. 'A purely hypothetical construction' along these lines was presented by Vlastos (1950), who writes: 'Any part of flesh is flesh . . . Yet any part of flesh does contain hair, bone and the rest . . . hair can arise out of flesh since the ingredients of flesh are also the ingredients of hair' (Vlastos, 1950: 339). As Strang remarks, one merit of this interpretation is that we don't have to account for stuffs twice, first in terms of E-substances in them, and secondly in terms of opposites. The weak point is that in fact it may, and in Vlastos' view, it does, involve an attack on Aristotle's evidence that stuffs are homoiomerous (or, as Vlastos puts it, simple). On this account, perhaps, stuffs are no longer truly homoiomerous.

As commentators point out, homoiomereity is a term of art coined by Plato in his discussion of the Unity of Virtues in the *Protagoras*, and subsequently taken up by Aristotle. As far as we know, the word itself was not used by Anaxagoras. But that does not, of course, necessarily make it inappropriate. Barnes, following Kerferd (1969), writes, surely correctly, 'Anaxagoras . . . did give some general characterisation of things, and that characterisation seems to Aristotle to fit his own notion of homoiomereity' (Barnes, 1979a: 19). Now a homoiomerous thing is a thing whose parts are of the same sort as the whole. If we cut up a bit of flesh, we have two bits of flesh. But if we cut up a bit of face, we do not have two bits of face, but a nose and a mouth, for example. Flesh is homoiomerous, but face is not. Now the strongest evidence that Anaxagoroas held a principle of homoiomereity is certainly Aristotelian. But Anaxagoras does say that 'the small contains as many portions as the large' (fr. 6). Strang comments that for Anaxagoras, 'structural complexity is not . . . a function of size' (Strang, 1963: 366).

It has been questioned whether the principle of homoiomereity is entirely compatible with the principle of mixture, and the principle of predominance. I shall simply here set out the case for the defence. Schofield, elaborating on an example of Kerferd (1969), discusses a cup of sweet black coffee (1980: 109). He asks,

> why do we call a cup of sweet black coffee "coffee"? Not

> simply because coffee is its major ingredient besides the water that we take for granted, but because it has the distinctive savour and smell and colour of the coffee-bean extract – i.e. because it has a certain set of predominant qualities.
> (Schofield, 1980: 118)

Schofield is here arguing for the view that for Anaxagoras the ingredients of things are substances, and not homoiomerous parts. But this example enables us to see that the principle of homoiomereity can be quite compatible with the principle of predominance. We need, essentially, to distinguish between actual, and theoretical division. Actual division, for Anaxagoras, will always give rise to homoiomerous parts. Theoretically, however, he can acknowledge that things must be composed either of E-substances or opposites as ultimate ingredients. So long as there is infinite divisibility, however (and Anaxagoras held that there was, see fr. 1), it may be impossible, in practice, ever to separate out the pure ingredients that compose C-substances.[41]

It would seem that Anaxagoras' theory is completely coherent. Let us summarise the main points. Things are, in several important respects, very much as we think they are. There is plurality, and there is change. But things are mixtures, in a much more thoroughgoing way than we would normally imagine – there is a bit of everything in everything. This is the underlying fact that makes change and plurality possible (here Anaxagoras is responding to the Eleatic excluders in just the way Nozick predicts). However, this principle does not itself account for change and plurality. The principle of predominance explains plurality – one stuff differs from another because different ingredients predominate in different parts of the world. And change occurs as local predominance conditions alter, through locomotion.

Anaxagoras does not argue for his physical system. It has the character of a philosophical 'picture' rather than a philosophical theory, to adopt a distinction of Kripke's.[42] Kripke remarks that a defect 'probably common to all philosophical theories' is that they are wrong (Kripke, 1980: 64). Philosophical pictures, by contrast, are only more or less satisfactory representations of how things are. And certainly, Anaxagoras has presented a set of interlocking ideas, which is highly resistant to direct challenge. But this is not to say that Anaxagoras' philosophical system is immune to criticism and counter-argument – for example, there may be something to the Aristotelian point that change is more regular than Anaxagoras makes out. And a philosophical 'picture' is always liable to be supplanted when a more attractive rival picture becomes available. A full assessment of the work of Anaxagoras would involve comparing his philosophical picture with the rival philosophical picture formulated for much the same purpose by the Greek atomists (for discussion see the following section).

Anaxagoras' response to the sceptical paradoxes of the Eleatics is a sceptical response, in Kripke's terms (see pp. 42–3 above). Anaxagoras concedes important ground to the Eleatics; and though in a sense he defends a common sense position, the upshot of his response to the Eleatic arguments is that we have to swallow some fairly unexpected theories in order to preserve our view that the world is plural and subject to change. Furthermore, even where Anaxagoras disagrees with Parmenides, he is more concerned with self-defence than with attack. Indeed, he makes no explicit reference to the work of the Eleatics.[43]

And yet Anaxagoras is essentially responding to the Eleatics, and it is only in this context that his views can be properly assessed. This is where philosophy starts to become professionalised: it is no longer possible to take an individual off the streets and tell him the truth about philosophy. Or rather: you can, perhaps, tell him the truth, and he will, perhaps, understand you. But he will see no reason to adopt the true viewpoint until he has first-hand experience of the power of the Eleatic position. This is not, of course, something we can hold against Anaxagoras. It is simply a (perhaps rather unfortunate) aspect of progress in philosophy – a topic to which we will have occasion to return (see Chapter 4).

We might, conceivably, hope for a more robust response to the Eleatics – for a direct attack upon their central theses, and a straight solution of their sceptical paradoxes.[44] As a sceptical solution to the paradoxes, Anaxagoras' system will be hard to surpass.

THE ATOMISTS

The ancient atomists, Leucippus and Democritus, philosophised widely. They spelled out a physical theory in great detail, and they came up with fascinating new ideas in cosmogony and cosmology. Democritus also wrote on ethics 'carrying on the work of poets and moralists before him' (KRS, 1983: 433), and on music and literature, amongst much else. As Guthrie remarks, 'how one longs to know more about this remarkable man than the scattered remnants of his achievement allow' (Guthrie, 1965: 477). Confining ourselves to those scattered remnants, we must conclude that the ancient atomists do not seem to have advanced any theoretical account of the nature of philosophy. And as to their practice of philosophy, for the most part, the atomists simply did rather better than anyone had done before, the same sort of thing as their predecessors. There is little that survives in the fragments of Democritus and Leucippus, or in reports of their work, that can help us understand better the nature of the philosophical enterprise.

There are, however, two exceptions to this generalisation. First, the atomists can help us to further our understanding of sceptical paradoxes and responses to them in so far as they present us with a response to the challenge of the Eleatics, which we can compare with Anaxagoras' response. And second, Democritus faces openly for the first time a deep question that is (arguably) latent in the Presocratic tradition, and which is still of interest to us today. That question is, how our everyday view of the world is to be related to the view that emerges from philosophical, or scientific, investigation. Ancient atomists are not at all like contemporary atomists, of course. As KRS say, the 'real nature and motives' of contemporary atomic theory are 'utterly distinct' from those of the ancient atomists (KRS, 1983: 433). Barnes spells it out: 'Leucippus and Democritus had not observed Brownian motion; they were largely ignorant of chemistry; they did not rest their atomism on a host of special observations' (Barnes, 1979b: 42). For all that, as we shall see, ancient and modern atomism pose much the same sort of challenge to our common-sense beliefs.

Before we investigate the nature of that challenge, however, let us first ask what sort of a response the atomists offered to the arguments of Parmenides and Zeno. Unlike Anaxagoras, they do not present several interlocking ideas that, taken together, serve to rebut the Eleatics. Rather they have one big idea, which is to allow notbeing a role within their system. They hold that atoms and void, the former to be identified with being, the latter with notbeing, exist alike. Thus Aristotle reports that: 'They say that notbeing exists no less than being, in so far as void exists no less than atoms' (*Metaphysics* 985b7–9).

KRS comment about the claim that notbeing exists, that 'it is hard to see how the atomists justified this paradox' (KRS, 1983: 415). However the paradox was justified, there is no shortage of ideas about the role that the notion of void may have played in the atomist system. Thus it has been suggested that void is what separates one atom from another; void is empty space; or void is absolute Newtonian space.[45] Hussey suggests that 'qualitatively, the "nothing" is distinguished from the "thing" simply by its lack of "thingness", by not being an individual with all that that implies' (Hussey, 1972: 143).

Whichever view of the nature of void is correct, what we have here is a case of 'straight' disagreement with Parmenides, and the first step along a path to parricide that Plato will later traverse.[46] On the atomist view, Parmenides is simply mistaken about notbeing; we can and should say that there is void (notbeing). But the atomists do not hold that Parmenides is simply mistaken *tout court*. In fact, they share a substantial amount of common ground with the Eleatics – and to this extent present a sceptical solution to their sceptical challenge. For when the atomists assert that there are indivisible, indestructable atoms (being), they are asserting the existence of tiny counterparts of the Eleatic One and endorsing the Eleatic conception of being. When they assert that never is there any mixture of atoms with void – that their association consists of mere temporary and random contiguities – they are agreeing with Parmenides that being does not associate with notbeing. The atomists may want to 'reconcile the evidence of our senses with Eleatic metaphysics' (KRS 1983 : 408), but this is not, for them, by any means a straightforward process. For the atomists, as much as for any philosopher or scientist, the commonsense view of what there is – the view that there are tables, chairs, and so on – stands in need of both contradiction and supplement.

On the atomist view, sensible bodies are formed of temporary amalgams of atoms that are interspersed with void. Atoms,

> collide and become entangled . . . [in so far as] some of them are angular, some hooked, some concave, some convex, and indeed with countless other differences and they cling to each other and stay together until such time as some stronger necessity comes from the surrounding and shakes them apart (fr. A37)

Such temporary amalgams of atoms, however, are still fundamentally composed of atoms which have not lost their individual unity, and which will disperse when necessity and chance so have it. A truly unitary body, one which will not split, is an individual atom.

We may wonder why individual atoms cannot be split. Of course, by the account just given, if we can split something, that something is not an atom (and the word 'atom' means 'that which cannot be cut'). But there is obviously more at issue here than the definition of the word 'atom'. Unfortunately, exactly why atomists thought that there were fundamental particles is unclear, given the state of the evidence.[47] Barnes concludes an interesting and persuasive discussion of the evidence as follows: 'solidity supplies the chief argument for the . . . atomicity of Abderite substances . . . a solid atom cannot have bits chipped off from it; and an atom with bits conjoined to it will never constitute a solid body' (Barnes 1979b: 49). It is thus physical necessity, in the view of Barnes, that renders atoms indivisible, eternal and immutable (or impassive) (Barnes 1979b: 50). Things could have been otherwise, so far as the dictates of logic are concerned. It seems perfectly possible to entertain the idea that atomic substances are splittable; and it seems perfectly possible to visualise an atomic substance, and then to visualise it splitting (atoms have extension); most substances we see can be split, and it would seem perfectly reasonable to conjecture that all substances are splittable (until and unless we encounter something that resists splitting, that is). But if it just so happens that there are unsplittable atoms, then we can answer the sceptical challenges of the Eleatics.

On this view, if void can get into something, it does; if void does not figure in something, that is because the something in question is an individual atom and void cannot get into it. There is nothing in which void could come to figure, in which it does not figure now. In this respect, the world is, as it always has been, and as it always will be. (Although in other respects, it is governed by chance and necessity; there is no grand scheme or order in the cosmos.) The atomists, on this view, move back into the realm of scientific conjecture. At the end of the day, either sensible bodies are composed of solid unsplittable atoms or they are not. Parmenides' idea of being has been taken over by the atomists; but once they allow being to be multiple and allow notbeing a role within their system, the Parmenidean idea of being can be put to the scientific test. Parmenides thought this was what being must be like; the atomists were conjecturing that being actually is like this.

For Democritus, as for most of the earlier Presocratics, much of our sensory experience is misleading. Parmenides had distinguished sharply between how the world is, and how the world seems to us. The latter is perceived by the senses; the former is judged by reason. But it is hard to rest content with a complete Parmenidean divorce between how the world seems to us and how the world is. We have seen that Anaxagoras, in response to this problem, distinguished between C-substances, which alone can be encountered through the senses and their pure ingredients (E-substances or opposites), which we cannot perceive. And even C-substances may not be accurately perceived by the senses: they are not pure specimens of what they are (predominantly); and the senses could never inform us directly that there is a portion of everything in everything. Plato will later attempt to resolve the problem with his view of the Form/particular relation. For Plato, Forms represent being and particulars represent seeming; particulars alone are perceived through the senses; they are seen either as images of Forms, or as 'partaking in' (having a share in) Forms.

Democritus, unlike Plato and Anaxagoras, distinguishes not between being and seeming, or between two sorts of being, but between convention and reality. Thus he contends: 'by convention sweet, by convention bitter, by convention hot, by convention cold, by convention colour; but in reality atoms and void' (fr. B 9). With this fragment, we may perhaps see the first attempt at distinguishing primary and secondary qualities.[48] Exactly how we should formulate this distinction is disputed. I take it that the core of the distinction is the idea that things have some properties in themselves (the primary qualities), but other qualities only in relation to us (the secondary qualities); and further, that a scientific account of the world will be given in terms of primary qualities only; secondary qualities will be explained in terms of primary qualities.[49] The primary qualities describe how the world is; the secondary qualities describe how the world seems to us.

If Democritus is making a distinction along these lines, the primary qualities are the qualities of atoms and void; the secondary qualities are the conventional qualities. It remains a moot point what his attitude is towards the secondary qualities – those that he calls conventional. To know what Democritus' view is, we would need to know more about his view of convention. That his view of secondary qualities is not completely dismissive, or that he is aware of the problems with such a view, is revealed when he writes 'Wretched mind, do you take your assurances from us [the senses] and then overthrow us? Our overthrow is your downfall' (fr. B125). This strongly suggests that we cannot use the evidence of the senses to establish a system which proceeds to undermine that evidence. Perhaps the idea is that we are in contact with reality through our senses, but the mind transforms those messages in producing a philosophical or scientific account of the world. There is a tension between convention and reality (between seeming and being), but a tension we must live with: the mind cannot overthrow the testimony of the senses; the senses cannot reach the truth if they work unaided.

An interesting recent discussion of this question is provided in Strawson's 'Perception and its Objects' (P.F.Strawson, 1981). Scientists convince us that there is much in the world that is scientifically basic, and that we cannot see with the naked eye. Furthermore, many of our untutored perceptions of the world (our perceptions of secondary qualities) can perhaps be explained scientifically (in terms of the primary qualities of things); but are they not also undermined? (Is my desk really coloured?) Are there simply, as Strawson suggests, 'two discrepant viewpoints' that cannot be blended, and of which we must recognise the relativity (as we do in standard cases of shift of viewpoint when we say both 'blood is really red' when viewed under normal conditions and 'blood is really colourless' when viewed under a microscope). P.F.Strawson reminds us that 'science is not only the offspring of common sense; it remains its dependant' (P.F.Strawson, 1981: 59) in a manner highly reminiscent of Democritus. We cannot pretend that Democritus sees the questions here as clearly as Strawson. But we only have fragments of Democritus, and he is approaching the problem for the first time. It is all the more remarkable that he sketches out the problem in very much the same terms that we see it today, and that he suggests a resolution of it that still seems defensible.

Such, then, is the final, and culminating, achievement of Presocratic philosophy. The Presocratics asked two central questions of philosophy, 'what is there?' and 'what can we know there to be?'. These questions matter to us: they determine our basic orientation towards the world, and they set the stage for the rest of our philosophical thinking. It matters to us whether there is a simple unified world of interconnected opposites, characterised by flux and by war, or whether there is a world of atoms and void ruled by chance. And if, in everyday life, we ordinarily think we know the right answers to these questions, our common sense views are very much open to philosophical challenge.

The Presocratics developed a variety of philosophical methods, ranging from the bold conjectures of the Milesians to the cryptic challenges of Heraclitus and from the deductive argument of Parmenides to the paradoxes of Zeno and the philosophical pictures of Anaxagoras and the atomists.

Not all the substantive philosophical views formulated by the Presocratics now seem very persuasive. Some have been rendered implausible by scientific progress; others were never very plausible in the first place. And not all the methods we have seen demonstrated are now employed by contemporary philosophers. Moreover, the range of questions discussed by philosophers in this period was not very wide. None the less, the Presocratics were not just the first philosophers but were the first great philosophers. The best philosophy invites the student to engage actively and personally with philosophical problems. And we can learn a great deal as philosophers – both about metaphysics and epistemology and about the nature of philosophy, from grappling with the work of the Presocratics.

2

SOCRATES: A METHOD OF DOUBT

It is widely agreed that Socrates represents a new departure in philosophy. But there is no real agreement as to the nature of this new departure. Aristophanes in the *Clouds* even doubts whether Socrates does differ from his predecessors. At least he represents Socrates as interested largely in physical questions, in the manner of the Presocratics. It may be significant here that Socrates in Plato's *Apology* complains about misrepresentation by a comic poet (18c). Certainly Aristophanes seems deeply misguided. To Dover, indeed, this portrayal of Socrates is so hard to understand, that he is driven to compare Aristophanes to those people who do not understand or care about the difference between Bach and Rachmaninov (Dover, 1968: 71). Plato in the *Phaedo* suggests that Socrates was the first philosopher to seek teleological explanations (96ff.). This claim too is rather surprising. It is true that none of the Presocratics (except arguably Anaxagoras) had displayed an interest in teleological questions. But Plato's comments still seem to relate more closely to his own theory of Forms, than to the historical Socrates. Aristotle's view is that Socrates' contributions to philosophy lay in his interest in definitions and in inductive argument (*Metaphysics* 1078b27). About this, we might say that Socrates does have these concerns, and is the first to do so; but these concerns do not seem central to his practice of philosophy. Cicero says that Socrates brought philosophy down from the sky (*Tusculan Disputations* 5.4.10). He tells us something important in this passage – but only that with Socrates we find the first sustained treatment of ethical questions.

Plato gives us perhaps the fullest and earliest account of Socrates' philosophical activity in his *Apology*. The story Socrates tells there is simple. His friend Chairephon consulted the Delphic oracle, and was told that no-one was wiser than Socrates (21a). Socrates found this hard to believe, and wanted to find out if it could really be true. (He tells us that he asked himself what the god was riddling, at 21b.) He set out as if to refute the oracle and find someone wiser than himself (21bc). He consulted widely, but he came to the conclusion that there was a sense in which he was wiser than those he talked to: he was aware that he knew nothing (23a). Thus he vindicated the oracle, without ascribing to himself great wisdom.

For Socrates, then, the practice of philosophy was, in part, the fulfilment of a personal quest. At the same time, Socrates was tried in Athens for corrupting the youth, and in the *Apology*, he does have some remarks to make about this. Had he, wittingly or unwittingly, corrupted the youth? Socrates was pleading not guilty. He claimed that in fact his enterprise had benefited Athens; and that he accordingly deserved free meals for life. Athenians needed a gadfly to stir them up to take care of their souls (29–30). And Socrates was engaged in an *elenchos tou biou*, 'an examination of life' (39c) – a painful process, from which the Athenians hoped to be released by their condemnation of Socrates, but one that is ultimately beneficial.

Plato portrays Socrates' impact on his fellow citizens in philosophical dialogues – employing a form of philosophical discourse in which he has had few successors.[1] It may seem, then, that Plato is concerned here with the intrinsic worth of Socrates as a human being and not simply with his philosophical views. And yet the life of Socrates as portrayed in the early Platonic dialogues is a life of philosophy. In Plato's account of the life and death of Socrates, we find Plato's first, and simplest, attempt to justify the life of the philosopher. This is what philosophy did for Socrates, it might seem.[2] Can it do the same for us? This question may seem especially pressing, and especially troublesome, in the light of the intellectualist cast of Socratic ethics. As Robinson remarks, 'Socrates was certainly a unique moralist if he hoped to make men virtuous by logic' (Robinson, 1953: 14).

There are several distinctive aspects of Socrates' practice of philosophy. His *disavowal of knowledge* gives the enquiry its starting point; it renders the *elenctic method* natural – the oracle leads to Socrates' examining others, and refuting, or undermining their claims to knowledge; and the elenctic method leads to *aporia* – the upshot of a Socratic dialogue is that the interlocutors find themselves at a loss as to how to proceed. In this chapter, I shall first discuss Socrates' elenctic method of enquiry, and ask how this enables him to achieve practical results in philosophy. I shall then examine an individual elenctic argument in detail. Finally, I shall ask about the merits of leading a life devoted to *elenchos,* or an 'examined' life.

The *elenchos* lies at the heart of Socrates' practice of philosophy. Socrates, like Descartes, believes in the value of a method in philosophy and in the value of a method of doubt – in his case this is the method of *elenchos*. Like the method of doubt, it is essentially first-personal. Unlike the method of doubt, it does not lead Socrates to a firm and secure foundation for his philosophy, but only to *aporia*. All Socrates' philosophical results derive from the practice of *elenchos* (or purport to do so); and it is the practice of *elenchos* that benefits human souls.

For Socrates, it would seem there is one great philosophical question – one neglected by Athenians – 'What is the right way to live?'. We might expect any answer to this question to involve discussion both of our desires and our beliefs. For Socrates, our desires do not need too much discussion: we all want the good, and no-one does wrong willingly (for discussion of this view of Socrates, see below). The difficult questions and the ones that need discussion concern our beliefs. Socrates asks 'what is the good?'; or rather, he asks more specifically, 'what is virtue?' and 'what are the virtues?'. (The idea is that virtue is what enables us to attain the good.) These are the questions which Socrates investigates with the aid of the *elenchos*.

Socrates believes that the answers to these questions will have practical implications for the everyday conduct of our lives. In the dialogues, Socrates asks mostly supposed experts in ethics about definitions of the virtues. But his view is that the answers to them matter to everyone, and that, in the memorable words of Burnyeat, we should not 'leave philosophy to those who are good at it' (Burnyeat, 1984: 246), but try to answer these questions for ourselves. The *elenchos* is universally prescribed.

Vlastos sees in this universal prescription of *elenchos* a 'failure of love'. He argues that Socrates' care for the soul is limited and conditional – 'if men's souls are to be saved, they must be saved his way' (Vlastos, 1958: 16). Plato sees other problems with the method. In the *Apology* itself, Socrates remarks that in the hands of the idle, rich youth of Athens, the *elenchos* can become a party trick (23c). In the *Republic*, Plato shows concern about premature exposure to the power of the *elenchos*, which he thinks can induce moral scepticism. He confines the practice of dialectic to philosophers and to trainee philosophers who are towards the end of their training course (see *Republic* 539).

Let us ask first about the *elenchos* as a method of investigating definitions of the virtues. As we have seen, Socrates thinks he does not know anything, big or small, himself. The obvious course of action then, if he wants a definition of a virtue, is to go and consult an expert on the virtue in question. Socrates does consult supposed experts. Employing Socratic irony,[3] he plays along with the supposition that he is speaking to experts in the field of ethics. He feigns not to believe the obvious explanation of his experiences of these discussions (though he tells us what conclusions he did draw from them at his trial – i.e. that his interlocutors knew nothing, 22a). Supposed experts are not what they seem. On examination, they prove unable to answer the questions of definition.

It may seem, then, that Socrates' interlocutors know nothing, and Socrates knows nothing. And this might seem to make any form of progress in Socrates' enquiries completely impossible. This problem is explicitly raised in Plato's *Meno*, where Plato responds to the difficulty by advancing his theory of recollection: the idea is that we do all know something, but that we have temporarily forgotten what we know. The question I want to ask here, though, is not how Plato, or the Socrates of the middle dialogues, would have resolved the problem, but how Socrates might have answered the question in the early dialogues.

Let us first consider the view of Vlastos (1983), who holds that in *elenchos*, Socrates aims not just to test his interlocutors' beliefs for consistency (which is one of the standard interpretations/criticisms of the *elenchos*)[4] but also to seek for truth. Basing his case largely on the *Gorgias*, Vlastos argues that Socrates aims to derive true conclusions for his interlocutors, on the basis of premisses to which they agree, and which Socrates holds to be true. The elenctic method is essentially deductive, not inductive. We deduce truths from premisses 'q' and 'r', to refute an initial premiss 'p'. Socrates disavows knowledge only in what Vlastos (1985) calls the 'strong' sense of knowledge; he does not disavow the knowledge (in the weaker sense) that results from *elenchos*.[5]

There are many attractions to Vlastos' view. In the first place, many of Socrates' arguments conform to the deductive pattern that Vlastos has set forth (we shall examine one such argument, from *Meno* 78, below). Second, this view explains the place in the Socratic system of the various Socratic paradoxes – no-one errs willingly, the unity of the virtues, virtue is knowledge, and so on. These theses constitute knowledge in the weak sense of the term, and are counter-endoxic conclusions (that is, conclusions that run counter to our pre-philosophical, or everyday, intuitions) arrived at deductively on the basis of endoxic premisses.[6] Finally, Vlastos' view explains why the method of *elenchos* is worthwhile. A successful *elenchos*, it would seem, increases our stock of true beliefs, or of knowledge in the weak sense.

But other features of Vlastos' view are less attractive. Socrates the system-builder seems a long way removed from the Socrates of the *Apology*. Socrates there is not concerned to help us increase our stock of knowledge, or true beliefs. The Socratic paradoxes are indeed counter-endoxic theses based on endoxic premisses (think of the relation of 'no-one willingly errs' to 'everyone wants the good', or of the relation between 'everyone wants the good' and 'no-one wants to be miserable and wretched'). But they have only the status of elenctic results – which is not knowledge, even in a weak sense. They could all be refuted tomorrow. (Perhaps not everyone does want the good.)

So let us examine another approach to the question of how we can hope to progress through the *elenchos* when we have no knowledge. Perhaps, following such authors as Geach (1966) and Burnyeat (1977a), we should question whether it is really true that we do not have any knowledge. Certainly, we may not have any knowledge of definitions, which is how Socrates sees knowledge. But we may have knowledge of examples, for all that. Otherwise, indeed, we would never be in a position to assess the merits of candidate definitions.

Several issues arise here. One is whether, in suggesting that we do not know what an X is unless we can define 'X', Socrates is simply practising a 'high redefinition' of terms here as when we say 'there are no physicians in New York', but mean by this only that there is no-one in New York who can cure any known disease within three minutes.[7] Burnyeat suggests, very plausibly, in response to Geach, that Socrates did not think that one should be able to produce a definition on demand. Socrates as midwife and Socrates in the *Meno* both think rather that one may hope to produce definitions after, and not before, *elenchos* (Burnyeat, 1977a: 391). Furthermore, according to Burnyeat, what Socrates seeks is philosophical clarity, and not everyday understanding (Burnyeat, 1977a: 389, but this distinction is unclear – Socrates hopes that 'philosophical' enlightenment will have some effect on 'everyday' life). Burnyeat suggests that theories and examples are surveyed together, with only a small core of central examples providing an agreed fixed core of reference. (Thus in the *Laches*, at 196, Socrates is prepared to revise ordinary usage by refusing to call animals 'brave'.) Socrates is, on this view, to be contrasted with for example G.E. Moore, who holds fast to the security of certain basic examples in epistemology above all. For Moore, nothing can be more certain than that 'here is one hand, and here is another'. Socrates, in the view of Burnyeat, provides the better model for epistemologists. He gives (at least in the *Theaetetus*) a rationale for adopting a revisionary attitude towards examples (as Wittgenstein, but not Moore, will later give a rationale for holding fast to the security of examples).

Burnyeat's view stands at a tangent to our current enquiry, in so far as he focuses on epistemology and not ethics,[8] and in so far as he is interested in one of Plato's later dialogues, the *Theaetetus* as well as the Socratic dialogues. Burnyeat's view of the role of examples in epistemology can be called in to question.[9] But let us here focus on his view of the Socratic *elenchos*.

Burnyeat's view of the *elenchos* is that it is quite straightforwardly intended to help us to formulate definitions. But there is a problem with this view, which is that the *elenchos* would seem to be essentially a method of refutation. For what Socrates actually does in the Socratic dialogues is to elicit a candidate definition from his interlocutor, to formulate it so that it is refutable, and then proceed to refute it by means of examples, by showing, for instance, either that it is too broad or that it is too narrow.[10] Socrates is not turning ignorance into knowledge, but supposed knowledge into ignorance.

If the Socratic *elenchos* is a method of refutation, it may be helpful to call to mind here Popper's account of the growth of scientific knowledge. On Popper's view, scientists proceed by a process of conjecture and refutation, and do not turn ignorance into knowledge (knowledge being unattainable). But the enterprise is still worthwhile. Scientists provide increasingly satisfactory working hypotheses, which are as yet unrefuted. Perhaps Socrates could make the same claim. He employs a method of conjecture and refutation. He too can hope to make progress – as he does in the formulation of his paradoxes. These may have the status of as yet unrefuted hypotheses (cf. Vlastos, 1958: 11).

The parallel with scientific method may also help us resolve an internal problem with the Socratic method in philosophy, set up by Irwin. Irwin remarks that some Socratic doctrines rest on the *elenchos*, and others rest on an analogy between virtue and craft (Irwin, 1977: 37), but that this is problematic: Socrates 'suggests no source of moral knowledge outside the *elenchos*' (Irwin, 1977: 96); furthermore 'he ought to use the systematic exposition proper to a craft' (Irwin, 1977: 97). Moral knowledge should be passed on like craft knowledge – which is not passed on through *elenchos*. This is an intriguing problem. But it can be answered – at least, if we distinguish (as do philosophers of science) between a method of enquiry and a method of teaching.[11] *Elenchos* might function as a tool for moral research, but not be the best method of teaching a fully developed moral system. Socrates, of course, does not have a fully developed moral system, so it is understandable that he should continue to employ the method of *elenchos*.

The main problem with the parallel is Socrates' apparent revisionism with examples. But here we might point out that scientists too sometimes think it right to reject apparent counter-evidence to their theories (and sometimes do so correctly). So perhaps the parallel between Socratic and scientific method may yet hold good.[12]

Let us now examine an individual elenctic argument in more detail. One of Socrates' most striking positions is his denial of *akrasia*, weakness of will, and his doctrine that *oudeis hekon hamartanei*, 'no-one willingly errs'. This position is defended in the *Protagoras* against the many, who hold that we all want the good, but that the good is the pleasant. It is also defended against Meno in the *Meno*, who agrees that no-one wants to be wretched and miserable, and hence is persuaded (against his initial intuition) that we all want the good. In short, the idea is, in both dialogues, that there is a single scale of value, and that all apparently akratic behaviour really arises from a mismeasurement of goods against this single scale of value. There is no scope for psychic conflict, nor for internal division in the agent.

Socrates' argument is thought-provoking, but inconclusive; we can always deny the relevant premiss (be it 'everyone wants the pleasant' or 'everyone wants the good'). It is typical, in this, of the *elenchos* at its best. But for all that, Socrates' claim that no-one does wrong willingly has functioned as a sceptical excluder for later philosophers, such as Aristotle, or in our own times, Davidson (1970) who asks 'how is weakness of the will possible?'. There is, in fact, still no agreement whether weakness of the will *is* possible.[13] Philosophers who believe that it can occur and does occur, must try to give some account of how it can happen. Plato and Davidson (1982) adopt the same approach to this task. Both think Socratic psychology is too simple and that our souls are more complex than Socrates makes out: different parts of the soul can function independently. On this (very persuasive) view, akratics suffer more from disordered souls than from a misguided claim to knowledge. It may not be true that other people differ from Socrates only in so far as Socrates has recognised his own ignorance, and they have not. They may need rather more than the intellectual understanding provided by the *elenchos* to resolve their problems in living.

An individual elenctic argument can be thought-provoking. But Socrates thought it worthwhile to devote his life to elenctic arguments. What are the benefits of devoting one's life to philosophy in this way? The claim that has been entered on behalf of Socrates' practice of philosophy, at this point, is that the philosophical way of life yields a worthwhile increase in self-knowledge (thus Burnyeat, 1977b: 9). I would like to explore this in parallel with a similar claim that Cavell has advanced, on behalf of the work of Austin and the later Wittgenstein, to the effect that the 'ordinary language' approach to philosophy can increase our self-knowledge.[14] In both cases, it is hard to know what to make of the idea that there is a worthwhile increase in self-knowledge to be gained through the practice of philosophy.

In most cases, when we speak of an increase in self-knowledge, it is clear why the knowledge in question is called self-knowledge, and also why acquiring such knowledge is a worthwhile goal. We might think, for example, of the self-knowledge gained by Jane Austen's Emma when she realises she is in love with Mr Knightley. Here it is clear in what sense the knowledge to which she gains access is knowledge of herself, and also why it is helpful for her to acquire this knowledge.

But the increase in self-knowledge that is supposed to arise from Socratic *elenchos* or from ordinary language philosophy seems to be very different in character. In the case of Socrates, Burnyeat points to Platonic texts which suggest that self-knowledge 'will limit the tendence to be overbearing to others and promote temperance'. Socrates helps people 'find out for themselves what they knew and what they did not'.[15] Pupils' 'awareness of their cognitive resources' is itself a 'vital force' (Burnyeat, 1977b: 12). This may well be true. But it is also true that for Socrates, ignorance is the human condition, not especially the condition of particular individuals. And it also remains unclear how becoming aware of our own ignorance will help us achieve the Socratic goal of care of the soul.

In the case of ordinary language philosophy, Cavell claims that we gain self-knowledge by answering questions like 'what should we say if . . . ?' or 'In what circumstances would we call . . . ?'. This is 'a request for the person to say something about himself, describe what he does' (Cavell, 1962: 66). The 'self-knowledge' in question is like the self-knowledge to be gained through psychoanalysis (Cavell, 1962: 66) and through Socratic enquiry (Cavell, 1962: 68). Cavell explicates his conception of self-knowledge when he writes that 'Knowing oneself is the capacity . . . for placing oneself in the world' (Cavell, 1979: 107). The idea is that this is a capacity that can be developed as we articulate, in the manner of the later Wittgenstein, or by paying reflective attention to 'what we say', the forms of life in which we participate. In this case, too, however, we are concerned, not with knowledge of our own individual characters, but with knowledge of local conditions, with our own form of life and its attendant use of language. And in this case too, the benefits of this 'self-knowledge' are unclear – many people seem to lead satisfactory lives in a condition of ignorance.[16]

The case for living the life of philosophy, the 'examined' life, has not been made out. It is arguable that we do all want to live well, and that we should engage in ongoing examination of our lives, if this will help us live better. But we may already be living well; and if we are not, it may be doubted whether repeated exposure to the Socratic *elenchos* will help us live better. For it is not just the mistaken claim to knowledge that stops us from living as well as we might: we may stand in need of emotional, as well as cognitive, therapy. For all that, the *elenchos* can be helpful. It can lead to the undermining of existing theories, to greater epistemological caution, and towards the formulation of tentative new (as yet unrefuted) conjectures. One can hope, using this method, to formulate answers to the great question of how we should live, and to the subsidiary questions of how to define the virtues. The hope will often be frustrated; and at best we will not know that we have achieved the right answers to these questions. But, as Socrates himself demonstrates, one may have a fair degree of subjective certainty about this, whilst recognising that one's beliefs are as yet only provisional.

3

PLATO: THE LIFE OF PHILOSOPHY

Plato's defence of Socrates and of the practice of philosophy in the early dialogues is direct and straightforward. His case is, as we have seen, that Socrates awakened Athenians to the care of their souls through the practice of *elenchos*, which made them aware of their own ignorance. As the early period gives way to the middle period, the picture becomes very much more complicated. First, Plato develops further his criticisms of our everyday perspective on life. He examines closely, and finds wanting, the claims to our attention made by art, rhetoric and eristic (eristic being a sort of argumentative logic-chopping; a perversion of philosophy in which we try to win arguments, and not arrive at truths). Plato also develops further his conception of philosophy. He formulates new ideas about philosophical method, new philosophical doctrines about the nature of knowledge and reality, and a new conception of the philosophical way of life.

Eristic, rhetoric and art are three disciplines that each lay claim to part of the domain properly occupied by philosophy. In this sense, they are the professional rivals of philosophy. Eristic mimics the technique of philosophy. We gather from the *Euthydemus* that the student of eristic learns to win arguments at all costs, to use any fallacy he can get away with, and has no personal commitment to his results. His motivation is not that of the philosopher: he has no 'care for the soul'. Rhetoric offers the rewards of success in life, and personal security. It presents itself as a craft of persuasion. The student of rhetoric learns how to speak persuasively when time is limited, when he faces a large audience, and when he must exploit the emotions and the existing beliefs of that audience. Art, finally, makes no claim to teach us how to argue, or how to get on in life. But artists do lay claim to expertise about the crafts and to wisdom about the meaning of life; and Plato argues in the *Republic* that if we believe the artists on either score we may be led astray. True knowledge of crafts resides in craftsmen, not poets, and true knowledge about the meaning of life results from the study of philosophy. Art is also dangerous because of its effects on the soul. Acting in plays fragments the soul, and watching plays nourishes the lower, non-rational, part of the soul. In studying philosophy, by contrast, we nourish the rational part of ourselves, and we promote harmony within the soul.

Plato formulates a new conception of the life of philosophy in his middle period works, along with new ideas about philosophical method, and new doctrines about knowledge, reality and the soul. The new method of hypothesis and the new doctrine of recollection are first mentioned in the *Meno*, and show us Plato coming to grips with some of the problems inherent in the Socratic *elenchos*. The new philosophical doctrines, about the nature of the soul and about the nature of knowledge and reality, follow soon afterwards in the *Phaedo*, and are more fully developed in the *Republic*. The philosophical way of life, in the *Phaedo*, is newly seen as a preparation for death. In the *Symposium*, the philosopher emerges as an expert on love, who spends his time in contemplation of the Form of Beauty. In the *Republic*, the philosopher can no longer spend all his life in contemplation, but is an expert on justice who must acknowledge his duty to rule the ideal state. In all three dialogues, Plato's conception of the philosophical way of life is ultimately based on his new theory about the soul and about knowledge and reality. It has become very important, for Plato's justification of the life of philosophy, that his substantive philosophical views hold good.

PHILOSOPHY AND ITS RIVALS

The Euthydemus: philosophy and eristic

At a crucial juncture in the *Meno* (80e), Socrates pauses to consider an *eristikos logos*, an eristical argument – that a man cannot search either for what he knows or for what he does not know. For you wouldn't search for what you know – you know it, and there's no need to search for it; nor would you search for what you don't know, for you don't know what you'll be looking for.

Before examining Plato's response to what has come to be known as the paradox of enquiry, let us ask first what claim it might seem to have on our attention. We might note, first, that it has the same character as the sceptical paradoxes of Zeno. We may or may not be able to spot the fallacy in the argument (a useful first move is clearly to point out that there are few subjects with regard to which we are completely ignorant, or completely knowledgeable, but that only in these two extreme cases is there any prima facie plausibility to the paradox of enquiry). But we know that there is a fallacy – we enquire successfully all the time. And, at least at first sight, it may seem that we need not be too concerned whether or not we can diagnose the fallacy completely or accurately. The paradox does not seem to raise issues that demand our attention. And it does not seem to be seriously motivated (this may be partly why it is called eristical).

Plato's response to the eristical *logos* may persuade us to take the paradox more seriously. On this occasion he certainly does take the paradox seriously. This would not seem to be because he in general believes in taking sceptical paradoxes seriously (he never says anything like this). Rather, Plato may take the paradox seriously in the first instance because it touches on a point of particular interest to him. In Socratic dialectic, as we saw in Chapter 2, Socrates disavows knowledge, and his interlocutors are certainly ignorant. It is a real question for Plato, then, how Socrates could hope to make progress from such a starting point. This is one of the serious issues raised by the eristical *logos* – and an issue to which Plato goes on to respond by advancing the theory of recollection. The theory of recollection, the question of how we learn a priori truths (as raised by the example of the slave, who, through questions, converts a state of ignorance about a geometrical problem into a state of true belief, if not into a state of knowledge or full understanding), the question of the immortality of the soul – all these questions can command our attention, if the eristic paradox itself does not. And they are questions which, as Plato sees, arise naturally from reflection on the eristic paradox.

The problem Plato faces in the case of eristic, then, is to distinguish arguments like the eristical *logos* from philosophical arguments, which are often paradoxical, and often leave us none the wiser, but which are intrinsically worth exploring. In the *Meno*,

Plato carries out this task by providing a philosophical discussion of the eristic paradox.

But eristic is only a passing interest of Plato's in the *Meno*. The dialogue he devotes to the exposure of eristic is the *Euthydemus*. In the *Euthydemus*, Socrates competes with the sophists Euthydemus and Dionysodorus for the attentions of a young man Kleinias, a potential client. Plato shows us here eristic at work. For the most part he leaves us to draw our own conclusions – conclusions, however, that will be very much easier for us to understand if we also have some knowledge of philosophy, as portrayed in other Platonic dialogues.

For most of the dialogue, Euthydemus and Dionysodorus display their wares. They ask questions such as 'do learners learn what they know or what they don't know?', and answer 'both'; they suggest that wanting Kleinias to become wise involves wanting to destroy Kleinias (who will no longer be who he is, or just no longer be)[1]; they produce arguments for the impossibility of falsehood, and the impossibility of contradiction; and they conclude with a number of arguments that depend on fallacies concerning relatives – such as that he who knows something knows everything.

Socrates occasionally comments on fallacies in the arguments (thus he complains at 278a that the first argument trades on an ambiguity in the Greek word *manthanein*). In two interludes in the dialogue, he converses with Kleinias himself (278–82, he argues that wisdom means we need not rely on good fortune in life, and is necessary for the right use of goods and skills – if it is teachable, then obviously, one must spend one's life in seeking to learn it; 288–93, Socrates distinguishes between the maker and the user of tools; he argues that word-making skill is a tool, that still needs its proper use, and that *politike* seems to be the kingly art needed for use of what other skills have created/hunted).

After the brothers' display is completed, Socrates comments that their performance has been a *tour de force* (303c); but that ordinary folk would rather be refuted by such arguments than use them to refute others (303d; cf. 304a: this is also true of Crito, who reports the dialogue). Furthermore, the bystander Ctesippus has picked up the brothers' stock-in-trade very easily and quickly (303e); so if it is to be a valuable commodity, tuition must occur in private (304bc). Finally, Socrates and Crito exchange some remarks outside the main framework of the dialogue. Crito tells

Socrates how a casual listener, a speechwriter, described the show as 'merely the sort of stuff . . . that you hear such people babbling about at any time – making an inconsequent ado about matters of consequence' (304e, Loeb translation). Socrates counters with an attack on speechwriters (who think they know some philosophy and some politics and so are better off than philosophers and politicans; but the truth is, they do neither properly, 306), and concludes with the advice to Crito that he make a personal trial of philosophy and sees how it goes (307b).

There is an evident contrast between the philosophical and the eristical sections of the dialogue. The contrast is not, however, one of subject matter. For Plato clearly believes that in fact all the problems raised by Euthydemus and Dionysodorus are properly treated of by philosophy. They are all treated of by philosophy in other Platonic dialogues. Thus Plato himself asks what learners learn when he raises the paradox of enquiry in the *Meno* and presents the theory of recollection in response to the paradox. Kleinias' becoming wise is perhaps to be accounted for in terms of his coming to partake in the Form of Wisdom (see, at any rate, *Phaedo* 96ff. for an analysis of how Socrates comes to be small). The *Sophist* will demonstrate the possibility of falsehood; the law of contradiction is discussed at length in *Republic* IV. Relatives are discussed in the *Charmides*.

Nor is it simply that Socrates' arguments are always sound, while the arguments of the brothers are always fallacious. It is hard to say how conscious Plato was of the nature of the fallacies in argument that he attributes to Euthydemus and Dionysodorus – although it is clear that he does have some interest in this topic; and it's also clear that the brothers don't produce a single persuasive argument in the course of the dialogue. The problem in this regard is that so many of Socrates' own arguments in the dialogues don't bear critical examination.

Perhaps, ultimately, then, the difference is simply one of motivation. If Socrates is concerned for the care of the soul, and wants to find out how best to live, then when one of his arguments is challenged, we can expect him to welcome the challenge, and try to mend his ways. The brothers show no trace of this motivation in their practice of dialectic. They practise dialectic for the sake of dialectic – or, as I should write, eristic for the sake of eristic. For eristic is a sort of distorting mirror of philosophy. Philosophise well, and you will learn the truth about all the subjects canvassed in the dialogue. Philosophise less successfully, and you may at least come to grips with these problems, and learn to appreciate your own ignorance. Study with Euthydemus and Dionysodorus and you will disgrace the good name of the subject. The layman will perhaps be unable to detect the precise nature of the fallacies they practise. But he will assuredly know that he is better off without contact with such charlatans. If he takes this for philosophy, he will give philosophy a wide berth. The contrastive picture of Socrates at work should serve to reassure him. But at the end of the day there will be no substitute for personal experience of the practice of philosophy.

It may be hard to philosophise when one is not guaranteed a successful outcome to one's enquiries. Plato will soon hope, however, for better things. Already, in the *Gorgias* we will find philosophy associated with the ideas of craft and knowledge, and contrasted with another of its images, rhetoric. And the rewards of philosophy are already pitched high: the philosopher is here said to be the only true politician. In both respects, the *Gorgias* shows us the shape of things to come in middle period Plato.[2]

The Gorgias: philosophy and rhetoric

In the *Gorgias*, Socrates discusses the nature of rhetoric, first with Gorgias, then with Polus, and finally with Callicles. The case against rhetoric is gradually filled out and strengthened, as Socrates' interlocutors attempt increasingly radical defences of their trade and their way of life. Philosophy slowly emerges as a rival discipline and a rival way of life that can deliver the goods that rhetoric can only promise. Three themes emerge as the discussion progresses – those of knowledge, power and punishment. The promise of rhetoric is that it will help us to maximise our power over others and miminise our own vulnerability (as manifested notably in our liability to punishment in the lawcourts). And the view of philosophy, as seen from the standpoint of rhetoric, is memorably charactised by Callicles: philosophy is a suitable enough activity for young men, but it does not fit one for action in the world. An older man who practises philosophy 'lives whispering with three or four boys in a corner', and deserves to be beaten (*Gorgias* 485cd, tr. Irwin). Philosophy as it sees itself is rather different: it is aimed at the acquisition of knowledge and virtue (which is based on knowledge). Philosophy will teach us that – contrary to what we might think – it is not important for us to maximise our power over others. What is important is the care of the soul. So punishment, being an aid to the care of the soul, should actually be welcomed by wrongdoers. Philosophy, which is based on knowledge, can deliver on its promise. Rhetoric, by contrast, cannot deliver on its promise; it is not a skill based on knowledge, but is a mere knack that panders to the worst aspects of the human being.

One of Plato's fundamental concerns in ethics is that the goal in life, of the man in the street, is the maximisation of his personal power. He wants to maximise his personal power so that he can live securely himself, but also so that he can, if he so wishes, act harmfully to others, and get away with it. Plato's most effective exposition of this worry occurs in the *Republic*, with the image of the ring of Gyges. The ring of Gyges would give me the power to become invisible whenever I want to, so that I could act unjustly towards others and get away with it. I would be invulnerable to others (they would not know the identity of their malefactor) but others would remain vulnerable to me. In the *Gorgias*, these concerns come to the fore in Socrates' discussion with Polus. The nub of Polus' position, as captured by Socrates at 466d, is that 'rhetors kill whoever they want to, like tyrants, and expropriate and expel from the cities whoever they think fit'. Socrates introduces the image of the the knife-man (469d, a fifth-century assassin) at this point, and Polus responds with the image of the tyrant (471ae). These figures, surely, have power. The knife-man holds any given other in the palm of his hand. 'If I think that one of the people you see should be dead on the spot, he'll be dead, whoever I think fit' (469d5). The problem with this, as Polus points out, is that the knife-man will be punished.[3] The tyrant Archelaus, however, behaved antisocially, and avoided punishment. In fact, he did away with all potential rivals: he killed first his master and uncle, Alcetas, together with his son Alexander, thereby, as Polus ironically remarks, 'becoming utterly wretched without noticing it' (471b); then he threw his brother into a well and drowned him.

Plato's attempt to refute Polus follows at 474b ff. Plato argues that characters are indeed utterly wretched: doing injustice and not paying for it is the greatest of all evils (479a). His argument is notoriously unsound (though the fallacy is hard to pin down). I do not want to examine the shortcomings of the argument in detail here, however,[4] but rather to discuss the broad contours of the positions Plato attacks and defends in this passage.

We may feel various misgivings about Plato's characterisation of rhetoric in this passage. First we may wonder whether rhetoric is not, as Gorgias has claimed, a power that may be used for good or for ill, as in the example he gives in 456. He has often persuaded a patient to drink a medicine or 'let the doctor cut or burn him', in cases where the doctors' own attempts at persuasion have failed. Second, we may wonder whether, even in those cases where the orator uses his power in the service of his own ends, he is really like the tyrant or the knife-man. If the Athenian Assembly, persuaded by an orator, condemns a man to death, they act as something more than an assassin's knife.

But perhaps this suggests something of how the orator sees other people – that is to say, that he sees them as means to ends, and not, for example as ends in a kingdom of ends. Rhetoric is, after all, simply a tool for persuading other people to do what one antecedently wants them to do. And to this end, the orator may, and perhaps must, exploit our imperfect natures. We may contrast Socrates' practice of dialectic. Socrates tries to perfect our imperfect natures (see for example 504de) to enable us to guide our conduct by reason. He hopes to encourage us to do what we (really) want to do ourselves. And he works to this end through a rational form of persuasion, which examines, and does not simply take for granted the truth of our everyday beliefs. The Socratic practice of dialectic does seem morally superior to the practice of the orator.

On the score of personal power, also, we may feel that there is some plausibility in Plato's general position. After all, what human being would want to become an assassin, or an Archelaus (or a Hitler)? We may not think such characters were utterly miserable, but we do think that there is something wrong with such people and that they have failed in the care of their souls. At the same time, we may perhaps feel that we would rather be Archelaus than his uncle Alcetas: we might not want this sort of power for ourselves, but nor would we wish to be vulnerable to this kind of power. It is, after all, real enough power.[5]

Plato acknowledges this point, when he reverts to this subject at 508d, though his response there is not competely persuasive. He initally makes a comparative claim that it is better to suffer injustice than to commit injustice: 'having my face pushed in unjustly is not the most shameful thing – nor is having my body or my purse cut. But to strike and cut me and mine unjustly is more shameful and evil . . .' This, of course, may well be true. But it would still be better for me not to have my face pushed in unjustly. Plato, however, does have a further response at this point. He suggests that in fact one faces a harsh choice in life:

> Then suppose some young man in this city thought, 'How might I win great power so that no one does injustice to me?' Apparently this is the road for him; he must accustom himself from youth to enjoy and hate the same things as the tyrant, and manage to be as like the tyrant as possible (510d).

We have here, obviously, the idea that power (tyrannical power) corrupts; and also that one decides as a young man what sort of person one will be, and then one is stuck with the consequences of one's decision. Rhetoric is not seen here as a skill that one can decide to employ on a given occasion at will; it is part of a way of life to which one must aspire as a whole. So Plato's position on vulnerability is that it is indeed possible to become invulnerable by becoming a powerful orator; but that all powerful orators have paid a price for their invulnerability – they are all unjust.

It may be helpful now to consider other cases in which we might seem to be confronted by an equally stark choice. We might perhaps compare the idea of trying to fight a just war against an aggressive opponent who has no intention of reciprocating in kind. Is one better off fighting a just war and losing, or fighting an unjust war and winning? There is no doubt what Plato's answer would be. And there is no doubt what Plato's answer was in the case of Socrates. Would it have been better for Socrates to have won his lawsuit, using an unjust means, or was it better for him to have been unjustly condemned to death? Socrates had claimed in the *Apology* at 41cd that nothing bad can happen to the good man, in life or death. In the *Gorgias* he says 'being put to death itself – no one fears that unless he's altogether unreasoning and unmanly; it is doing injustice that he fears' (522e). For the good man, it would seem, there is no need even to inhabit the best of all possible worlds. Everything is for the best, even in the actual world. He will be able to handle all that the world can throw at him, by way of problems and disasters. It is only committing injustice that he need fear, and avoiding this lies within his own power.

This position seems counter-endoxic. And in some respects it really is counter-endoxic. We do not normally think that it is unmanly or unreasonable to fear being put to death, or being physically injured. And it would require very strong argument to persuade us to the contrary. But it is possible to mount a defence of what is perhaps the core of Plato's thinking here. For what seems right about Plato's view is that it will be impossible to violate the personal integrity of the good man: the good man's goodness will remain intact, come what may. His life will be all of one piece, for he will have no bad impulses; for he will have firmly established within himself a source of good actions. And Plato clearly thinks that those who have once firmly established the good inside themselves, just cannot act badly. Thus Gorgias agrees with Socrates at 460bc that: 'the man who has learnt just things is just; and the just man will never want to do injustice.' (Of course it is not clear what right Plato has to think this; as commentators point out, this is a very questionable claim, if justice is to be seen as a craft – see Irwin, 1979: 127.) There is no source within the good man for bad actions to issue forth from. And if the good man never acts wrongly, he will never have cause to reproach himself for what he has done. He will never experience any form of 'agent-regret'. And this, it would seem, is the single, necessary and sufficient, condition of happiness. The happiness of the good man would seem simply to consist in his awareness that he has had the internal resources to meet the temptations and challenges presented to him by the world justly; and in the absence of any ground for self-reproach.

This is why punishment is so important for the good man, if he should by any chance act wrongly. It is imperative that his soul remain entirely good, if he is to stand firm against the world. Hence Plato's argument for the thesis that it is better not to get away with wrongdoing, but to be be punished for it. Socrates argues that what is most important for us is the care of the soul, and that deserved punishment is part of care of the soul. Just as we care for the body (and try to avoid other evils, such as sickness and poverty), so we should care for the soul. If our soul needs flogging, a fine, prison or death, we should in fact denounce ourselves to the courts, and do our best to make sure that this is what we get (480cd).

Mackenzie suggests that we must distinguish here between ideal, and actual, penal codes (Mackenzie, 1981: 181–182). Perhaps one might be better off for undergoing some ideal form of punishment; that does not mean one wants the retribution that masquerades as punishment in all actual states. And certainly whether or not one wants punishment, when one has done wrong, may depend on what is on offer. One might not want six years in jail. But in Athens, it was always possible for a wrongdoer to denounce himself to the court and try to set himself an appropriate penalty.[6]

It would seem, then, that we all do care about our souls, and we might in some circumstances opt for punishment after wrong-doing. Perhaps too, we would all rather learn dialectic than rhetoric if we had to choose. But we may not be all that convinced that we do have to choose; and we may not be convinced that if we learn rhetoric we will become like tyrants. The thought may still remain, that rhetoric can, and should, be used as a supplement to philosophy, as necessary.

This is where we need to take a careful look at the claims of rhetoric to be a discipline at all. The idea that rhetoric, by contrast with philosophy, is not a craft, is one that runs throughout the dialogue. It first surfaces at 453, where Gorgias says that the orator deals in words and persuasion. We immediately wonder, 'don't other crafts also deal in words and persuasion?'. Is there room here for rhetoric? There are two sorts of persuasion, says Socrates, one based on knowledge, the other not. Arithmetic, for example is persuasive about the odd and the even on the basis of knowledge (453e-454a). Undeterred, Gorgias soon claims that you need only learn rhetoric, and you need never lose [arguments] to other craftsmen (459c). The scene is now set for Plato's first discussion of his distinction between crafts and knacks.

Plato first introduces this distinction at 463ab. Rhetoric, Socrates claims, is 'a practice, not of a craftsman, but of a guessing, brave soul, naturally clever at approaching people; and the sum of it I call flattery'. Other knacks are cookery, cosmetics and sophistry, we learn. All four are part of flattery; and rhetoric in particular is 'an image of a part of politics' (463d). Socrates agrees with Gorgias that he has said nothing clear yet (463e). But as the dialogue progresses, Socrates continues to work at the distinction between knacks and crafts, and towards the conclusion of the dialogue, at 521d, feels able to conclude that he himself is in fact the only true politician among contemporary Athenians. Still, to revert to 463ff., crafts, we learn, are grounded in knowledge while knacks are grounded in people's uncertain and changing tastes. Knacks and crafts are competitors; that is why Plato describes knacks as images of crafts. This is true both in the care of the soul and in the care of the body: 'cookery impersonates medicine, then, and pretends to know the best food for the body' (464d); and 'cosmetics is disguised as gymnastics in the same way' (465b). The soul alone can tell the true craft apart from the impersonator, as the true craft possesses a *logos*, 'rational account' (465c). Children, and men as foolish as children cannot recognise healthy food (464de); similarly the body cannot succesfully 'discriminate [cookery from medicine] by guesswork from the gratifications to it' (465d) This is further explained in the dialogue at 501: knacks aim at pleasure, and pleasure is tied to the body.

These last remarks follow the extensive discussion of pleasure that occupies much of Socrates' discourse with Callicles. Pleasure is an important topic for middle period Plato. Art gives us pleasure, and that has to do with what is wrong with art. The body gives us pleasure, and that has to do with what is wrong with the body. And here knacks give us pleasure, and this has to do with what is wrong with knacks.

Let us postpone discussion of Plato's view of pleasure until we have surveyed more of the evidence. Let us remark here simply that Plato's ideas about crafts and knacks may seem to be rather narrowly tied to fifth century BC Greece. The fact that an activity is pleasant does not mean that it cannot be taught. One can, after all, buy cookery books, or places on cookery courses, today. We now see cookery as a skill that can be taught (up to a point). There seems to be room for crafts of the pleasant. And there seems to be less room for impostors in the domain of the rational than Plato would imply: even the boldest advertising agency would not try to persuade or dissuade us of the truths of arithmetic.

But the main themes of the *Gorgias* do not lack contemporary relevance. We do not, today, worry overmuch about the power of the orator[7] (we do not live in a direct democracy). But there are contemporary figures who seem to have great power over us – to hold the other in the palm of their hand. Thus Malcolm Schofield has suggested to me that today we have comparable fears about technology and those who manipulate it. And Irwin, in his commentary on the *Gorgias*, at one point compares the orator to the ad-man (Irwin, 1979: 130–1), a contemporary figure who might also be thought to satisfy people's desires (and who seems to be of increasing importance in political life). Irwin makes the point, by means of a quotation, that the ad-man might also be thought to create our desires, and to appeal to our ids in encouraging us to satisfy them.

We might take this comparison a stage further, and look at the ad-man as a persuader. If you are persuaded by an ad, what sort of persuasion is going on? The answer must be that it is persuasion that is supposed to be effective at all costs, that it is addressed to a mass audience, that it plays on the (less noble) emotions of that audience, and that it accepts the beliefs of that audience as it finds them. This all seems very reminiscent of Plato's view of rhetoric. Of course, ads do not persuade you about the truth or falsity of philosophical doctrines. But then philosophical doctrines are at least not immediately at issue in the lawcourts either, where rhetoric gets to work. And Plato's idea is that the correct technique of persuasion in any context is the Socratic one. If this is ill-fitted to successful self-defence in the law courts, or successful persuasion by television advertising, this is so much the worse for the society that tolerates such institutions.

The dialogue raises deep issues about the nature of a satisfactory human life. Other disciplines, such as psychology, developmental psychology, and psychoanalysis, may now make an essential theoretical contribution to our understanding of this area. But there is still a role for philosophy as practised by Plato. One's conception of the good life still needs to be fully characterised and spelled out, and then criticised and evaluated. And this is a task for the philosopher. In fact, the images of the life of philosophy and the life of rhetoric are memorably characterised in the *Gorgias*. The problem with the dialogue is not that Plato's project is in any way misconceived, but that the case he develops for the philosophical life rests on too many dubious premisses and fallacious arguments.

Philosophy, poetry and the meaning of life

Dubious premisses and fallacious arguments also coexist with deep philosophising in Plato's discussion of art in the *Republic*. It may at first sight seem surprising that Plato is interested in art in the *Republic*. After all, the place of art in the state is not nowadays a burning topic in political theory (at least it was not, prior to Iran's death threat against Salman Rushdie). But the question is natural in the Greek context, and in the context of Plato's claims on behalf of philosophy. For Plato (and indeed Aristotle) are engaged in a competition with the tragedians for supremacy in Greek cultural life and the Greek educational system. And the tragic poets may also seem to compete with Plato as philosophers: they offer their readers a philosophy of their own (in loose terms), and try to answer the question 'how should one live?' The tragic poets see a religious dimension to human life. Plato and Aristotle rather see human life in relation to ultimate philosophical truths.[8] And even today, of course, we might see poets and philosophers as rival purveyors of truths about the meaning of life.

So why does Plato banish art (all art or most art) from the ideal state? In this section, I shall simply first set out, and then discuss, Plato's three main lines of objection to some, or all, art. One of Plato's lines of argument has to do with the consumer of art, the second has to do with the producer of art (the artist or the actor), while the third concerns the nature of the art-work itself.

First, where the artist or the actor is concerned, Plato is troubled by the effect of art on the character. The problem here is not so much that art is connected to the wrong, or lower, parts of the soul (when Plato expresses these concerns about art, he has not yet, in fact, introduced the view that there are parts of the soul), as that the fact of *mimesis* – personating other people must be part of this – is dangerous. It is dangerous in two ways. First, there is the problem of becoming like the people you personate (this is a problem when they are bad, 395c). And second, there is the problem that the ideal person is a coherent personality over time. In Plato's view, it is not good to change all the time, and nor is it good to appear different in different contexts. This leads to fragmentation of the self (397e).

Second, where the nature of the art-work itself is concerned, Plato expresses the view that it is a simple copy of what there already is in the world; and that an art-work is the sort of thing you get by pointing a mirror at the world (596e) (just as things in the world are themselves a sort of copy of Forms, 596–7). Not only do actors personate others; art-works too are guilty of personation.

Finally, and perhaps most significantly, Plato is concerned here with the effect that viewing tragedy has on the soul. In *Republic*

II-III, Plato discusses the role of art in education, suggesting that it is important that children learn true opinions (392) and see true stories about gods and heroes (377 – that is, stories in which gods and heroes are good and behave well). The idea is more fully worked out in *Republic* X, however, when Plato returns to this theme. Plato holds that the soul has three parts (or perhaps, in *Republic* X, two parts), and that it is the lowest part, the emotional part, that enjoys tragedies – and to which art (and the false views about life it embodies) addresses itself. Just as mimetic art produces a product that is far removed from the truth, it associates with the part in us that is remote from intelligence (603ab).

Plato develops this theme with reference to a case-study in *Republic* X: how should one mourn the death of one's son? (introduced by Plato at 604e). A good and reasonable man will be moderate in his grief, alleges Socrates. And he will be more likely to resist his grief in the presence of others (604a). Plato here diagnoses conflict between the parts of the soul. The reasoning part will encourage us to feel nothing in human life is of great concern, it does us no good to take these things hard, and we don't actually know what is good and what is bad in these matters. (That is to say, it will encourage us to feel small and powerless and ignorant in the face of the universe.) The irrational and idle part encourages us to remember the experience, and lament it. One moral follows immediately for Plato: we should not cultivate the lower part of the soul.

This leads directly to the greatest accusation against art – that it can corrupt even the best among us (606a – though philosophers are protected against its ill effects by their knowledge, 595e). In Homer, or in a tragic poet, a hero in a state of grief will give vent to long speeches of lamentation, and we will enjoy this, even though we think it right to restrain ourselves in times of affliction. But our soul will suffer for it if we pity the hero in his grief: it will be that much harder for us to hold our own grief in check. Similarly, we enjoy buffooneries in comedy that we would ordinarily think it wrong to practise ourselves. But once we fail to detest them as base in the context of art, our guard will slip more generally: we will be more inclined to act the buffoon ourselves, when we have a mind to; and similarly with the representations of sex, anger, and all pleasures and pains (606d).

In the case of bereavement, we can say authoritatively that Plato has got hold of the wrong end of the stick – that it is important for the bereaved to express their grief (see Parkes, 1986). But what of Plato's more general case against art? All Plato's arguments against art are of great interest, and deserve close attention. All are, in fact, closely bound up with central themes of Platonic philosophy. But all can be understood independently of this background.

Plato is not alone in thinking art at least potentially harmful. The potential harmfulness of art for its consumers is a well-documented literary theme – from *Don Quixote* through *Northanger Abbey* to *Madame Bovary*. The idea is that if you lead your life in accordance with what you read, you may well behave in a manner inappropriate to your actual circumstances. Quixote is not Amadis of Gaul. Catherine Morland is not a Gothic heroine. Madame Bovary is not destined for a life of romance. All are influenced and, arguably, harmed, by their reading.[9] This poses the question whether it is enough to say, of art, 'I enjoy it'? It suggests that we need to be able to say, at least, what sort of enjoyment it gives us, and where this enjoyment fits into our lives.

The idea that art might be harmful for its practitioners is also not unparalleled. There is a certain unease about the idea of becoming *pantodapos*, a man of many parts. Compare the view of Rousseau as reported by Trilling (1972). For Rousseau, as for Plato, it is not just that the soul of the actor 'is deteriorated by identification with such morally inferior characters as he impersonates', but that 'by engaging in personation at all the actor diminishes his own existence as a person' (Trilling, 1972: 64). Jane Austen expresses similar concerns in *Mansfield Park* (also discussed by Trilling). Stepping out of character when acting is the first step towards living out of character. The self must remain within its own bounds if it is to preserve its integrity. Of course, it could be argued that it is beneficial to act alien roles. This need not lead to fragmentation of the self; but it may increase our behavioural repertoire, and help us in understanding ourselves and others. Furthermore, a consideration of alternative developmental paths may be helpful to the individual. Plato might counter this argument, however, by claiming that if we know the best path of development for human beings, we should concentrate on that.

Finally, what is a work of art? Here Plato's thinking looks very unpersuasive. Even in the case of the most 'realistic' novels, we are far from dealing with a mirror pointed at a 'slice of life'.[10]

And it may well be that Plato's criticisms of art derive partly from a misunderstanding of the nature of art-works.

But of course, Plato's view of art-works and his case against art are both founded on a number of dualisms that are deeply rooted in his thought – the dualisms between pleasant and good, between seeming and being, between what can be believed and what can be known. Art gets its grip on us in the actual world, if we do not know the good, if the *logistikon* does not consistently rule in the soul, and if we are affected by what seems, rather than what is. And if we judge the world by the yardstick of the pleasurable, art scores very highly. But this, for Plato, is the wrong yardstick. It predominates in the inferior part of the soul, in children and fools, who cannot tell appearance from reality, and also (605b7–8) in the bad element in a state. Most of us, in Plato's view, judge life by the criterion of reality most of the time, but in the case of art, we let our guard slip. We regard art as a special case, where the usual criteria do not apply. Philosophers, by contrast, judge art by the yardstick of reality – and exclude art from the ideal state.

But the whole of life will be very different in an ideal state organised by philosophers who know the good. In the ideal state, there will be no tragic dimension to human life. Socrates incurred a fate that seems tragic to us only because he did not live in the ideal state but in fifth-century BC Athens. (And of course, given the Socratic/Platonic worldview, it is debatable whether his fate really is tragic. After all, as we have just seen, Plato and Socrates think that nothing can harm the good man, that it is better to suffer injustice than to commit injustice, and so on . . .) And if there is no room left for tragedy in the ideal state, and no room for agent-regret in the life of the good man, then it is not really surprising if there is no room left for tragic art – especially if art mirrors life.

Belfiore (whose analysis I have followed at several points) compares Plato's view of art with that of Freud (Belfiore, 1983: 65, n.31). Freud too thinks that art creates a special context in which we liberate, temporarily, the child within us – though unlike Plato, Freud does not disapprove of this. Here, perhaps, we touch the core of the problem. We can accept, perhaps, with Freud, that the mind is not unitary; and further, perhaps, that part of the mind is rational and part is not. But in this case we are likely to believe, not that it is best for us to cultivate exclusively the rational part of our being, and to ward off and disown our irrational impulses, but that it is better for the self to be most fully integrated, and for our rational and irrational parts to live in harmony. To achieve such integration may call for sacrifices from our rational selves as much as from the irrational. Within this context, we may welcome a chance for the child within us to achieve self-expression, and the nourishment this may bring to our irrational selves. We may not wish to keep it permanently under wraps.

Further, we are perhaps more open to the idea that there is an irreducible plurality of value than Plato was. We do not expect works of art to be all-embracing in their vision. Nor do we feel we must wholly endorse the creative vision of the artists – I can enjoy reading Hardy, for example, without being persuaded of the truth of his 'pessimism'. I can read, and enjoy reading, Céline, but positively dissociate myself from his anti-Semitism and his Fascism. The explanation for this phenomenon (if it needs one) is that we may find a new and partial insight into the world intrinsically valuable. Céline's disgust with humanity, with the First World War, with colonial exploitation, with 'taylorism' (the production line at Ford's), with the powerlessness of medical science in the face of disease – all this can cast everyday experience in a new light. For Plato, however, there is just one true perspective from which we can view the world, the perspective of the philosopher-king with knowledge of Forms.

It is from this perspective that the philosopher judges that the messages of art are false and that the wisdom which artists lay claim to is a mere image of the real thing. It is from this perspective that the philosopher endorses the judgements of the *logistikon*, and rejects the verdicts of the emotional part of the soul. So let us now turn to examine this perspective in more detail.

THE LIFE OF PHILOSOPHY

Philosophy and the fear of death

Popper suggests, as we saw in Chapter 1, that in a sense we are all philosophers, because we must all take up an attitude towards life and death. And the question of the appropriate attitude towards death retains its interest for professional philosophers today.[11] Perhaps the first philosophical exploration of this topic occurs in Plato's *Phaedo*, where he argues that the fear of death is misplaced – especially for the philosopher. The philosopher in particular should not fear death because of the life he leads, which is a life of *melete thanatou*, cultivation of, or preparation for, death.

In this dialogue, Socrates is talking to his friends in the hours immediately before he drinks the hemlock. Early in the dialogue, he defines death as dissolution of the soul and body (64c – he takes this to be uncontroversial), and then proceeds to argue that 'those who practise philosophy aright are cultivating dying' (67e). This is because the philosopher is not keen on the pleasures of food and drink, or sex (64d), nor does he value smart clothes and shoes or other bodily adornments (64e). Further, the body is no help, but is a hindrance, in the pursuit of wisdom (65b). Wisdom, Plato hints, has to do with Forms (65de), and we do not get access to Forms through the senses. So it would be absurd for a philosopher to be resentful when death comes: for he has lived his life 'as close as he can to being dead' (67d).

This is Plato's initial statement of his view of philosophy in the *Phaedo*. The dialogue will consist hereafter partly in reflections about the nature of the life of philosophy and partly of arguments about the nature of the soul and arguments for the immortality of the soul.[12]

Thus Cebes responds to the initial description of philosophy as a cultivation of death by suggesting that maybe the soul perishes as soon as it is separated from the body (70a). And Socrates in reply presents three arguments for the immortality of the soul, from *palingenesis*, from his theory of recollection, and from *homoiosis*.[13] After presenting these arguments, Plato elaborates upon the theme of death and the philosopher. Upon death, the body is liable to be dissolved (80c); but the soul that is kept pure by *melete thanatou*, the cultivation of death, departs to the divine and immortal and wise (81a). If it is polluted, impure, and interspersed with a corporeal element, however, it will roam among tombs and graves, pending reincarnation in animal forms (81dff.). Pleasures and pains bind the soul to the body, and make the soul take the sensible things that affect it to be the most real. This, in fact, is the most serious evil of the non-philosophical life, and not 'being ill, for example, or spending money to satisfy one's desires' (83c). Philosophy, Plato hints once more, has to do with Forms (the soul 'thinks of any of the things that are, alone by itself' 83a). The life of philosophy cannot be combined with the life of sensual pleasure – that would involve binding and unbinding the soul to the body, like weaving and unweaving Penelope's web (84a).

But Plato recognises that we may still be unconvinced by his view of the soul. The account of *melete thanatou* again leads to a rejoinder. Simmias suggests that maybe the soul survives a few uses by various bodies, like a cloak, but is worn out and dies at last. Cebes adds that maybe it is like an attunement in a lyre, which is noncorporeal, but which does not outlast the lyre. Socrates responds with a discussion of hypothesis and explanation, and with the final argument for the immortality of the soul, which depends on the hypothesis that there are Forms, which explain being and coming-to-be in the sensible world.

Plato seems to acknowledge that even this argument may not be ultimately coercive: Socrates and Simmias agree that the final argument could do with more examination (107ab). But they have run out of time and Socrates must now face his death as a philosopher. He tells a myth about the afterlife, then drinks the hemlock.

For all Plato's stress on the question of the cogency of the arguments, I do not propose here to examine the individual philosophical arguments in detail, and seek out their shortcomings.[14] Rather, I shall ask more generally why Plato thinks that we should cultivate death instead of cultivating life.

To this end, let us ask first, why we face a choice between paying attention to the body and paying attention to the soul. After all, given that we are in fact amalgams of soul and body, we might perhaps expect that we should listen to the reports about the world of both body and soul with equal respect, and pursue the pleasures of both body and soul. Both sorts of pleasure might be components of the good life; they might even reinforce one another (thus Nussbaum mentions the possibility that a moderate, or even a high, degree of sensual indulgence might be required instrumentally, to foster philosophical growth – Nussbaum, 1986a: 151). Plato argues, however, first, that servicing bodily desires leaves us with no leisure to do philosophy (66d), and second, that philosophy leads us to disregard reports of the senses (and hence the body) (83a).

As human beings, then, we must either practise life, accept the reports of the senses and pursue bodily pleasures, or practise death and lead the life of the philosopher focusing on the soul's view of the world. There is no middle way. And this is still Plato's position in the *Republic*. By the time of the *Republic*, Plato has elaborated his theory of the tri-partite soul. We face there, not a choice between body and soul, but a choice between different parts of the soul (see, for example, the end of Book IX)

Given that we face a choice between cultivating death and cultivating life (or between cultivating the higher, or the lower, part of the soul) Plato gives us two reasons for choosing the former option. He argues that the senses present us with misleading reports about the world; and that bodily pleasures are inferior to those of the soul.

Let us first look at Plato's case against the pleasures of the body. Nussbaum draws together the threads of several relevant Platonic discussions in Chapter 5 of *The Fragility of Goodness* (Nussbaum 1986a). In the *Gorgias*, Socrates mentions as representative examples of pleasures itching/scratching and passive homosexual activity. Nussbaum characterises Plato's point here in terms of the 'need-relativity' of bodily pleasures. A closely related set of ideas recur in the division of worthwhile activities in *Republic* II: some activities are valued as instrumental means to ends (such as exercising, undergoing medical treatment when one is sick, making money), others are valued intrinsically (such as happiness and pleasure), while a third group is valued on both counts (such as sight, hearing, intelligence and health, 367c). In *Republic* IX, Plato contrasts with these bodily pleasures the purity and stability of the activity of philosophising, and of the objects studied by philosophy, and its claim to tell us the truth about the world. The pleasures of philosophy are accordingly more real than the pleasures of the body.

Plato's attack on bodily pleasures is not entirely successful. Nussbaum writes persuasively about the pleasures of scratching as follows:

> What we find ridiculous about scratching as an activity is not exactly its need-relativity. The source of our condemnation lies elsewhere. It is an indication of bodily disease or poor hygiene; it is futile, because it never completely relieves the annoying pain, but usually makes it worse; and it provides a constant very strong distraction, devoid of all positive pleasure, from other important life-activities like work and sleep. What is more, the activity lacks any positive aesthetic side; we cannot imagine an art of it, or connoisseurs of it.

> It is, finally, socially unacceptable and embarrassing. Eating isn't like that. Sex isn't like that.
>
> (Nussbaum 1986a: 153)

We might add that the pleasures of scratching are, in the terminology of von Wright (1960), mere passive pleasures: they comprise simply pleasant physical sensations. Active pleasures – those that involve the enjoyment of an activity – are clearly valued as ends in themselves, as well as for pleasure or happiness. And of course most, even, of our passive pleasures (though not, perhaps, the pleasure of scratching an itch) we invest with personal meaning. Furthermore, we may feel that the pleasures of the body are basic to human life, and that their reality can hardly be questioned. Few would want to live a life wholly restricted to the pleasures of the mind.[15]

For all that, Plato's case against bodily pleasures certainly has its strengths as well as its weaknesses. Nussbaum argues persuasively that there are cases, such as that of perverse sexual desire, that Plato's analysis does fit, and that appetite can distort our view of the world, and act as an obstacle to true judgement (Nussbaum, 1986a: 155). It is hard to see how we could hope to derive any meaningful overall life-plan simply from devoting ourselves wholly to bodily pleasures, and from satisfying our instinctual desires for food, drink and sex. A creature who leads such a bodily life would be very much at the mercy of his environment; even at the best, his life would be uninteresting.

But if Plato's case against the pleasures of the body seems to have some substance, his case against the reports of the senses is more difficult to defend. Plato discusses the shortcomings of the senses' reports on the world most clearly in *Republic* 523–5 and in *Republic* X. In *Republic* 523–5, he tells us that the senses report inadequately on a finger that is large and small, telling us that there is some single entity mingled together. In order to clarify the senses' report, the mind must separate the big from the small. In *Republic* X, the senses tell us, when seeing a straight stick in water, that it is bent. The mind must correct this report. More generally, the senses fail to inform us that there are Forms. This is a truth accessible to the mind alone. None of these complaints about the senses, however, seems very cogent. In the case of the finger that is big and small, there is no good reason to think that the senses are misleading us – the finger *is* both big and small in different contexts; in the case of the bent stick, perhaps the senses do mislead us, but the deceit in question is local in extent, and the misleading reports are easily corrected on the basis of further sensory evidence; in the case of Forms, it would appear that the senses are correct in their report – there are no Forms.

It would seem, then, that Plato's case against bodily pleasures has some substance, but that his case against the reports of the senses about the sensible world is much more suspect. But there are, of course, two sides to Plato's case. Plato hopes to convince us not only about his view of the body, but also about his view of the soul – that there is a perspective on life, that of the soul, from which the cultivation of death seems appropriate.

It is not difficult to argue that there is a standpoint on the world which is other than that of everyday life (the standpoint from which Plato thinks we value the pleasures of the body). This idea has, for example, been developed very persuasively by Nagel, with his concept of the 'view from nowhere'. Nagel develops a polarity betwen subjective and objective views we might take of various philosophical questions, as follows:

> At one end is the point of view of a particular individual, having a specific consititution, situation, and relation to the rest of the world. From here the direction of movement [is towards] a conception of the world which as far as possible is not the view from anywhere within it.
>
> (Nagel, 1979: 208)

Nagel thinks that 'We must admit that the move towards objectivity reveals what things are like in themselves as opposed to how they appear' (Nagel, 1979: 212). To that extent, objectivity is preferable. But it is not clear that we always need to step back to the objective viewpoint. As Nagel points out, there seem to be elements of the subjective viewpoint that it is hard to accommodate within the objective viewpoint. A satisfactory integration between the two standpoints is thus a worthwhile goal (Nagel 1986: 6).

For Plato, unlike Nagel, the objective view of the world is always preferable to the subjective one. This is because the everyday subjective view of the world is a sort of distorted reflection of the philosophical, objective view of the world. Particulars give us some idea (but not a very clear idea) of what Forms are like. Seeming is a guide (of a sort) to being. And the pleasures of the many are a sort of distorted image of true (i.e. philosophical) pleasure (*Republic* 586b).

Plato's conception of the content of the objective standpoint on the world differs from from that of Nagel. For Plato, we occupy the objective standpoint whenever we philosophise. For Nagel, however, tensions between the subjective and the objective standpoints arise within the practice of philosophy. (Philosophers are tempted to espouse both viewpoints – to believe both in free will and in determinism, for example.) Nagel himself sometimes takes it that the objective view is the scientific one; at other times it is simply the view he thinks emerges when we shrug off our local and particular concerns. There is not necessarily any tension between these two conceptions of the objective – it may be that the scientific view of the world is what emerges in certain fields when we shrug off the local and particular. Obviously, the scientific conception of the world was not available to Plato. But the objective standpoint on the world still deals in things as they are, and not as they seem to be; and the philosopher does abstract from the personal as he abstracts from the bodily.

The real question, then, is how effective Plato is in giving substance to his own conception of the objective standpoint, to his view that this is occupied by the philosopher who lives in communion with Forms and who sees life as a practice for death. This is where we need to assess the direct philosophical arguments for soul/body dualism and for the immortality of the soul.

The crucial arguments are the argument from recollection and the final argument, which rests on the hypothesis that Forms explain the sensible world. The first of these arguments purports to show that the sensible world is not all there is; the second argument rests squarely on the view that there are Forms as well as sensible particulars. We must ask whether we can reply to the questions 'can we stock our mind from the sensible world?' and 'can we explain being and coming-to-be in the sensible world?' without invoking the theory of Forms. It may be sufficient to remark here that there is general agreement that these are difficult questions, but that we are unlikely now to appeal to the theory of Forms as a way of resolving the difficulties to which they may give rise.

In Plato's view, to be a human being is to be a temporary amalgam of an immortal soul with a body that is subject to generation and decay. If that view were correct, Plato might indeed stand some chance of delivering us from the fear of death and of transforming our attitude towards life. For we might become convinced that our souls will simply become separated from our bodies at death, and will move on to higher things. In that case, the prospect of real death, after a lifetime of cultivation of death, might indeed seem quite welcome. As things stand, the *Phaedo* presents us with a challenge, in the portrait of Socrates in life and in death. Socrates makes out an impressive case for his way of life. But his confidence in the immortality of the soul would seem, as he himself describes it, to be a 'noble risk' (114d). It does not seem anything like a certainty.

Plato on love

We have seen that in the *Gorgias*, Socrates makes a claim to expertise about politics, remarking that he is the only true politician in Athens. This claim is surprising for many reasons, but not least, because of Socrates' limited involvement in the political life of Athens. In the *Symposium*, Socrates makes an equally surprising claim to expertise about love – a claim that is surprising, both in the light of Socrates' restrained sexual behaviour (as reported in the Socratic dialogues, and in the *Symposium* itself, by Alcibiades), but also because Socrates is a philosopher, and we do not take the study of love to be a natural part of philosophy. It will transpire, however, that Socrates takes expertise about love (like expertise about politics) to be closely linked to expertise in philosophy.

Socrates tells us in the *Symposium* that he knows nothing except about love (177d6). The claim to know nothing reflects the general Socratic disavowal of knowledge; and indeed later in the dialogue (198d2), Socrates recalls his earlier claim to be *deinos ta erotika*, to be 'skilled in matters of love', and now says that he knows nothing about the subject. He soon recants again, however, and says that he was taught in matters of love by Diotima, a priestess from Mantinea, who was wise both about this question and about others (201d); and he offers to share Diotima's wisdom on the subject with his listeners.

It in fact transpires, as we share in Diotima's wisdom, that philosophers have a lot in common with the god of love, Eros. They share with him a sort of intermediate status, desiring, but not yet possessing, the beautiful (wisdom being one of the most beautiful of all things). Neither the wise man nor the ignorant man philosophises, but those who are aware of, and wish to make good, their own lack of wisdom. (204a) Love is an important aspect of the life of the philosopher. Diotima's theory of love is that we desire good and beautiful things when we lack them and are aware of the lack (204a); one of the things we want and lack is immortality (207a), and we try to make good this lack through creation, *tokos en kaloi*, 'generation in the beautiful', a creation which may be either of physical, or better, of intellectual, children. There are higher and lower forms of love; we ascend from the lower to the higher forms of love in the following order, if we wish to go about the business correctly: we start out in life by loving an individual beautiful body (but trying to generate from that body beautiful thoughts); then we become lovers of all beautiful bodies; next we ascend to love of souls – of beautiful thoughts, of laws and institutions, and finally to the love of the sciences and (ultimately) of the Form of Beauty. This, the life spent in contemplation of the Form of Beauty, is the life to be lived by man (210–211).

It is very soon apparent that we will not want to accept Plato's view about the relation of love to philosophy. The philosopher's claim to expertise about love is based on the claim that he alone contemplates the Form of Beauty, and that this is the highest form of love. But if there is no Form of Beauty, then these claims are based on an illusion (see pp.122–123 below for a further account of the theory of Forms). None the less, as we shall see, a study of Plato's views on this subject can stimulate us to think for ourselves and help us towards the truth, both about the nature of love, and about the nature of philosophy.

Three aspects of Plato's theory of love are of particular interest – all of which were originally discussed in a classic paper by Vlastos (1969). First, there is the question whether, when we are in love, we are concerned primarily with the welfare of the person we love. We have already seen (in Chapter 2) Vlastos' view that Socrates manifested a 'failure of love'. In this paper, Vlastos explores various surprising aspects of Plato's view of love. One of Vlastos' central claims, put very roughly, is that whereas we think (and Aristotle thought) that when we are in love with someone, or more generally care for someone, we wish that person well for his own sake, Plato thinks, by contrast, that the primary object of love is the Form of Beauty. We obviously do not wish the Form of Beauty well for its own sake. Nor do we wish our lovers well for their own sake if we see them (as Plato may do) as mere stepping-stones towards love for the Form of Beauty.

Second, there is the question whether love as described by Plato will tend to promote in us a more truthful vision of the world. Vlastos holds that whereas we standardly idealise the one we love, Platonic love is not like this. We may see our lover as a mere image of the Form of Beauty; but we see how he falls short of the Form of Beauty. So we can see him steadily and see him whole.

Finally, we must ask whether Vlastos is right when he praises Plato for realising that not all love is love for individuals: Vlastos holds that Plato recognises, and deserves credit for recognising, that we can also care passionately about ideas.

Let us first ask about the twin issues of loving others for their own selves, and idealisation of those we love. It would be nice to think that we care about other people as they really are. Perhaps we sometimes achieve this in friendship, as Aristotle thinks. Idealisation of the loved one seems relatively frequent, however. And this may interfere in our loving another person for that person's own sake. Indeed it may even interfere with our perception of those we love. For example, Proust, in *A L'ombre des jeunes filles en fleur*, describing the narrator's adolescent love for Gilberte Swann, writes:

> My imagination had isolated and hallowed in social Paris a certain family, just as it had set apart in structural Paris a certain house, whose entrance it had sculpted and its windows bejewelled. But these ornaments I alone had eyes to see . . . [my mother and my father] saw nothing unique in it. . . . For in order to distinguish in everything that surrounded Gilberte an indefinable quality analogous in the world of the emotions to what in the world of colours is called infra-red, my parents would have needed that supplementary sense with which love had temporarily endowed me.
>
> (Proust 1918: 450)

A second point familiar to us is that love may sometimes involve an identity confusion or fusion. Indeed, on some theories of love, the loved one can represent a past loved one, as well as existing in his or her own right. Thus Freud says that all finding of an object is in fact a re-finding (quoted by Santas, 1988: 123); and

Hardy can write, in *The Well-Beloved*, a story about a man who loves first a woman, then her daughter, then her granddaughter.

Plato also thinks that illusion is relevant to the discussion of love. After all, he thinks our whole lives are filled with illusion. We mostly live in a dream-world, taking sensible reality for true reality (see *Republic* V). This is what we do, if we take equal sticks for the Form Equal (and *Phaedo* 73–4 suggests we sometimes may). The prisoners in the cave take the shadows of puppets for reality (see *Republic* VII). It would be unsurprising then, if the Platonic lover were to take illusion for reality, and idealise his lover, mistaking him for the Form of Beauty. There is at least scope for idealisation, and for identity mistakes or confusion, at the lower points in the ascent of desire. Plato comes closest to discussing the question of idealisation at *Phaedrus* 251. Here Plato says of the lover that 'did he not fear being taken for a madman, he would offer sacrifice to his boy-love as to a holy image and a god' (251a). Vlastos remarks that 'the ontology of the paradigm-form' enables the best lover to 'keep his head clear even when his senses are inflamed' (Vlastos, 1969: 29). With Santas, however, (1988: 71),[16] I believe that Plato is clearly recognising the phenomenon of idealisation here – and giving some account of it. It is really the Form of Beauty that we see in our lovers, and the Form of Beauty towards which we direct our worship when we idealise our lovers. The best Platonic lover may differ from the everyday lover in understanding better his own behaviour. But for all of us, those we love represent for us something over and above their own persons.

Vlastos remarks that it is a 'sterling asset' of Plato's view that it 'makes for a more truthful vision of the part of the world . . . we love' (Vlastos 1969: 30). But in fact I doubt if Plato really deserves this praise. Vlastos later remarks that Plato's theory 'does not provide for love of whole persons' (Vlastos 1969: 31). Here we touch on the crux of the issue of idealisation. The ordinary lover loves a person, idealising that person, and taking the part that is perfect for the whole. The Platonic lover realises that he loves only a part of an object – that part that represents the Form of Beauty in the loved one. Thus by comparison with the ordinary lover, he may appear clear-sighted. But there is a third alternative, not considered by Plato. This is centrally important in Melanie Klein's view of human development. Idealisation is a primitive mental process that interferes with our perception of others (and ourselves), and with our caring for others for their own sake. It is as we mature into what Klein calls the depressive position that we form a picture of ourselves and others as whole persons, that we understand how good and bad coexist in ourselves and in others, and that true concern for others, accurately perceived and unidealised, can emerge.

These ideas are completely foreign to Plato. He does not think that the highest phase of human development is perception and acceptance of people as they are. Rather, he believes that opposites should be kept apart by the mind, and that what is wrong with the sensible world is precisely their universal compresence. Santas aptly remarks that 'the Form of Beauty cannot be overestimated' (Santas, 1988: 175). We cannot idealise it, or form too high an opinion of it. It actually delivers what we all, perhaps, want from an object of love.

Vlastos refers in this context not just to idealisation, but also to what he calls 'the tyranny that even the unidealized love-object can exercise over a lover' (Vlastos, 1969: 30). This too, he thinks, could exist only on the very lowest rung of the ladder of the Platonic ascent of desire. Vlastos mentions as a case in point Swann's love for Odette (in Proust's *Du côté de chez Swann*). He claims that Swann loves Odette long after idealising her and that his love 'disabled his spirit for the rest of his life' (Vlastos 1969: 30). We should note that this is wrong: Swann is already a failed aesthete when he meets Odette. His love drives him back (temporarily) to his study on Vermeer and for the duration of his unhappiness (which is perhaps coextensive with the duration of his love), he lives on a higher level of morality (Proust, 1913: 375).

Vlastos, interestingly, gives no account of where the tyranny arises from. One idea here might be that when we are in love, we tend to lose our own boundaries, and merge with the loved object, who can thus seem like an uncontrolled (and potentially tyrannising) part of the self. On this story, Swann might remain tyrannised by Odette, because their identities had merged, even when he had begun to see her more accurately. This account would form a natural extension of the idea mentioned in the speech of Aristophanes in the *Symposium* that Zeus formed human beings by splitting their ancestors in two, as one might split an egg in two. Human beings then tried vainly to reunite with their missing halves, and often gave up on life and died. Zeus took pity on them, and rearranged their sexual organs, so that intercourse and generation became possible. Since that time, love has naturally existed in human beings, 'that reconciler and bond of union of their original nature, which seeks to make two, one, and to heal the divided nature of man' (*Symposium*, 190–1,).[17]

Diotima's theory of love is clearly incompatible with that of Aristophanes (as Diotima remarks in 205a, her theory is that we all love the good, not that we all love part of ourselves), although both are full of interest. On Aristophanes' theory, we are all interested in 'restoring an earlier state of affairs' (Santas 1988: 161).[18] The motivation for love comes from within ourselves and from our own personal histories. On Diotima's theory, by contrast, we perceive and are attracted to what we think good. The motivation for love comes from without. On Aristophanes' theory, the lover is very much at the mercy of chance. On Diotima's theory, the lover can rest secure that the Form of Beauty is there and waiting for him.

Let us now turn to the extension of love beyond the individual. It is natural here to contrast Plato's theory of the ascent of desire with Freud's theory of sublimation. On Freud's theory, we come to care about intellectual pursuits when some of our libido (sexual energy) is diverted, or sublimated, from its natural aim or goal. Freud's concept of sublimation is part of his more general theory of sexuality, and represents an important aspect of his extended conception of sexuality. (Other extensions are from adults to children; and from the genitals to the mouth and the anus.) Plato is sometimes thought to anticipate some of these ideas. (Thus for example, in *Republic* 571–2, he suggests that the shameless man, but not the good man, will dream of sleeping with his mother.)[19] Following Santas, we should note some important differences between the views of Plato and those of Freud. For Plato the process of ascent is conscious, whereas for Freud the process of sublimation is unconscious. For Plato the ascent of desire leads to more satisfactory fulfilment of the original desires; sublimation would seem, however, to lead to less satisfactory fufilment of those desires. One point of similarity should be noted, though: 'generation in the beautiful' sounds as though it is still sexual in character. One does not generate ideas alone.[20]

What have we learned about philosophy from pursuing Plato into his discussion of love? First, something of how a set of beliefs in metaphysics and epistemology can bear directly on the conduct of our everyday lives: if there is a Form of Beauty, and if love for the Form of Beauty is a natural extension of, or indeed, an ascent from, our love for individuals, then the goal of our lives should clearly be to ascend from our love for individuals to love of the Form. Second, we have perhaps learned something about the scope of philosophy. Expertise about love is not today the mark of the philosopher. Plato's *Symposium* shows that this could be a mistake. Philosophical discourse is one possible route to enlightenment about love – alongside some of the other forms of discourse exemplified in the *Symposium*.[21] Plato has charted new ground for philosophy. At the same time, his actual philosophical theories are not wholly convincing. They do however, show us one way to integrate the phenomena we look at under this heading; and challenge us to formulate a rival, more persuasive, theory of our own.

Plato on philosophy and the ideal state

In the *Phaedo* and the *Symposium*, Plato tells us how the philosopher will live in fifth-century Athens: he will cultivate death and contemplate the Form of Beauty. In the *Republic*, Plato turns his attention to the life of the philosopher in the ideal state. The picture that emerges is, unsurprisingly, somewhat different. The subject of philosophy first crops up in the *Republic* when Plato tells us in Book V, at 473bd, that the smallest change in the status quo that we would need to bring into existence the ideal state is that philosophers should become kings or kings should become philosophers. In this section, I want to focus on books V-VII of the *Republic* in which Plato defends and develops this claim.

There are three main parts to of the discussion. First, Plato argues that philosophers alone have true knowledge and true understanding; and that philosophers alone, then, are experts in justice, and philosophers alone should rule (he deploys the analogy of the ship of state at 488ff.) Second, Plato sets out his vision of the human condition in the similes of the sun line and cave, and of the route we must traverse if we are to become philosophers. Finally, Plato sets out the ideal educational curriculum for the student of philosophy in the ideal state.

Plato's first claim, that there is such a thing as political expertise, and that such expertise is to be acquired through philosophy, is argued for directly at the end of Book V. But the argument is exceptionally unconvincing, and I do not propose to discuss it here.[22] Rather, I propose to focus on a portion of the text that is less dependent on the correctness of a philosophical argument, namely the vision of the sun line and cave, and the account this gives us of the philosopher's progress.

Plato here paints a memorable picture of the human condition – the sort of picture that Dennett calls an 'intuition pump', one of the 'enduring melodies of philosophy, with the staying power that ensures that they will be remembered by our freshmen, quite vividly and accurately, years after they have forgotten the intricate contrapuntal surrounding argument and analysis' (Dennett 1984: 17). Dennett cites Plato's cave as an example, along with the geometry lesson in the *Meno*. An intuition pump, for Dennett, is a sort of thought experiment. The point is 'to entrain a family of imaginative reflections in the reader that ultimately yields not a formal conclusion but a dictate of "intuition" ' (Dennett, 1984: 12). They are 'powerful pedagogical devices', but they can 'mislead as much as they instruct' (Dennett 1984: 18). Their use in philosophy shows that philosophy is not a science; but they help us 'enlarge our vision of the possible' and 'break bad habits of thought' (Dennett, 1984: 18). The role of intuition pumps in philosophy need not embarrass us, claims Dennett, if, for example, we accept Wittgenstein's view that 'philosophy is a battle against the bewitchment of our intelligence by means of language' (Wittgenstein, 1953: §109).

There is no denying the power of this image to pump intuitions. It is often asserted, in various unlikely contexts, that we do live in the darkness of Plato's cave.[23] The image, once summoned up, is hard to dissipate. We shall examine the source of its power later. First let us look at the image more closely, in its immediate context in the *Republic*.

Plato says, in the image of the cave, that we are prisoners bound in a cave, who can see only shadows of puppets. We are desperately in need of release, if we are to see the world as it is. Fortunately, a guide is available, and also a route by which we can leave the cave, and gain access to the external world. When we are first freed from our chains, we will suffer pain and *aporia* (515d6); and the guide will never be popular with the prisoners within the cave. The prisoners in the cave would kill someone who tried to enlighten them, if they could (517a). And if the philosopher had to dispute in the lawcourts about justice or about the statues the images are of, with the prisoners who have never seen the real thing, he will be at some disadvantage (517d). It is hard to avoid the conclusion that Plato has in mind the life and death of Socrates.

The cave shows us something of the first stage of our journey towards enlightenment. The image of the line tells us something about a later stage of our journey. Mathematics is a helpful study, in so far as mathematics makes it easy to realise that the sensible world is not all there is – that we use sensible diagrams as images of a non-sensible reality.[24] Mathematicians, however, do not realise the true nature of the non-sensible reality in question. And they hypothesise the odd and the even, and so on, but do not ask, after the manner of Socrates, 'what is the odd?', 'what is the even?', and so on. The image of the sun, finally, tells us how the world coheres at the highest level. All knowledge, and all Forms, fall under the Form of the Good; and it provides the medium through which we may attain to knowledge of the Forms (508de).

The three images introduce Plato's account of the educational system he proposes for the ideal state, a course of study that will draw the mind 'from what is becoming to what is being' (521d). Would-be philosophers should study first plane geometry, then solid geometry, astronomy and harmonics before finally graduating to dialectic, the grasping at the good itself. Dialectic lies like a coping-stone on top of the other sciences (535a); in the image of the cave, it represents the philosopher's progress from the moment that he first looks at the real things outside the cave (532ac).

It is important not to embark on dialectic too early (539). One is brought up with certain moral beliefs which one respects as a child respects its parents. Being asked Socratic questions, and suffering defeat in dialectical debate is like discovering that one's supposed parents are not one's real parents. It is all too easy at this point to conclude that nothing is fine rather than disgraceful (538e1), and to turn from traditional beliefs to the way of life that flatters (the life of pleasure). However, when education proceeds at the proper pace, the effect on the character is highly beneficial. At the start of Book VI, Plato tells us how the character of the philosopher is formed by his love of, and contemplation of the Forms. He will love truth (485d) and the pleasures of the mind (485de). His mind, being used to the contemplation of all time, and all being, will not consider human life a great thing (486a8–10).

He will have many desirable qualities. The key to his character, however, is that he will become like what he contemplates (500a).[25]

The conception Plato now has of philosophy is very different from that of the Socratic dialogues. Plato's view of the man in the street has not changed: he is a dreamer, or he is a prisoner in the cave. Nor has his view that the practice of philosophy is a form of care for the soul, and leads the philosopher to his personal happiness. But the soul is now tripartite; and happiness consists in justice. This consists, in turn, of knowledge of Forms, on the one hand, and a soul whose parts are in harmony, on the other. And Socratic *elenchos* is no longer the only method recommended to philosophers. Dialectic, now identified with the method of hypothesis, is the coping-stone of the sciences, and the culmination of a long period of study. It is not freely available, but is confined to the over-40s. The theory of Forms bulks large in Plato's conception of philosophy. Philosophical enlightenment is to be achieved through recollection (or quasi-recollection) of the Forms.[26] And the theory of Forms now fills out the claim that virtue is knowledge. It rebuts scepticism about ethics, and it underlies Plato's new picture of the human psyche. The truth the *logistikon* lays claim to is the truth about Forms.

The theory of Forms is a metaphysical doctrine with consequences – if we accept it – for the everyday conduct of our lives.[27] If we do not accept the theory of Forms, however, we might as well stay on in the cave, continue to enjoy the poets, fear death, and lead the ordinary human life. There is nothing to back up Plato's vision of a brighter world outside. Plato's conception of philosophy and of the philosophical life, is wholly bound up with the success of this particular philosophical doctrine.

But even if we do not accept the theory of Forms, Plato's *Republic* retains much of its value as philosophy. This is partly because of the fundamental nature of the questions Plato asks, and partly because of his development of certain fundamental responses to those questions. Thus in political philosophy, Plato asks the question 'who should rule?', answers that the best should rule, and then sets up an educational system and a state that will produce the best. Perhaps here the response of Popper is necessary: the initial question is what is misguided. (See Popper 1945: 120–121; he suggests that we should replace the question 'who should rule?' by a new one: 'How can we so organise political institutions that bad or incompetent rulers can be prevented from doing too much damage?') In moral philosophy, the theory of Forms can be seen as an answer to scepticism about ethics. Here it is interesting to note two claims of the contemporary moral sceptic, Mackie (1977). Mackie believes that 'ordinary moral judgements include a claim to objectivity' (Mackie, 1977: 35), but that this is an error. About the theory of Forms, however, he says that it gives 'a dramatic picture of what objective values would have to be' (Mackie, 1977: 40) – that is, 'a very central structural element in the fabric of the world', 'eternal, extra-mental, realities' that are at once objective and prescriptive (Mackie, 1977: 23). Mackie here pays tribute to Plato: he offers an impeccable development of a natural line of thought about ethics, and one to which we must address ourselves. If, at the end of the day, we reject Plato's answer to this question, our engagement with Plato's view will have led to an increase in our philosophical understanding (if not our philosophical knowledge).

Moreover, as we have seen, the *Republic* also has an effectiveness as philosophy that transcends the effectiveness of the individual arguments. Plato's images of the human condition continue to pump intuitions, even when they are cut free from his arguments about knowledge and reality. We may feel that, paradoxically (bearing in mind Plato's view of art), Plato's picture of the human condition has the same sort of persuasiveness as great literature. These images retain their power, because they capture part (but only part) of the human condition. It is impossible to look around the world and feel that, morally speaking, everything is in order as it is. Plato had seen representative Athenians condemn Socrates to death for teaching philosophy (or for corrupting the youth and believing in strange gods). The moral understanding of most individuals is rather limited.[28] It is his sense of this limitation that Plato has expressed very forcibly with the image of the cave.

The philosopher today does not lead a distinctive lifestyle; he does not practise for death; he does not prove himself an expert on love through his contemplation of the Form of Beauty; he does not rule in the ideal state; nor, typically, does he accept the truth of Plato's central philosophical doctrines about knowledge, reality and the soul, or Plato's views about the life of philosophy. But there is much that we can still learn from Plato. Plato addresses the central questions of philosophy; he shows us the significance of these questions, and how they are related to each other. His philosophical position on most of these questions is attractive, but fatally flawed. His general vision of the world, however, we are unlikely ever to forget. We may rebut many of Plato's arguments; but his vision expresses central truths about human life.

4

ARISTOTLE: PHILOSOPHY, METHOD, BEING AND THE GOOD LIFE

INTRODUCTION

Plato was the first philosopher to found a philosophical school. Aristotle was a student of Plato's for nineteen years in his school years. But when Plato died, he was succeeded as head of the school, not by Aristotle, but by his nephew Speusippus. Aristotle left Athens, and studied not just philosophy but also biology for a time in Assos and in Mytilene, before becoming tutor to Alexander the Great in Macedonia. When Aristotle did return to Athens, he founded his own philosophical school, the Lyceum. He withdrew from Athens again shortly before his death, on being prosecuted for impiety. (He would seem to have been innocent of impiety, but guilty of Macedonian connections at a time when this made him unpopular.)

Ross suggests that in Plato's philosophy, Aristotle 'found the master-influence of his life' (Ross, 1949: 2). Certainly, this is true of the three aspects of Aristotle's conception of philosophy that I propose to explore in this chapter – his view of philosophical method, his view of the organisation of knowledge (and the doctrine of being on which this view ultimately rests) and his conception of the role of philosophy in the good life.

Aristotle's conception of philosophical method is remarkably 'anthropocentric' (Nussbaum, 1986a: 242). Unlike Plato, Aristotle does not expect us to remodel our lives, starting from scratch, but rather to deepen our existing understanding of the world. According to Aristotle, we do and we should start our philosophising from where we are – from our existing beliefs and our existing perplexities. We cease to philosophise when we have resolved our perplexities. In the course of our enquiry, our understanding of the world will have increased; we will have moved from what is more intelligible to us to what is more intelligible in itself. We may be helped in this process by reflecting on the work of our philosophical predecessors. The best approach, when faced by an *aporia* or perplexity, is, in general, to examine the views of the many and the wise (past philosophers), and see if we can construct a solution that satisfies us, but that builds on the insights of others. It will be apparent that Aristotle's account of philosophical method is refreshingly independent of his substantive philosophical doctrines. I shall examine its merits further below (pp. 108–20).

Aristotle's method of philosophical enquiry yielded philosophical results; and he also achieved valuable work in science. In fact, Aristotle's writings range widely: they occupy twelve volumes in the Oxford translation. Aristotle discussed the movement of animals and the movement of the heavenly bodies; he discussed rhetoric, tragedy and the Athenian constitution; and he discussed most of the central questions of philosophy – ethics, metaphysics, philosophy of science, philosophy of mind. An important question for Aristotle, then, as the head of a philosophical school, was how those results should be categorised; and how they should be passed on to students.

Aristotle advanced views about the structure of a completed science. The propositions that fall within a given field follow deductively from its first principles (see *Posterior Analytics* I.2 and 4). In teaching a science, we demonstrate these deductive links to students. In enquiry, however, we use the method of dialectic; we do not proceed from first principles, but towards them (cf. Owen, 1986: 154).

Aristotle also divides thought according to its subject matter. He claims at *Metaphysics* 1025b–6a that all thought is either practical or productive or theoretical (1025b25); theoretical thought is further subdivided into physics, which deals with changeable things; mathematics, which deals with things *qua* 'immoveable and separable from matter' (1026b10); and theology, which deals with 'things which both exist separately and are immoveable' (1026b16).

In the (late) *Metaphysics* Γ, Aristotle holds that there is a single overarching discipline which unites the various departmental branches of knowledge, namely the study of being *qua* being, or first philosophy. Earlier, however, Aristotle had criticised Plato's view of the relation between the sciences on the grounds that 'being' and 'good' are homonymous, and that there is no single overarching study which is the study of being and good. Aristotle's view of being seems to change as his thought matures. I shall examine Aristotle's doctrine of being below (pp. 120–9), and argue that in this case Aristotle's practice of philosophy is reasonably in accord with his view of philosophical method.[1]

Aristotle also presents us with a new conception of the role of philosophy in the good life – or perhaps, two new conceptions of this. One is that of the 'harmonious' life (as it has been termed by Lear 1988), in which philosophical contemplation plays little part, but man fulfils his own human, social, nature. The other conception, that of the 'disharmonious' life, is one in which man tries to become immortal, so far as in him lies, and devotes his time to philosophical contemplation, to understanding, and to self-understanding. I shall examine below (pp. 129–38) Aristotle's view of the good life, and the role of philosophy in the good life.

PHILOSOPHICAL METHOD

Aristotle held influential and interesting views on the subject of philosophical method. But he wrote no treatise on the subject, nor any chapter of any treatise. And it is (rather surprisingly) very unclear how Aristotle came to formulate his ideas on this subject. Certainly, he did not pick them up as a student in Plato's Academy. Equally certain is that he did not employ his philosophical method in order to formulate, or even expound, his view of philosophical method. (In fact, if he had done this, he might have reached rather different conclusions about philosophical method.) Rather, he just tells us every so often, almost in passing, what he thinks he is doing when he philosophises. (And, as we shall see, it has sometimes been thought that his theory of philosophical method does not, in fact, correspond all that closely even to his own practice in philosophy.)

The most famous of Aristotle's remarks about philosophical method occurs in his discussion of weakness of will. He writes:

> As in the other cases, we must set out the appearances (*phainomena*), and first go through the puzzles (*diaporesai*). In this way we must prove (*deiknunai*) [Owen, 1961: 114, translates 'indicate'] the common beliefs (*endoxa*) . . . ideally, all the common beliefs, but if not all, then most of them

> and the most important. For if the objections are solved, and the common beliefs are left, it will be an adequate proof.
> (*Nichomachean Ethics* 1145b2–5 tr. Irwin)

Phainomena here was translated 'the observed facts' by Ross; but according to Owen (1961) we need to understand it closely with *endoxa* with which it is coupled; it means 'what would commonly be said on the subject'; and when Aristotle says that Socrates' view conflicts with the *phainomena*, he means that it conflicts with what would commonly be said, and not that it conflicts with the observed facts – he does after all agree with Socrates in a way (1147b15), and he can't hold that his own view is in conflict with the observed facts.

Aristotle says a litte more about the process as a whole in *EE* I.6:

> For it would be best if everyone would turn out to agree with what we are going to say; if not that, that they should all agree in a way and *will* agree after a change of mind; for each man has something of his own to contribute to the finding of the truth . . . beginning with things that are correctly said, but not clearly, as we proceed, we will come to express them clearly, with what is more perspicuous at each stage superseding what is customarily expressed in a confused fashion. (tr. Woods)

He comments further in *Nichomachean Ethics* 1095b2:

> For while we should certainly begin from origins that are known, things are known in two ways; for some are known to us, some known unconditionally. Presumably (*isos*) then the origin we should begin from is what is known to us.

The idea may be that confusion gives way to perspicuity as we work towards principles that are unconditionally *gnorima*, 'intelligible'.[2]

In *Metaphysics A*1, Aristotle tells us that wisdom is knowledge about certain principles (*archai*) and explanations (*aitiai*) (982a2) and that it is knowledge of universal explanation that we seek particularly (982a20). This text also sheds more light on Aristotle's view of our motivation to philosophise. Here Aristotle links the discovery of *aporiai* with the sense of wonder which he says first led men to philosophise:

> For it is owing to their wonder that men both now being and at first began to philosophise; they wondered first at the obvious difficulties, then advanced little by little and stated difficulties about the greater matters ... And a man who is puzzled and wonders thinks himself ignorant ... therefore since they philosophised in order to escape from ignorance, evidently they were pursuing science in order to know, and not for any utilitarian end (982b12–22).

Another important text is *Metaphysics* B1. Here Aristotle tells us that it is helpful to *diaporesai kalos*, 'go through the puzzles well', for those who want to *euporesai* ('have their doubts resolved'; Lear suggests more literally, 'have easy passage', Lear 1988: 4). Aristotle adds some images to explain this point: you cannot untie a knot unless you know how to tie it; you cannot set out before you have settled on a destination; and you need to hear the arguments on both sides of a question before you can be a judge of it (995a24–b4). The point about *euporesai* and *diaporesai* is repeated in *De Anima* I.2, and linked there to Aristotle's approach to philosophy through history of philosophy: one must learn from the opinions of one's predecessors and avoid their mistakes (403b20–24).

In general, Aristotle views philosophy as a co-operative enterprise in which he builds on the achievements of his predecessors who have each grasped some portion of the truth. The views of the wise are also a source of *endoxa* (*Topics* 100b21–23). Furthermore, in all cases of discovery, and all crafts (*technai*) such as rhetoric, progress tends to be cumulative (*De Sophisticis Elenchis* 183d18–27).[3] But his predecessors, he thinks, have contributed to the subject, not just through the true views that they have advanced, but also through the false views they have put forward. He says at *Metaphysics* 993a11–18:

> It is right that we should be grateful, not only to those with whose view we may agree, but also to those who have expressed more superficial views; for these also contributed something, by developing before us the powers of thought (*hexis*) ... from some thinkers we have inherited certain opinions, while the others have been responsible for the appearance of the former.

It is not, however, Aristotle's view that one must approach philosophical questions from a historical perspective. He says in *Metaphysics A*3 that it is not necessary to expound the doctrine of the four causes historically. It has already been discussed sufficiently in the *Physics* (983a34–b1). None the less, he says, a survey of the views of his predecessors will give greater confidence that there are no causes over and above the four causes that he has isolated in the *Physics* (983b4–6).

In fact, in this particular case, one might suspect that Aristotle is being a little disingenuous. The full account of the four causes offered in *Physics* B4 is, indeed, not directly based on the analysis of past philosophical theories. Rather it is derived from a different set of *endoxa*, from a study of *posachos legetai aitia*, in how many different ways we speak of 'cause' (or 'explanation') (195a3–4). In *Physics A*, however, Aristotle has presented already his view of form and matter (two of the four causes) in the context of an analysis of his predecessors' attempts to explain change in the world. Moreover, the theory as a whole is clearly intended to answer certain antecedently existing philosophical questions; there would be no point in simply cataloguing what we say about explanation.[4]

Whatever we may think about this individual case, however, the general outline of Aristotle's view of the natural course of a philosophical enquiry has become clear: in philosophy, we start from wonder, or from a perplexity – in either case this involves ignorance on our part; we work through the *endoxa*; we also work from and try to resolve the *aporiai* that trouble us. In fact, we cannot hope to get clear about philosophical problems if we do not work through the difficulties for ourselves, and explore the problems to the full. In the course of our work, we will generally find that it is profitable to study in some detail the views of past philosophers. In our attempt to resolve our problems, we will be guided by a concern to preserve or vindicate all, or most of, or the most important of, our common conceptions about that subject. The state that we work towards has something in common with Rawls' conception of 'reflective equilibrium'.[5] We aim, certainly, to achieve an equilibrium between those views of past philosophers and those of our common conceptions that pass the test of philosophical analysis. At the same time, it is not just equilibrium, but philosophical understanding that we seek, and this may mark an important difference between Aristotle and Rawls.

Aristotle's view of philosophical method is also very different from that of most of his philosophical predecessors. We may, for example, think here of Socrates' attitude to *aporia* (for him the goal – or at least the outcome – of philosophical enquiry) and the *endoxa* (which are, for him, the subject of *elenchos*). We may also contrast Aristotle's view of philosophy with that of Parmenides (and Descartes). There is no quest here for first principles from which to start our enquiry and from which our results will follow with certainty. Rather, such principles as there are will emerge, or will fail to emerge, from our enquiry as it progresses.

There are, it would seem, three main areas where Aristotle's account needs filling out. First, Aristotle does not say enough about the question of the origin of philosophical perplexities; he does not tell us how it comes about that philosophers sometimes tie themselves in knots. And yet this is surely an important question. Philosophical questions may arise from our sense of wonder, as a condition of the human lot (the view canvassed in Chapter 1). Or they may arise only as a result of misunderstandings (philosophical misunderstandings) of the world, as Wittgenstein thought. It makes quite a lot of difference which view is right – whether in philosophy we are seeking a systematic understanding of the world or piecemeal resolutions of philosophical misunderstandings.[6]

Second, Aristotle says nothing about the apparently interminable nature of philosophical disputes. If philosophical problems once solved, were solved for good, then there would need to be an ongoing supply of fresh philosophical problems, if philosophers were not to run out of work. It is nowadays clear that philosophical problems are very rarely resolved once and for all. And even in the Greek context, there was some evidence that philosophical questions are hard to resolve definitively – we have seen in Chapter 1, how the paradoxes of the Eleatics resisted definitive solution. And some ancient conceptions of the nature of philosophy allowed for this – we saw in Chapter 2 that the Socratic *elenchos* cannot be expected to yield definitive results.

A third problem is that Aristotle has nothing to say about an obvious potential line of criticism of his philosophical method – namely that it cannot be expected to bear much fruit by way of *new* philosophical truths – that it is 'hopelessly flat, tedious, underambitious' (Nussbaum, 1986a: 241).[7] Can we hope to add to the existing stock of wisdom, if we hold fast to the *endoxa*?

And will the method place a constraint on what views we can examine?[8]

There are also problems in reconciling Aristotle's theory of philosophical method with his actual practice of philosophy. We might call to mind Lear's discussion of Aristotle's response to sceptical paradoxes (summarised in Chapter 1 above). According to Lear, Aristotle's response to Zeno's paradox of the arrow is largely based on his own, already formulated, positive theories of time and place. The presenting *aporia* is dissolved, but only in the light of Aristotelian theory, and only for the audience of Aristotle's lectures. It is not dissolved for Zeno himself, or one who accepts his views. And Aristotle does not present Zeno's paradox to us as a starting point from which we can gradually work our way towards the truth. Similarly, Lear (1981) has argued, when Aristotle presents a dialectical defence of the law of contradiction, he does not aim to convince the sceptic about the law that he is wrong. Nor does he think there is any insight in the sceptic's views that can help us in formulating the truth about the law of contradiction. The sceptic just enables us (if he says something) to convince ourselves that we are right and he is wrong. This exercise helps us to better understand our own thinking and our own presuppositions; it does not involve learning from the claims of our opponents. We can only conclude, I believe, that in his practice of philosophy, Aristotle does not always follow his theoretical recommendations about philosophical method.[9]

Aristotle is the first great philosopher to believe in the value of a systematic historical approach to the problems of philosophy. And I now propose to compare and contrast Aristotle's view of the relation between philosophy and history of philosophy with a number of rather different accounts of this relation that have been offered in recent years. Philosophers today have more history of philosophy to contemplate; and in their contemplations, they are able to take more account of historical process. To this extent, their accounts of the relation between philosophy and history of philosophy are likely to be more sophisticated than that of Aristotle. But this is not to say that we will necessarily find that Aristotle's account of the relation is unsatisfactory. Many philosophers today doubt the value of studying history of philosophy as a way of studying philosophy. I shall suggest that on this score Aristotle's view may turn out to be more satisfactory than its rivals.

First, though, I want to consider a view that would endorse an approach to philosophy through history of philosophy – the view that in philosophy we have a choice between rival theories about certain major unchanging philosophical questions (thus, for example, Russell, 1912). On this view, history of philosophy will be worth studying in so far as past philosophers will sometimes have advanced the right philosophical theories.

Sometimes it is thought, additionally, that it is worth studying philosophical views from the distant past in cases where philosophy has subsequently taken a wrong turning that has been very influential. Thus Williams holds that Greek ethics is attractive and persuasive precisely because it is pre-Kantian, and there is no trace there of the categorical imperative, or of the idea of duty. And in philosophy of mind, Aristotle is sometimes thought to be particularly well worth studying because, unlike modern philosophers, he has only Platonic, and not Cartesian, dualism to contend with.[10] This view takes its most extreme form when a philosopher is praised simply on the grounds that he has not encountered problems later faced by his successors, and so has advanced the correct theory, which his successors have then lost sight of. Thus Sorabji holds that it is a merit of Aristotle's philosophy of mind that it prevents the problem of other minds from arising. He writes that:

> It never occurs to Aristotle to raise doubts about other minds. Such doubts would fit badly with his teleological attitude . . . doubts about other minds would also fit badly with his dialectical method, the method of starting from opinions that have been accepted by others. . . . For Aristotle, seeing is physiological process. . . . One can in theory observe the fact that another person is seeing.
>
> (Sorabji, 1974: 88)[11]

The claim that we can learn from Aristotle in this case is not very plausible. Those who are troubled by the problem of other minds are unlikely to be satisfied by Aristotle's general ideas on how to philosophise, or by his specific views on the eye-jelly. To put the point in Aristotelian terms: you have to learn how to tie a knot before you can hope to untie it. And in general, the view that philosophy is a matter of choice between rival theories is not very persuasive. If a past philosopher advanced the correct answer to a philosophical question, it is hard to understand why his theory has not been universally embraced.

Sometimes it is thought, however, not that we can hope to adopt the views of past philosophers wholesale, but that we can learn a great deal from their general outlook on philosophy (thus Rorty, 1984). For example, MacIntyre, in his book *After Virtue* (MacIntyre, 1981) argues that there is much to be learned from Greek ethics, and in particular from Aristotle's ethics. But he thinks that there are three aspects of Aristotle's ethics that in particular need modification: Aristotle's teleology, which presupposes his metaphysical biology, needs to be replaced by a form of teleology that is not metaphysical; we will need to advance the concept of a shared practice to replace the reality of the *polis* in Aristotle's ethics; and we will need, also, to improve on Aristotle's account of moral tragedy (MacIntyre, 1981: 152–3 and 183–4). But what MacIntyre thinks we can learn from Aristotle is something about the right way to approach ethics in general – that is, that we should take, not the individual, but a community as our starting point in ethics, and that we will then, and only then, give due weight to the virtues in our account of ethics (see also note 32, below).

If we ask how later philosophers came to overlook these insights of Aristotle's, MacIntyre has a ready answer. The history of philosophy, he thinks, is often to be accounted for in terms external to it – in this case, by facts concerning the nature of the societies in which philosophers have lived (not everyone has been fortunate enough to live in a *polis* or an Oxbridge college).

The view that we cannot write a coherent 'internal' history of philosophy is one that we must explore further in due course. Next, however, I want to look at another view which might lead us to doubt the value of the study of history of philosophy as an approach to the study of philosophy. This is the logical positivist view that philosophy tends to contract.

According to this view, philosophical problems are those that resist solution either by empirical study or by formal analysis. Once empirical study or formal analysis gets to grips with a field, progress is made; and once progress is made, any remaining problems in the field become problems for the professional, and not problems of the philosopher. So philosophy, and philosophers, on this view, should gradually wither away. Schlick writes:

> Thus the fate of all 'philosophical problems' is this: some of them will disappear by being shown to be mistakes and misunderstandings of our language and the others will be found to be ordinary scientific questions in disguise.
>
> (Schlick, 1932: 51)

Philosophy, on this account, is not equipped to deal with the world at all (this is the province of science), but only with certain confusions we have about language. There will be no valuable truths to learn from our philosophical forebears. In so far as past philosophers have been successful, the problems that they dealt with will have disappeared. At best, I suppose, we might learn something about philosophical method from the study of past philosophers.

Today logical positivism no longer seems an attractive philosophical position. And so no-one is likely to take a purely logical positivist view of history of philosophy. But there are still philosophers who hold that philosophy either does, or should, tend to contract. Thus Rorty, in *Philosophy and the Mirror of Nature*, holds that philosophy does contract, but that nothing fills, or should fill, the gap left vacant by the demise of philosophy. Discussing Quine's view that epistemology can be 'naturalised' as part of science, Rorty writes that, 'after arguing that there is no line between science and philosophy, he tends to assume that he has thereby shown that science can replace philosophy'. But on Rorty's view, there is no 'area left vacant' to be occupied. In epistemology, 'we can have psychology or nothing' (Rorty, 1978: 228).[12]

As to the nature of a philosophical question, Rorty's view of one famous philosophical problem, the relation of mind to body, is that our intuition that some things are mental but other things are physical 'links up with no issues in daily life, empirical science, morals or religion' (Rorty, 1978: 22). About other problems, he has similar views: 'to solve "the problem of induction" . . . would be like "solving the problem of fact and value"; both problems survive only as names for a certain inarticulate dissatisfaction' (Rorty, 1978: 341). On this view of the nature of a philosophical problem, it is hard to see why we might want to approach the subject historically. The problems discussed by past philosophers will nowadays not be problems, or not be philosophy at all.

Another commonly held view about philosophical problems is

that their origin lies outside the discipline of philosophy itself, and that for this reason, it is not possible to write a coherent 'internal' history of philosophy. One exponent of this view is MacIntyre, as we have seen above. But there are, in fact, many different reasons why the history of philosophy is sometimes held to be discontinuous. One common view is expressed by Popper, when he claims that famous philosophical doctrines arise from contemporary developments in science and mathematics. For Popper, Kant's metaphysics is, fairly straightforwardly, an attempt to come to terms with Newton's physics. Plato's theory of Forms is, somewhat less plausibly, all about the Pythagorean discovery of irrational numbers (Popper, 1958). Philosophy is, in Locke's phrase, the handmaiden of science. On this view, past philosophy cannot be understood on its own; it can only be understood once it is related to developments in science and mathematics.

Another reason why it might be difficult to write a connected, 'internal' history of philosophy is suggested by Kuhn (1962). Kuhn's view is that in philosophy, as in science, different practitioners work within different, and incommensurable, 'paradigms' – but with this important difference, that in philosophy, unlike science, one paradigm is not (eventually) supplanted by a successor, but all remain in circulation. Professional philosophers do not tend to reach a unanimous consensus about the merits of philosophical theories.

This is not because, or not simply because, facts and experiments are available to the scientist but not to the philosopher. Scientific facts and experiments do help science to progress, but not, as Kuhn emphasises, through straightforward refutation of current paradigms. It is always possible (and quite frequently correct) to patch up an old theory in the light of new experience. New paradigms arise in science, and supplant old paradigms, because research under the old paradigms has become stultified, and the new paradigm offers new problems and new research possibilities.

Kuhn runs the risk of making science seem deeply irrational, despite its apparent links with the world through evidence and experience. What hope, then, is there of making sense of history of philosophy on such a model? Here it is not at all clear that new facts or new observations are brought into play. Does one free-floating paradigm after another simply arise and remain current? This seems to be the view of Rorty, who writes that 'Aristotle's remarks about knowing do not provide answers, good or bad, to Locke's questions, any more than Locke's remarks about language offer answers to Frege's' (Rorty, 1978: 263). Conversely, 'no revolution in philosophy can succeed which employs a vocabulary commensurable with the old, and thus none can succeed by employing arguments which make unequivocal use of terms shared with the traditional wisdom' (Rorty 1978: 58, n.28). 'New philosophical paradigms nudge old problems aside' (Rorty 1978: 264).

In so far as we cannot write a continuous and coherent 'internal' history of philosophy (whether this is because philosophy is linked with sociology, or because it is linked to science and mathematics, or whether it is simply because each major philosopher works within a new paradigm of his own making), it will obviously not be sensible to approach philosophical questions, in the manner of Aristotle, by looking at the views of past philosophers. Past philosophers will probably have been studying problems that no longer trouble us.

MacIntyre (1984) has responded forcefully to this view of history of philosophy, arguing that even in the case of revolutionary crises in science, one can write a narrative of the crisis. Perhaps there is an important incommensurability between the views of Einstein and Newton, making the comparison of one component of Einstein's system with one component of Newton's problematic; none the less, there is a very general and unspecific question 'what is the world like?', to which both produce rival and competing hypotheses. Similarly, in philosophy, there are some highly general questions to which philosophers produce competing answers. The questions that we have examined so far that might seem to fall into this category are 'what is there?' and 'how should I live?'. A problem that is internal to a philosophical paradigm might be the so-called problem of misuse, that arises only on the Socratic conception of virtue as a craft.[13]

There is one other view about the nature of philosophical questions we should consider at this point – the view of Nozick, outlined in Chapter 1 above, that philosophical questions typically assume the form 'how is it possible that p?', a question we formulate when we encounter a sceptical argument that seems to contradict a known truth. On this view of the nature of philosophical enquiry, it will make sense to study history of philosophy.[14] For one will thereby come to be acquainted with the current state of philosophical theory. It will be necessary to learn about past apparent excluders, rebuttals, and so on, in order to make one's own, new, contribution to the debate. Philosophy, however, will once again be parasitic on the results of scientific enquiry. Scientific questions, of the form 'is it true that p?', would seem to be the really important questions; and the history of philosophy will consist of a growing stock of arguments about apparent excluders of scientific, or everyday, truths.

We may doubt, however, whether this really does justice to the nature of our interest in past philosophical arguments. Some philosophical arguments are indeed naturally seen as excluders of known truths and rebuttals of those excluders. But we study past philosophers to gain some idea of what range of outlooks is possible in a given area. And their arguments, when we accept them, yield something like data which we must organise into a unified philosophical theory. We may expect further data to emerge which will affect the shape of the theory that we are ultimately prepared to accept. Wittgenstein is surely close to the mark when he writes that 'every new problem which arises may put in question the *position* which our previous partial results are to occupy in the final picture' (Wittgenstein, 1958; 44). Wittgenstein compares arranging books in a library. Following up this image, we might think that some acquisitions to the philosophical library will need replacement; mostly, however, the library will need supplement and recataloguing in the light of new theory as to how the books can be most perspicuously arranged on the shelves.

None of the accounts of the relation between philosophy and history of philosophy that we have examined is free from difficulty. And yet perhaps they all, as Aristotle would seem committed to maintaining, contain an element of truth. Progress in science and mathematics can and does throw up philosophical problems. Philosophical problems may sometimes take the form of sceptical arguments that seem to exclude known truths. Sociological factors can sometimes explain some aspects of the development of philosophy. Occasionally, a philosophical problem arises, or seems to arise, only because we have adopted a particular philosophical 'paradigm'.

A final account of the nature of philosophy would take account of these points. Our present question, however, concerns Aristotle's view of the relation between philosophy and history of philosophy – whether it needs supplement, whether it needs correction, or whether it should be abandoned. And we can get clearer about this question (and about the strengths and weaknesses of Aristotle's philosophical method more generally) if we examine an area where Aristotle actually applies his theory of philosophical method in practice. We have seen that Aristotle does not always or for the most part apply his method in practice. But in his account of 'being' (to be examined on pp. 120–9 below) and his account of the role of philosophy in the good life (to be examined on pp. 129–38 below), we will find that Aristotle does employ the philosophical method he recommends as the correct one. I shall ask in these sections how Aristotle's views on these questions are related to the *endoxa*; and to what extent Aristotle is working within the same paradigm as his predecessors and his successors in this field.

BEING AND THE SCIENCES

We have mentioned that Aristotle's school enquired into many domains of human knowledge, and that Aristotle formulated various views about the structure of knowledge. In this section, I want to discuss just one of Aristotle's ideas in this area – his view that the sciences are autonomous. And I want to focus on the theory of being that suggests this view to Aristotle. I shall suggest that Aristotle's theory of being derives in large part from reflection on Plato's theory of being, and that Aristotle here employs the philosophical method we have sketched in the previous section in his treatment of a philosophical problem. I shall ask how satisfactory Aristotle's method turns out to be in this particular case.

Owen has argued that Aristotle worked out his view of the autonomy of the sciences in reaction or response to the view of Plato. Let us summarise Owen's position, which is persuasive and widely accepted.[15] Plato had held, in his middle period, that all knowledge was knowledge of Forms and that all Forms were explained, in their turn, by the Form Good, in some way. And Plato had held this view, because of his doctrine of 'being': only Forms, on his middle period view, exemplify pure being; the sensible world exemplifies being mixed with notbeing, and for this reason, it cannot be known. Now Aristotle, in his youth, formulated a doctrine, the doctrine of homonymy, according to which there could be no single science of 'being', because the term 'being' is 'said in many ways' (i.e. it is ambiguous). Most importantly, 'being' is 'said of' items in all the different 'categories'; there are, accordingly, different varieties of being. Aristotle remarks in *Topics* I.9 that 'someone who signifies what a thing is, sometimes signifies substance, sometimes quantity, sometimes qualification, sometimes one of the other predications'.

It is an important fact that there are substances, quantities, qualities and so on (or that we can classify the world in terms of substances, qualities, quantities and so on) because substance, as we shall see later, enjoys priority over the other categories, and substantial being is prior to (and also different from) nonsubstantial being. As time went by, however, Aristotle developed a more subtle view about the homonymy and non-homonymy of words. He no longer saw a simple either/or dichotomy here, but realised that words could be used with relation to a 'focal meaning'. Initially, he applied this idea in connection with words like 'medical'. There are, for instance, medical knives, medical minds, medical hands and medical operations; and these uses of the term 'medical' are not unrelated, but are 'said' in relation to a single focus (*EE* 1236a13–22). Later – in *Metaphysics* Γ – he came to see 'being' too as a case of focal meaning (1003a33). Its primary use was of items in the category of substance; but its secondary uses, of items in other categories, were focused around the primary use, and were not completely distinct from it. Thus he writes that 'some things are said to be because they are substances, others because they are affections of substance . . .' (1003b6–7); so that 'it will be of substances that the philosopher must grasp the principles and causes' (or 'origins and explanations', 1003b18–19). There are as many parts of philosophy as there are kinds of substance (1004a2); and there is a 'first philosophy', which will investigate unity, being and their contraries:

> For if it is not the function of the philosopher, who is it who will inquire whether Socrates and Socrates seated are the same thing, or whether one thing has one contrary, or what contrariety is, or how many meanings it has? (1004b1–4).

On Owen's view, Aristotle's early theory of being represents a reaction against Plato's teaching; while his mature position – that expressed in *Metaphysics* Γ – represents a return towards the position of the Academy. In this section I want to focus on Aristotle's earlier view, that 'being' is homonymous in so far as it is said of items in different categories, and on the role that his study of Plato's theory of being played in helping him to form this view. I shall suggest, by contrast with Owen's account of Aristotle's response to Plato, that Aristotle's early position does not represent a simple rejection of Plato's doctrine of being, but that Aristotle also learns from Plato. In particular, Aristotle was at all periods of his life concerned to preserve what he took to be an important insight of Plato's (I shall refer to this as the Platonic *endoxon*) – that there is a crucial difference between predications such as 'Socrates is a man' (Owen calls this 'strong' predication) and 'Socrates is pale' (Owen calls this 'weak' predication).

This *endoxon* is to be preserved, although it need not lead us to accept Plato's view that we cannot know the sensible world and that all knowledge is knowledge of Forms.

Plato's own theory of being relates directly to his main contrast between Forms and sensible particulars. Plato holds, centrally, that sensible things both are and are not, whereas Forms just are (see, for example, *Republic* 479a). What he means by this is partly that sensible things change, whereas Forms do not, and partly that sensible things take on different properties in different contexts, whereas Forms do not. What today is a tree may next year be a desk; a large mouse is a small animal. To turn to more Platonic examples: my fourth finger is both big and small – big in relation to my fifth finger, but small in relation to my third finger (see *Republic* 523–5); or again, repaying debts is and is not just – in most cases it is just, but if somone lends a knife to a friend, then goes mad, then asks for the return of the knife, it is not just to repay the debt (see *Republic* I).[16] Sensible things, according to Plato, cannot be known – cannot be the object of *episteme*. But we do have knowledge, and so there must be objects of knowledge. These are the Forms, pure, unitary, and unchanging – and not subject to the coincidence of being with notbeing. The Form Just (unlike repaying debts) is in no way unjust; the Form Big is no way small.

Plato also remarks that sensible particulars are like images of Forms (for example, in the images of the line and the cave in *Republic* VI and VII). Here the point is different, and is related to the claim that we can only understand the sensible world if we see it in relation to Forms. Sensible particulars 'partake in', or have a share in Forms, and it is from this relationship to Forms (however it should be spelt out) that sensible things in fact derive such being as they can lay claim to.

Plato's doctrine of being, on this account, is not a doctrine about what there is, although it is closely linked to a doctrine about what there is (the doctrine that there are Forms). Plato's doctrine of being is rather that there are different sorts of being, and that one sort of being – which is pure being, is both metaphysically and cognitively superior to the other sort of being – which is impure being mixed with notbeing. Impure being is a sort of degraded copy of pure being, and it is unintelligible if we do not see it in relation to pure being.[17]

Now Owen takes it that Aristotle's early theory of being – his theory of the different categories of being, and his contrast between 'strong' and 'weak' predication – is to be contrasted with Plato's theory of being, and derives from critical reflection on Plato's theory of being. Thus Owen cites as a piece of corroborative evidence to 'certify the anti-Platonic provenance of the whole account' (of 'strong' predication and the doctrine of substance) a contrast between Aristotelian substances and Platonic Forms, Aristotelian substances being 'mutable things such as a man or a horse, able to house contrary attributes at different times, but never identical with the contraries they house' (Owen, 1966b: 139), whilst Platonic Forms are precisely immutable specimens of such contraries.

And yet there is a remarkable degree of accord between Plato's views about satisfactory predicates and satisfactory predications, and those of Aristotle, and between Plato's theory of Forms and Aristotle's theory of substances. For Plato, a satisfactory predication is one where the predicate is uncomplicated by the possible presence of an opposite; and possibly it is always an essential predication, where the presence of the predicate excludes the presence of an opposite *ab initio*: 'the Form Big is big', or less controversially, 'this finger is a finger'. (Contrast 'this finger is small'.) For Aristotle, a satisfactory predication is a predication in the category of substance: 'Socrates is a man'. (Contrast 'Socrates is pale'.) Such predications also exclude the presence of an opposite, being essential predications. Substances, Aristotle tells us in *Categories* 3b24, have no opposites: there is no not-man on a par with man. And it is particularly characteristic of substance, Aristotle tells us, that it is able to receive contraries, whilst remaining numerically one and the same (4a10–11). We can say 'man is both pale and dark', meaning that some men are pale while others are dark, or that one and the same man may be pale at one time and dark at another time. But to raise the question of the coincidence of opposites, we must first mention the coincidence of a nonsubstance with a substance. If we think about the world simply in terms of substances, we shall not experience these problems.[18]

Plato thinks it is a problem that under some descriptions of the world (descriptions involving nonsubstantial properties), the world seems prima facie contradictory and hence unknowable and unintelligible. For Aristotle, it is enough that there is a description of the world (a description involving substance terms only), under which it can be known and understood. Being is not all of one piece; and descriptions of the world involving nonsubstantial terms do not impinge on, or infect, the primary description of the world in terms of substance.

We can set out the areas of agreement and disagreement between Plato and Aristotle as follows. Aristotle agrees with Plato about the nature of a primary and satisfactory predication and about the nature of primary and satisfactory being. Aristotle differs from Plato when he holds that there are different categories, and that terms used in different categories, such as 'being', are *ipso facto* homonymous. Aristotle's doctrine of being allows him to locate specimens of primary being – and being that is knowable and intelligible, in the perceptible world (or at least in a certain human construction of the perceptible world); and leads him away from the theory of Forms.

This account of Aristotle's relation to Plato cannot be defended here. But it can be filled out somewhat, if we examine some of Aristotle's criticisms of Plato's theory of Forms.

Let us look first at some of the criticisms Aristotle makes of the Form of the Good in *NE* I. Several of these have a direct relevance to his criticisms of the Platonic view of being. Aristotle complains here that there should not be Forms of things that admit of priority and posteriority; but that 'good', being predicated across categories, does admit of priority and posteriority (1096a18–23). Second, Aristotle claims that 'good' is homonymous, in so far as it is predicated in as many ways as 'being', and so there can be no common, universal, good (1096a23–30). And – for our purposes, finally – Aristotle points to the difficulty of deciding in what way a Form differs from a particular. *Qua* good, or man, the Form Good and the Form Man would seem to fall under the same definition as particular goods and particular men. The only, and rather unpersuasive, way in which Plato suggests that the Form differs from the particular is in so far as the Form always is what it is (good, or man) (1096a34–b5).

Aristotle here rules out all Forms of terms that are predicated across categories: there is no common, universal, 'being'. And Aristotle criticises Plato for failing to see how being in the primary sense differs from being in the secondary sense: Plato has no good account to offer of the priority of the Form F over the particular F's. Secondary forms of being differ categorically from being in the primary sense, and not as an image differs from an original, or as an impure specimen of a stuff differs from a pure specimen. Plato's view that the Form F is always F whereas the particular F's are not always F seems deeply misguided.

Aristotle makes some further relevant criticisms of the theory of Forms in *Metaphysics* A. First, he remarks there that positing Forms is like doubling a number of things that we want to count (990b1–8). Second, he remarks that certain of the more accurate arguments for Forms yield Forms of relative terms, 'of which we say that there is no *kath' hauto genos*', no *genos* in itself (990b15–17). Third, there is the rather more lengthy argument that (a) there seem to be Forms both of substances and of non-substances, but (b) both according to necessity and according to (Platonic) opinions about Forms, there should just be Forms of substances: but then (c) there is a problem concerning the relation of Forms to particulars (990b22–991a8).

The central point here, which is made in a number of ways, is that for Aristotle, there is no upgrading the metaphysical status of non-substances, by creating Forms for these terms. If particular F's are substances, the Form F will be a substance. If the particular F's are not substances, the Form F will not be a substance. This is why Forms merely duplicate the sensible world. The being of Forms is supposed to be prior to the being of particulars: but then, how can there be Forms of relatives? There *should* be Forms just of substances; but then how are we to ascribe priority to the Form F over the particular F's, when F is a substance term? Both already exemplify being in the primary sense.

Aristotle's writing here is compressed; but it would seem that Aristotle understands very well both Plato's theory of Forms and Plato's theory of being. Aristotle has embraced the Platonic *endoxon*, and given an account of it within his own theory of being. He here shows us why Plato's own account of the Platonic *endoxon* is inadequate.

This view of Aristotle's relation to Plato is further confirmed by the nondialectical account he gives of 'being' in *Metaphysics* Δ7. We learn here that 'being' can signify what is true (1017a31ff.), or what is potentially or what is actually (1017a35ff.). We learn also that 'being' may also be used either coincidentally or in its own right. Examples of coincidental being are

(a) someone just is cultured

(b) a man is cultured

(c) someone cultured is a man (1017a9–11).

These examples are then explicated with reference to a clearer example of the coincidental (but one which is not an example of coincidental being)

(d) a cultured man builds.

Aristotle's point about (d) is simple: it is that there is no connection between being cultured and building. A cultured man may build; equally well he may not build; and when a cultured man does build, it just so happens that the two predicates 'cultured' and 'building' both hold true of one and the same thing. So, in the case of being, the problem with

(a) someone just is cultured

will be that it is all too readily paralleled by

(e) someone just is not cultured.

Aristotle adds that 'being' has as many significations in its own right as there are categories (1017a22–4).

I have suggested above that nonsubstantial forms of being differ categorically from substantial being and, for the young Aristotle, are completely unrelated to substantial being. In this passage, Aristotle draws our attention to a further form of being, coincidental being, which is formed from the union of a substance with a nonsubstance, as when a man is cultured. If we now ask why we should take substances, rather than such coincidental cross-category compounds as metaphysically basic, the answer, I believe, is that if we proceeded otherwise, we would have great difficulty in coming to know or understand the world. We cannot take as epistemologically basic the building of cultured men, or cultured just individuals, or the fact that Coriscus is cultured or that a man is cultured.[19] (Aristotle explicitly says that we can have no knowledge of the coincidental at *Metaphysics* 1026b4–5.)

In one central area of philosophy, then, Aristotle's practice in philosophy is very much in line with his theory. And Aristotle's philosophical method, as applied in this case, does not seem 'flat, tedious and underambitious'. A new and interesting theory of being has emerged from Aristotle's reflections on the views of Plato – one that takes into account the Platonic *endoxon*, but is also in accord with our *endoxa* more generally – with the views of the many about what there is as well as the views of the wise. Aristotle's stance in metaphysics is somewhat Parmenidean: he tells us how the world must seem to us if we are to know it – we must see it in terms of substances. Aristotle's theory is more adequate than any of the ingredient *endoxa*, however, in so far as it encompasses them all, and encompasses them comfortably.

For all that, however, we are unlikely to adopt Aristotle's theory of being today. This is not because we do not share Aristotle's *endoxa*. The relation between epistemology and metaphysics remains contested in philosophy – and Aristotle's position on this issue remains defensible. The common sense view about what there is has not changed much since the time of Aristotle – and Aristotle's view remains reasonably compatible with it. The Platonic *endoxon* also seems perfectly defensible: it might seem to represent a basic linguistic intuition that we still share with the Greeks. There does seem to be an important difference between 'Socrates is pale' and 'Socrates is a man.' But this difference is one that today will not incline us to accept Aristotle's doctrine of being. We capture the intuition if we distinguish between necessary and contingent truths, or essential and accidental properties; and some would further explicate these distinctions by saying that Socrates is a man in all possible worlds, but is pale in some worlds but dark in others.[20]

In fact, no philosopher today, within the analytic tradition, is likely even to present a theory of being (though we should note that the concept of being is central to the philosophies of Heidegger and Sartre). If we were challenged to present an account of being, however, there are two basic approaches we might adopt, one through logic, the other through anthropological-cum-historical investigation of our linguistic practices (and those of other societies). So let us see how these approaches compare with that of Aristotle.

To take logic first. We do not now think that there is a different sense of being for each of the different categories. Rather, we think there is identity, predication, and existence. Identity is symbolised by =; predication by F( ); existence by the existential quantifier. There is also class inclusion: ϵ. And we recognise that in Greek, *einai* also sometimes carries a veridical sense. This analysis of being is thought of as philosophical progress. Thus Wittgenstein in his Lectures for 1934–5 says that 'no ordinary person mixes up the meaning of "is" in "the rose is red" and "2+2 = 4" ' (Wittgenstein, 1979: 98). For all that, the logical symbolism of Frege and Russell 'removed the temptation to treat different things as identical'. The temptation is one to which philosophers, in Wittgenstein's view, but not ordinary people are prone. And sometimes, it has been thought that this is a temptation to which ancient philosophers in particular gave way.

A defence of the philosophical practice of the Greek philosophers in this respect has been mounted by Kahn, however. His work illustrates well the other main approach we might adopt towards the question of being. He is concerned to analyse the actual use of the Greek verb *einai* by ancient Greeks. Kahn concludes that 'It was not a mistake to believe that predication, truth and existence (or reality) belong together in a single family of concepts' (Kahn, 1973: 372). As he later explains: 'There must be something there to talk about; there must be something to be said about it; and there must be some fitness or agreement – some truth or "satisfaction" between what is said, and what it is said of' (Kahn, 1973: 406). Kahn in fact thinks there is no distinct use of *einai* to mark identity. In the example 'Hecuba is Priam's wife', what determines whether or not this is an identity is not the use of the verb, but facts about the society. If the society is monogamous, 'Priam's wife' is a definite description, and we have an identity. Otherwise it is not.

Kahn's approach is more sympathetic to ancient philosophical theories of being. But it is unlikely to lead to their reinstatement. For in so far as they are a response to problems that go beyond the simple question 'what is there?', it might seem that these problems now admit of more perspicuous formulation. Thus Vlastos, in his discussions of Plato's doctrine of being, talks of the theory as a theory of 'degrees of reality',[21] and sees the theory as an early attempt to distinguish between the empirical and the a priori. If this is indeed the nub of Plato's thinking, clearly Vlastos' presentation of Plato's view is more perspicuous than that of Plato. Similarly with Aristotle's theory of being: advances in logic have led to an increase in clarity here.

Perhaps what has happened is that we have seen progress in the *endoxa*.[22] This is not necessarily to say that we now work within a different philosophical paradigm. We can still understand what Aristotle is saying about being; and there is a degree of commensurability between his philosophy and our outlook. But if, when we philosophise today, we start from different *endoxa*, then of course we should not expect now to replicate Aristotle's philosophical results by employing his philosophical method.[23] This is, in a way, a great tribute to Aristotle's conception of philosophical method: it leaves room for philosophical progress. At the same time, it means that his philosophical results (such as his views about being and about the departmentalisation of philosophy) cannot all be expected to stand the test of time.

As to whether philosophy is, or should be, departmentalised, we should, perhaps, keep an open mind. Some philosophical systems – those of Plato, Aristotle and the Stoics, for instance, offer a remarkably unified and coherent world view. On the other hand, this should not blind us to the value of piecemeal contributions to philosophy (such as Zeno's paradoxes of motion). Whatever the truth about this question, however, it is certainly unrelated to Aristotle's doctrine of being; and it is almost certainly unrelated to *any* doctrine about being.

PHILOSOPHY AND THE GOOD LIFE

We saw in Chapter 3 above that for Plato, the ideal life is the life of the philosopher. In the *Phaedo*, this life is seen as a cultivation of death; in the *Symposium*, the philosopher generates in the beautiful, and loves the Form of Beauty; in the *Republic*, the philosopher divides his life between politics (a sort of applied philosophy), and philosophical contemplation. Writing about the good life for man in the *Nichomachean Ethics*, Aristotle does not directly address these views of Plato's (he simply criticises, in Book I, the conception of the good from which these ideas are derived). But he does develop his own, rather differently based, view of the role of philosophy in the good life, the life of *eudaimonia*, 'happiness' or 'human flourishing'.

According to Kenny, the structure of Aristotle's answer to the question 'what is the good life for man?' is as follows:

> In books I and X of the *NE*, Aristotle behaves like the

> director of a marriage bureau, trying to match his clients' description of the ideal partner. In the first book, he lists the properties which one believes to be essential to happiness, and in the tenth book, he tries to show that philosophical contemplation, and it alone, possesses to the full these essential properties
>
> (Kenny 1966: 30)

Some commentators doubt whether the description of the contemplative life offered in Book X of the *NE* really does accord with the description of the life of *eudaimonia* outlined in Book I and described in Books II–IX. Thus Nussbaum (1986a) argues that book X.6–8, in which Aristotle recommends the life of contemplation, is out of step with the rest of the *Ethics*, though clearly written by Aristotle.[24] The good life is the life of practical wisdom described elsewhere in the *NE*. And Lear (1988) holds that, for Aristotle, human beings, who are composed of form and matter, must choose between living a harmonious life (the life of practical wisdom) that accords with their composite nature, or a disharmonious life (the life of theoretical contemplation) that accords purely with their form. The disharmonious life does not seem valuable from the human perspective; but then nor does the life of Gauguin, who abandoned his family and his life as a bank clerk in Paris to go off to the South Seas and become a great painter;[25] yet such lives have a different kind of value – an absolute value rather than a human value.

On Kenny's view, it is ultimately a coincidence that the life of philosophy constitutes the good life for man. The match between the life of philosophy and the good life for man is effected essentially through the description of the good life for man that emerges from the discussion in *NE* I. The good life is self-contained, continuous, reasonably secure from bad luck, and involves self-understanding; so too is the life of philosophy. So Aristotle must persuade us both about his view of the good life and about his view of philosophy if we are to accept that the good life is the life of philosophy. We may contrast the case of Plato: for Plato, it follows naturally from his central views in epistemology and metaphysics that the life of philosophy is the good life for man.

In this section, I shall look first at Aristotle's discussion of *eudaimonia* in *NE* I and then at Aristotle's discussions of friendship (an important part of the practical life) and contemplation. I shall suggest that philosophy has a dual role for Aristotle: it can help us to place ourselves as human beings in the grand scheme of things; but also the life of philosophy can constitute the good life.

In Book I of the *NE*, Aristotle makes at least three fresh starts (at I.i, I.iv, and I.vii); much of the discussion in these chapters is based on the *endoxa* (1098b25); but the content of the *endoxa* is not always manifest at first sight, and needs to be drawn out; finally, having presented an argument based on a philosophical analysis of man's *ergon*, 'function' or 'characteristic activity', in I.vii, Aristotle returns to the *endoxa* in I.viii, as a check on his results.

Some of the basic *endoxa* that emerge may be summarised as follows: we all aim for the good or the apparent good, and apparent goods are nested (I.i: for example, bridle-making is subordinate to horsemanship, horsemanship is subordinate to generalship); we all aim at *eudaimonia* or living well, but have different conceptions of this end (I.iv; pleasure, honour and mind are mentioned). The good is complete, self-sufficient and non-additive (I.vii); external good fortune plays a role in whether or not we achieve *eudaimonia*, but not a commanding role (I.viii)[26] (the activities that express virtue 'seem to be more enduring even than our knowledge of the sciences', 1100b15, tr. Irwin).

The *endoxa* are bolstered by an analysis of the human *ergon*, 'function' or 'characteristic activity'. Aristotle argues that we humans should do what is human; we will live well if we perform well the human *ergon*. What is characteristically human is thinking. Man is a rational animal (I.vi). At the end of this argument, Aristotle concludes not just 'that the human good will be the soul's activity that expresses virtue' (1098a16–17), but also that, 'moreover it will be in a complete life. For one swallow does not make a spring, nor does one day; nor similarly does one day or a short time make us blessed and happy' (1098a17–20).

It would seem that for Aristotle, as for Socrates and Plato before him, living well has to do with the inner world and personal integrity. The good man carries his security round with him; his character is stable; come what may, 'he will never do hateful and base actions' (1100b35). Changes in the external world will indeed affect us – no-one could be *eudaimon* who was being tortured (1153b16–21). But the better we become, the less vulnerable we are to luck.[27] Furthermore, in Irwin's terms, the agent sees himself as 'temporally extended'; given time he can right a reverse inflicted on him by the world; that is why it is tempting (if not finally correct) to think we can call no man happy until his life is complete.

But while the harmonious inner world of the *eudaimon* may afford him some protection against external misfortune, he still stands in need of external goods. One cannot flourish as a man of practical wisdom without the appropriate relations with other human beings; and these are always to some extent a matter of chance. As a social animal, one must live in a *polis*; one must have friends (cf. Nussbaum, 1986a). And a human being cannot flourish securely and continuously through contemplation in so far as one has human needs and human limitations. Thus both the life of practical wisdom and the contemplative life are to some extent fragile.

We achieve harmony with our fellow human beings through membership of a *polis*, but more particularly, through friendship. MacIntyre has remarked that 'friendship has become for the most part the name of a type of emotional state, rather than of a type of social and political relationship' (MacIntyre, 1981: 146–7). For Aristotle, the need to live in a *polis* and the need for friendship are linked. Aristotle remarks early in his discussion of friendship that 'friendship would seem to hold cities together and legislators would seem to be more concerned about it than justice' (1155a24–5, tr. Irwin).

Why does the good life involve friendship? Towards the end of *NE* IX, Aristotle argues that friends are 'the greatest of external goods'. To quote Irwin's summary:

> We need friends for us to benefit; solitude makes happiness impossible ('a human being is political, tending by nature to live together with others', 1169b17); we can observe the actions of virtuous friends (and thereby our own – our friends are to be seen as second selves); friendship provides pleasure (it makes continuous activity easier); it encourages virtue; it realises human capacities.

The conclusion follows, according to Irwin's summary, that friendship is needed for self-sufficiency. Aristotle simply says in conclusion that 'anyone who is to be happy must have excellent friends' (1170b19).

Cooper, analysing this passage and its counterparts in *EE* and

MM, finds essentially two arguments here, which both 'emphasise human vulnerability and weakness' (Cooper, 1977: 331). One is that friends are necessary for self-knowledge or self-understanding; the other is that 'only by merging one's own activities and interests with those of others can the inherent fragility of any human being's interests be overcome' (Cooper, 1977: 329). He quotes *EE* 1245b18–19: 'god is his own good activity, but human good consists in relationship to others'.

Friendship, however, is not to be seen simply as a means of overcoming human vulnerability and weakness. This is brought out very clearly in Cicero's discussion of friendship, when he remarks that friendship is not based on need. If this were so, then 'just in proportion as any man judged his resources to be small, would he be fitted for friendship; whereas the truth is far otherwise' (*De Amicitia* §29, Loeb translation). Aristotle agrees with Cicero about this, as we can see from his discussion of the three forms of friendship.

Aristotle thinks that some friendships are based on character, some on pleasure and some on business relations. Pleasure and business friendships are less beneficial to the individual than are character friendships. In pleasure and business friendships, a need based relation underlies the friendship (although the friendship is real enough – we wish our friends well for their own sake); and the friendship is accordingly fragile (my friend becomes ugly; he does his business elsewhere). Where the friendship is not need-based, it becomes maximally fulfilling, and far less open to luck. (Character is much more stable than are needs.) Wishing pleasure or business friends well may in some cases be wishing the friendship to end (my friend, for example, gets a job in Australia, which he very much wants, but which is incompatible with our continued friendship). I can wish character friends well almost unreservedly (we will both have the same view of the nature and importance of the friendship; and we will both form the same view about whether or not he should go to Australia). There is only one respect in which I will refrain from wishing well my character friends: I will not want them to become gods (1159a4–12).[28]

In friendship, we aim at the good – for ourselves and for our friends, we become more self-sufficient, our activities seem more continuous to us, and our self-understanding increases. So friendship would seem to be an important component of the good life.

Aristotle advises us in *NE* X, however, to 'immortalise ourselves as far as possible', and to live a life of philosophical contemplation. Let us ask first what it would be like to succeed completely in this goal, and resemble Aristotle's God, the 'Prime Mover', whose life of contemplation is described in *Metaphysics L*. Lear (1988) has advanced an intriguing account of the philosophical significance of the Prime Mover for Aristotle. According to Lear, Aristotle is here tackling problems of objectivity and subjectivity that he shares with Wittgenstein and Kant.[29] The Prime Mover shows us where understanding, and self-understanding, are ultimately to be located. Lear conjectures that 'the order of the world as a whole is an attempted physical realization of God's thought' (Lear, 1988: 296). God understands himself directly; that is why he can spend his time thinking himself, or 'thinking of thinking'. Being human, of course, we cannot immortalise ourselves completely. Lear holds that being enmattered, we need actualised forms to activate our thinking. Still, we can attain self-understanding by coming to understand the world (and ourselves as part of the world). This involves a re-enactment of God's thinking. In carrying out this re-enactment we lead, not the best life for man, but the best life *tout court*.

In *NE* X, Aristotle's arguments in favour of the contemplative life (in X.vii) run as follows, in Irwin's summary:

> Contemplation is most pleasant, and you can do it continuously, and you need no-one else to help you with it (whereas you need other people if you are to manifest practical wisdom). It aims at no end beyond itself; it involves leisure; it is a god-like life; and it realises the supreme element in human nature.

So Aristotle here recommends contemplation for much the same reasons as he had earlier recommended friendship. Both promote continuous and self-sufficient human activity and self-understanding. It will be hard to advise the client at the marriage bureau whether to pursue the practical or the contemplative life. In either case, he will be pursuing the goals of self-understanding, self-sufficiency, and self-completion, that seemed important for *eudaimonia* in the discussion of Book I. It will be an empirical question whether these goals are best achieved in the life of philosophy or in the life of practical wisdom.

Philosophy also has a second role in Aristotle's ethics, however.

It is the means by which some of us can perceive the truth about *eudaimonia*. But Aristotle is rather pessimistic about the power of philosophy to alter the lives of all and sundry. In book X, he remarks that argument alone is not sufficient to make men virtuous (1179b5ff.) – the many respond only to fear of punishment. It is impossible, or not easy, to alter by argument what has long been absorbed by habit (1179b17–18). Aristotle seems here to anticipate Williams's conception of the 'limits of philosophy' (Williams 1985).

Philosophy will be impotent in relation to the *akolastos*, the 'licentious man' – although it will show us, the students of philosophy, that the life of the *akolastos* is less than fully satisfactory. The *akolastos* has an overall conception of flourishing. But he thinks, mistakenly, that 'it is right in every case to pursue the pleasant thing at hand' (1046b24). The problem with this life is that the *akolastos* is fixated at the child's level of understanding. The child differs from the *akolastos* in that the child has no conception of himself as an agent extended in time; and no conception of overall flourishing. But all children initially value the pleasant, before learning through habituation to value the noble, and finally the good (see Burnyeat, 1980a). The *akolastos* has never learnt to value the noble or the good. He enjoys his life, without doubt: his life is full of pleasurable sensations;[30] but it does not offer the rewards of *sophrosyne*. Aristotle suggests that:

'No-one would choose to live with the child's [level of] thought for his whole life, taking as much pleasure as possible in what pleases children' (1174a3).[31]

A figure who has progressed further with his habituation is the politician. Indeed, the politician seems to us to lead an attractive, fulfilled life. And Aristotle himself sees ethics as an introduction to politics. But as one who values the noble, rather than the good, the politician too will not be open to philosophical argument. And, as we learn from Book I, the pursuit of honour depends on there being others prepared to honour us; and we may be motivated towards this life in order simply to convince ourselves that we are good (1095b22ff.) And we learn eventually from X.7 (1177b10–15) that the politician's actions require trouble; and being undertaken to promote *eudaimonia*, are distinct from *eudaimonia* itself. The politician leads a worthy life; but in the end it is less fulfilling than the life of contemplation. The politician relates to others, but in a needy and fragile kind of way. (It is as if he is engaged in a business or pleasure friendship rather than a character friendship.) He *may* succeed in self-actualisation; but his achievement will be precarious. He will always be highly vulnerable to reverses of fortune, because his life is not maximally sufficient and complete.

There are some, however, who can be helped by the study of philosophy in their quest to lead the good life. Aristotle tells us in Book I that the student of the *Ethics* knows the *hoti*, the 'that', but needs to discover the *dioti*, the 'because'. (That is to say, he knows the right thing to do, but not why it is the right thing to do.) In studying philosophy, he will learn the *dioti*. And as he learns the *dioti*, his understanding of his nature and his character will increase, and his quest for self-actualisation and self-completion will be fulfilled. He will lead the good life as he learns about the good life.

Aristotle's theory of the good life, like Aristotle's theory of being, is new and exciting. It is based on *endoxa*, but it transcends the *endoxa*; it is greater than the sum of its parts. But it does not represent the only building we can construct from these particular building bricks. And it is not a building we can inhabit today – even if we share many *endoxa* with Aristotle and are committed to an endoxic method. We can see this most clearly, if we examine a contemporary account of ethics that shares some common ground (some *endoxa*) with Aristotle's – that of Williams.[32]

Williams, like Aristotle, approaches ethics by asking about the nature of a satisfactory human life.[33] (He takes a determinedly ancient view of the central questions in ethics.) A satisfactory life is all of one piece, and demonstrates the quality of integrity; it closes, at the end of its natural term, with readiness for death; enough of one's personal projects will have been fulfilled and enough human possibilities explored. For Williams, as for Aristotle, human motivation arises from deep within the settled character-structure of the agent; one decides what one must do in the light of who one is. And there is an important social dimension to ethics: only a few life-plans are possible for a given individual in a given society. But Williams rejects Aristotle's *ergon* argument: maybe there is no shared human *ergon*, and maybe Aristotle's selection of the human *ergon* is arbitrary (Williams, 1972: 73).[34] Williams thinks that a satisfactory human life consists in the fufilment of personal projects. Williams endorses a phrase of D.H. Lawrence's: 'find your own deepest impulse and follow that', when first expounding his ideas on this topic (Williams, 1972: 93). Aristotle thinks we all have the same deepest impulse, that of actualising the human *ergon*. For Williams, the forms of human authenticity will be diverse. The hazards of the good life will be also more diverse in Williams' view than they are for Aristotle. The human agent will be liable to what Kenny (1986) has termed constitutive bad luck as well as executive and situational bad luck. It is not just that Gauguin's actions may have unforeseen consequences (executive bad luck), or that the boat may sink on the way to the South Seas (situational bad luck); he may arrive and discover that he is not a great painter (constitutive bad luck). And while Williams' method in ethics is in an important sense, intuitionist (and thus follows the *endoxa* we share about ethics) he is suspicious of the claim that philosophy can present us with a systematic moral theory (Williams 1988). And Williams, as we have seen, shares Aristotle's scepticism about the power of philosophy to reach all and sundry. At best, philosophy plays a part in teaching us how to combine truthfulness to and existing self and society with reflection, self-understanding and criticism (Williams 1985: 200); but the issues here will be personal and social, and not solely philosophical.

It would seem, then, that we are no more likely to embrace Aristotle's account of the good life today than Aristotle's account of being. We share most (though not all) of our *endoxa* with Aristotle, and at least some *aporiai*. And some philosophers will employ modified versions of Aristotle's philosophical method. But we cannot now adopt Aristotle's philosophical results, and treat them as our own. There is progress in philosophy. The stock of *endoxa* and *aporiai* has been enriched across the centuries; and we will now build different theories on the basis of some of the same building bricks.

Aristotle's achievement in philosophy was immense. He presented an all-embracing theory of the world, of which the parts are none the less autonomous. As we have seen, he has a theory about what there is, and what it is like – his theory of 'being', as given in his doctrine of the categories and his doctrine of the homonymy and focal meaning of 'being'. He has a theory about the nature of human beings, and the nature of the good life for human beings – this involves living a social life in a small community with our friends, or alternatively, living a life devoted to philosophical contemplation. And he has a theory about the nature of philosophy – it is through philosophy that we come to understand the world and through philosophy that we come to understand our own nature. The life devoted to philosophy may be the life of the gods; but the impulse to philosophise is also deeply rooted in human nature.

Aristotle's worldview would form a fitting conclusion to the history of ancient philosophy. New philosophical questions, and new philosophical answers, however, were to arise in the Hellenistic period – to which we now turn.

5

THE HELLENISTIC PHILOSOPHERS: PHILOSOPHY, NATURE AND THERAPY

INTRODUCTION

Philosophy first assumes its well-known contours as a discipline in the Hellenistic period. Or so, at least, it has been argued. Thus Long and Sedley claim that in the Hellenistic period, 'philosophy became for the first time pared down to something resembling the specialist discipline it is today' (Long and Sedley, 1987: 2). They point to the fact that specialists in what we now see as peripheral disciplines moved, in this period, from Athens to Alexandria, where they were well funded. Plato's Academy had housed research mathematicians as well as philosophers; Aristotle's Lyceum had contributed to zoology, political history and literary theory. The Hellenistic schools of philosophy, by contrast, house only philosophers.

This is a sociological observation; and it is a historical observation that when Cicero wrote his well-known philosophical works, he chose to concentrate on expositions of the different Hellenistic philosophies.[1] Both observations help explain why Hellenistic philosophy can sometimes seem closer to contemporary analytic philosophy than does the philosophy of Plato and Aristotle, or the Presocratics. A further sociological fact may also be relevant: the Hellenistic philosophies flourished at a time when the *polis* or self-governing city-state no longer seemed a viable institution. Philosophers now sought personal fulfilment by withdrawing from meaningful contact with the world (sceptics), or by forming a separate philosophical community of friends (Epicureans) or by orienting themselves in relation to nature as a whole (Stoics).

Nature is an important theme for all three main philosophical schools. All three schools promise personal happiness to the philosopher. All three (but especially the Epicureans and the sceptics) see their philosophy as a form of therapy. I shall suggest that these two themes are linked: it is those who understand nature, and in particular human nature, who are in a position to offer therapy for the human soul.

THE EPICUREANS

According to Sextus Empiricus, 'Epicurus used to say that philosophy is an activity which by arguments and discussions brings about the happy life' (25K). For Epicurus, there is no doubt that philosophy is supposed to do you good. Thus:

> Empty are the words of that philosopher who offers therapy for no human suffering. For just as there is no use in medical expertise if it does not give therapy for bodily diseases, so too there is no use in philosophy if it does not expel the suffering of the soul. (25C)

If philosophy is therapy for human suffering, what is the cause of human suffering? Epicurus talks of fears based on mythology (25B) and of the virtue of 'embarking on philosophy while still untainted by any culture' (25F). Another text tells us something of the content of human suffering. The upshot of philosophy, according to Epicurus, is that 'God presents no fear, death no worries. And while good is readily attainable, evil is readily endurable' (25J).

Long and Sedley believe that it is possible to misunderstand the significance of the medical analogy here, that it can 'foster the impression' that Epicurus 'assigned a purely negative, instrumental role to philosophy' (Long and Sedley, 1987: 156). They point to the words of Epicurus himself in refutation of this view: 'in philosophy enjoyment keeps pace with knowledge. It is not learning followed by entertainment, but learning and entertainment at the same time' (25I).

But there is also some evidence to support the view that Epicureans, if not Epicurus himself, did take an instrumental view of philosophy. Nussbaum (1986b), drawing largely on evidence from Philodemus, paints a very different picture of Epicurean philosophy in practice. She suggests that, if we see philosophy as therapy, we might expect to find and we do find, that their conception of philosophy is geared towards:

(1) practical causal efficacy
(2) value-relative procedures
(3) attention to the particular case
(4) relativity to the individual
(5) an instrumental role for reason
(6) no intrinsic respect for the virtues of rational discourse
(7) a non-mutual, asymmetrical relation of pupil and teacher
(8) a lack of interest in alternative views

These features (especially 5, 7 and 8) explain why the Epicurean school, uniquely, sees a role for memorisation, confession and informing in its therapy of souls (Nussbaum, 1986b: 48).

The characteristics Nussbaum discusses are not those traditionally associated with the practice of philosophy. But, as she remarks, Epicurus

> deals with many of the traditional concerns of philosophy-nature, the soul, the value of ends. It therefore seems to Epicurus appropriate to give this saving art the name of philosophy; and furthermore to insist that this saving art is what, properly understood, philosophy *is*.
>
> (Nussbaum, 1986b: 36)

Nussbaum contrasts Epicurus' view with that of Aristotle.[2] Aristotle holds, in common with Epicurus, that philosophy, like medicine, is practical, value-relative and particular. But he sees philosophy as 'gentle, complicated, reciprocal, and quite unlike force and drug treatment' (Nussbaum, 1986b: 60). She thinks that the difference between Aristotle and Epicurus on this point may have to do with more general theses about value. Aristotle sees philosophy as concerned with the clarification and articulation of ends. Epicurus, however, finds his concept of the good in the untutored behaviour of the child.[3] The child, for Epicurus, lives the life of unalloyed pleasure (just as, she thinks, black people play this role in Russell's *The Conquest of Happiness*, Nussbaum, 1986b: 71). We should learn from the child in this respect. It is not that we should return to the life of the child: the child sees the end clearly, but the adult is better placed to attain the end (for example, the adult, unlike the child, can summon up pleasures of retrospect and prospect, and this can help us achieve the happy life –

Nussbaum, 1986b: 33–34, note 3). But no harm will be done if we treat our errant students as children, who need our help. They do not, primarily, need an initiation into the techniques of rational argument: this is not part of the good, as seen by the child.

Nussbaum contrasts the view that philosophy is like medicine with the modern approach to ethics which sees ethics as a science (Nussbaum, 1986b: 71). If ethics is seen as a science, Nussbaum claims, it 'ceases to have the right sort of practical engagement with human lives' (Nussbaum, 1986b: 71). The importance of Aristotle is that he shows us that we do not face a choice between 'nonpractical mathematics and Epicurean reasoning as models for ethical reasoning' (Nussbaum, 1986b: 72). The tasks of the philosopher (seen by Nussbaum as 'assessing arguments, detecting inconsistencies, describing the historical alternatives in a clear, thorough, perspicuous way', Nussbaum, 1986b: 72) may have no necessary connection with the 'essential medical virtues of perceptiveness and responsiveness' (Nussbaum, 1986b: 72). But she suggests that 'it is not accidental that the character who contributes to the improvement of practice through discourse that surveys the alternatives is a character who puts in a lot of time practising the critical assessment of arguments' (Nussbaum, 1986b: 72). The tasks of the philosopher are internally interconnected and they are practically useful.

Several aspects of Nussbaum's account call for discussion. I shall first discuss the medical metaphor itself. Then I shall ask about the scope for rational discussion in the Epicurean school and in philosophical schools generally. Finally, I shall discuss the relation, for Epicurus, of theory to therapy.

First, then, let us ask about the medical metaphor itself, and its relation to our conception of ethics. It is, of course, quite true that ancient ethics is practical, where much modern ethics is theoretical. And it is also true that the idea that philosophy is like medicine is fairly common among the ancient philosophers.[4] However it may well be that the ancients' interest in practical questions (such as 'how should I live?' or 'what is the best life for man?') accounts for their use of the medical analogy, and not that their use of the medical analogy accounts for the practical nature of ancient ethics. When we ask practical questions today, such as 'should we eat animals?', the philosopher will return a practical answer. But for the most part, philosophers today do not ask practical questions; and this is one reason why we do not now see philosophy as the medicine of the soul.[5]

It may further be significant that the student Nussbaum considers is seeking admission to, and membership of, a philosophical *school*. It has been argued, by Popper, that philosophy is concerned with the critical examination of widely-accepted theories (see p. 11), but that such critical examination cannot flourish within a philosophical *school*. About schools in general, Popper writes,

> Far from being places of critical discussion they make it their task to impart a definite doctrine, and to preserve it, pure and unchanged. It is the task of the school to hand on the tradition, the doctrine of its founder, its first master, to the next generation, and to this end the most important thing is to keep the doctrine inviolate. A school of this kind never admits a new idea . . . should a member of the school try to change the doctrine, he is expelled as a heretic.
>
> (Popper, 1958: 149)

A school, for Popper, is rather like a small-scale example of what he calls a 'closed' society (which he contrasts with an 'open' society):

> a closed society is characterised by the belief in magic taboos, while the open society is one in which men have learned to be to some extent critical of taboos, and to base decisions on the authority of their own intelligence (after discussion)
>
> (Popper, 1945: 202.)

In a 'closed' society, as in a school, critical discussion is unwelcome.

Popper's view accords well with the picture of the Epicurean school that Nussbaum has built up. The teachings of Epicurus may not be magical taboos; but they are not open to question. There is no scope for the student to base decisions on the authority of her own intelligence. Popper's view offers a rationale for this state of affairs: Nussbaum's student has signed on for instruction in one particular philosophical system, and no other. And members of a school may reasonably enough try to guard and pass on to their students their own distinctive doctrines and their own distinctive inheritance. If this is so, it may indeed be the case that the free play of philosophical enquiry (of reason and argument, that is) would threaten the very *raison d'être* of such a school. For reason and argument must indeed play a merely instrumental role in such environments.

Furthermore, whereas critical discussion is aimed at establishing truths, therapy for human suffering may or may not be based upon the communication of truth from therapist to patient. So if therapy is the be-all and end-all on Epicurus' view of philosophy, then we may expect to find that he employs any method that works in his writing and teaching. All that will matter is that it should bring peace of mind.

We might compare the relationship of truth to therapy in psychoanalysis. In this case, Freud holds a number of theories about the course of human development, and about the structure of the human mind. He also has a technique of therapy, which does not consist in conveying to the patient the various theories Freud has come up with. Rather, he proceeds by encouraging free association, and offering transference interpretations. In this case, it may be that method is fundamental, and does not fully determine theory.[6] Moreover, therapy does not consist solely in the communication of truths about the world (or the truths of psychoanalytic theory) from analyst to patient. What the analyst says to the patient will be influenced by the shape the patient is in, and what truths about himself he is ready and able to cope with. The therapist may think it best to withhold certain truths from the patient, or delay the communication of some truths until the patient is ready to formulate these truths about himself and for himself.[7] But there are thought to be truths about human development, which are the same truths for everyone, and therapy is guided by theory in this sense.

Now let us ask about the Epicurean view of these questions. We shall find, I believe, that Epicureans do make a claim to truth about their theories – a claim that these theories will withstand critical scrutiny (by Stoics, or philosophical opponents) and aim to communicate these truths to the world at large. We will see that philosophical argument is presented as therapy – and that it may be that Epicurus is more successful at philosophical argument than at therapy.

So let us ask now 'what are the beliefs that we need to cure us of our suffering?'. In fact, the answer to this question is not so simple as one could wish. It is difficult to interpret the overall structure of Epicurean philosophy; and it is also difficult to decide to what extent (if at all) Epicurean philosophy is reductive in character. (That is, to what extent there are a few basic simple truths to which all other truths can ultimately be reduced.)

In fact, there seem to be two main views about the structure of Epicurus' philosophical theories. One is that they are focused on the study of the child, as suggested by Nussbaum, or on the reports of the senses, as is suggested by Long (1974) (the two views are akin, as we shall see); the other is that atomic theory plays the fundamental role in philosophical cures.[8] What the pupil/patient needs, when sick, is, on the first view, to rely more on the evidence of his senses; on the second view, it is to correct his view of physics. In either case, it may be that an apparent diversity of experience (perhaps a bewildering and illusory diversity) is reduced to a simple certainty: the ultimate truths are truths about atoms, or are truths about my sensory experience.

Let us now consider some examples of Epicurean therapy, and see how these ideas work out in practice. Let us first consider Epicurus' treatment of the fear of death. This might seem, *prima facie*, to support the view that what we need, in order to be happy, is a correct view of physics. For it might be that prior to one's encounter with Epicureanism, one fears death because one has the mistaken idea that one will survive the death and dissolution of one's body, and that this may be a misfortune (punishment may await in the afterlife). What philosophy does for such an individual is to convince him that he is an amalgam of atoms, and that he will not survive his death. And this, hopefully, will cheer him up. It may be better for us not to spend our lives hoping for the impossible. And physics teaches us what is possible and what is not.

When we look at Epicurean arguments on fear of death in more detail, however, we find that these do not simply focus on physical theory. Epicurus' first move is certainly to deploy physical arguments to the effect that the soul is mortal. Thus Epicurus argues that 'death is nothing to us. For all good and evil lie in sensation, whereas death is the absence of sensation' (24A). Lucretius too concludes,

> So death is nothing, and matters nothing to us
> Once it is clear that the mind is mortal stuff
> (iii. 830–1, tr. Sisson)

But the argument from physics is only Epicurus' and Lucretius' first move. Another important argument is an expression of Epicurus' belief in the primacy of the senses, and of the view that we should be concerned only with the sensations that fall within the limits of life – and, I would think we should add, only with what falls within the limits of our own life. This is the argument that the limits of life are birth and death (24C3). As I understand this, it is an almost Kantian point. The past and the future periods of non-existence cannot be striven for, any more than (for Kant) one could hope to attain knowledge of *noumena*. It is part of the human condition that it is lived between these two termini, and human beings should apportion their lives accordingly. Desires aimed at the impossible are empty, and should be eliminated. The Wittgenstein of the *Tractatus* does not moralise; but he seems to express a position quite close to that of Epicurus when he writes

6.431 'So too at death the world does not alter, but comes to an end'.

6.4311 'Death is not an event in life: we do not live to experience death'.

Epicurus claims that even a future replica of ourselves would be of no concern to us. Initially this looks surprising, but in fact it makes good sense. Today we might ask whether we would be concerned about the fate of possible replicas of ourselves on twin earths (where this is construed as a question about exact counterparts). I think the answer is 'no'. If they are not spatiotemporally continuous with us, their fate will not concern us in the same way as our own fate does.

Epicurus' arguments here rely both on his physics and also on the view of the primacy of our sense-impressions. If we accept both views, we are committed to a thoroughgoing re-evaluation of our way of life. Therapy will have been effected.

We should note the extent to which Epicurus hopes to revise our everyday beliefs. We would not normally think that we should be, or that we are, concerned only with what falls within the limits of our own lives. We have what Williams (1973) calls 'non-I' desires, as when we make our wills (the idea is that we may be keen to see certain states of affairs realised, even though we are fully aware that we won't be around to witness their realisation). We can suffer misfortunes which remain outside the domain of our consciousness. Nagel (1970) presents the example of betrayal: it may be a misfortune of mine if a friend betrays me, although I may never become aware of this betrayal. Then there is the open question whether there are ever 'external' reasons for action: these also exist outside of consciousness, if they exist at all (see Williams 1980, Nagel, 1972). Finally, there is the question of other minds: we normally think that we can perceive and feel concern at the pain of others; but Epicurus seems to think this is ruled out a priori. So if Epicurus' views about life and death are right, quite a number of our everyday beliefs will need extensive revision.

In other cases, too, Epicurus hopes to overturn deeply held everyday beliefs and convictions, and to do so by means of a combination of arguments from physics and arguments from the primacy of sense-impressions.

Lucretius, for instance, in his poem on the nature of things, argues that we are afflicted by a great number of false beliefs about love and sex and he believes that a correct understanding of these topics will lead to a happier life. Lucretius starts by telling us about the biology in question, how the 'seed is excited within us' and must be drained away. But he also claims that we should beware of the power of the imagination, and avoid love. One central false belief is that 'the body which causes this ardour/Will prove the best instrument for quenching the flame' (IV. 1087–8). In fact, however, this is quite contrary to nature: 'There is nothing to take in and enjoy but a pack of images' (1095–6) The experience is like trying to drink in a dream;

> So in love Venus plays with her lovers in images;
> they cannot be satisfied by looking at bodies
> nor can they scrape off bits of delicious limbs
> but think they might and roam all over the body
> (IV, 1102–4)

Furthermore, being in love can cause the lover to lose his perspective on the rest of life; there are the pains of jealousy and the blindness of love, both of which can involve false beliefs; and there are also 'couples who are the evident victims/Of mutual pleasure, though they find their chains a torture' (IV, 1201–2).

Lucretius here shows clear reductionist tendencies: his view is that there is a physical basis of sexual behaviour, but that there is nothing in the nature of things – in physics, or in our sense-experience, narrowly construed – that can account for the human experience of love. Lucretius does not conclude 'so much the worse for my theory of the nature of things', but rather 'so much the worse for the human experience of love'. It is based on false belief, and should be rooted out. We would all be happier if we did not superimpose works of the imagination upon the facts available to reason. But Lucretius gives no account of how human beings have become subject to communal illusion on this score. It is hard not to conclude that he has just missed something out from his account of human experience because it does not fit easily into his view of the nature of things.[9]

In the case of received religion and the gods, physical theory once again destroys common conceptions, but does not determine Epicurus' own theory. The problem with religion as commonly conceived is that its claims are all false, and that they bring a lot of misery to human life. We do not need to appeal to the existence of the gods in order to explain the movements of the heavenly bodies (or other workings of the natural world); and we certainly do not need to practise rituals like the sacrifice of Iphigeneia at Aulis (memorably described in Lucretius I).[10]

Reflecting on the role of atomic theory in Epicurus, Long and Sedley conclude that, whereas Democritus is a reductionist atomist, Epicurus, by contrast, is a non-reductionist atomist (Long and Sedley, 1987: 109). A reductionist atomist may be expected to argue in favour of scepticism and determinism: phenomenal properties, the 'self' and its volitions will be seen as (mere) human constructions – reality itself consists just of atoms and void. Epicurus, however, affirms the reality of phenomenal properties, and of the self and its volitions. He is a non-reductionist atomist who believes that atoms sometimes swerve unpredictably because he believes in free will (and not vice versa).[11] For Epicurus, ethics is prior to physics. Epicurus' remarkable philosophy of science (his suggestion that many explanations of for example the movement of the heavenly bodies are equally acceptable) also arises from this source: any explanation that is compatible with the phenomena and that helps us to be happy will do. We need not try to solve these problems in order to get a grip on our lives. Knowledge of physics can help us dismiss certain false beliefs; and it underlies and supports true beliefs about the world. But the way to proceed in philosophy is not to first establish the truth about physics, and then proceed on that basis to work out the truth about, for example, the relation of mind to body.[12] Rather, we must examine the evidence of the senses to determine the truth about the world. Epicurus believes that all perceptions are true, and that all scientific theses that accord with the testimony of the senses are acceptable. But the most important truth he believes that we learn from our senses, and from our study of the behaviour of the child, is that pleasure is the good.

Epicurus' idea that we can learn something about the the good by looking at the natural behaviour of the child is, as Striker (1983) has pointed out, completely novel in Greek ethics. The idea of studying, and learning from, the behaviour of the child is nowadays taken very seriously by developmental psychologists (cf. Kohlberg, 1981). But the idea nowadays is not that we should follow in the footsteps of the newborn; but rather that we should study the course of the child's moral development and (maybe) help children to achieve the final and most mature stage of moral development that we can discover. From this perspective, it seems very strange to take the newborn infant as the exemplar for adult human development.

On the other hand, if we are going to take the deliverances of the senses as the core of our philosophy, then it does make sense to look to the child, whose senses are in perfect working order, and are uncorrupted by the world. As Long and Sedley point out, the deliverances of the child's senses have the same sort of authority for Epicurus as the deliverances of reason for Descartes (Long and Sedley, 1987: 122). The question that faces us here, then, is whether we should take the deliverances of our senses as the starting point in philosophy. Epicurus, unfortunately, never explains why he thinks this should be the starting-point in philosophy. The problem is that the starting point is rather far removed from where we now find ourselves. We have learnt to mistrust our senses in the course of life, and to think that they are not the sole, or the most reliable, guides to right conduct or to the truth about the world more generally. We must unlearn all this, to become good Epicureans. Is it all worth while? We can only, I think, decide how to answer this question by looking at the conclusions Epicurus is able to draw from this starting point. (Contemporaries of Epicurus, of course, had more to go on: they could look at the community of real live Epicureans in the garden, and see for themselves, directly, if this life was the best for man.)

Epicurus' idea that pleasure is the goal in life may seem unpersuasive. In the context of Greek philosophy, hedonism had been very thoroughly examined and attacked by both Plato and Aristotle, and for the most part, Epicurus does not try to meet and counter their arguments.[13]

Furthermore, we may find the idea that pleasure is the goal in life unpersuasive. Tolstoy (1882) tells a story about a traveller in the steppe who is overtaken by an infuriated beast; he jumps into a waterless well, but at its bottom he sees a dragon who opens his jaws in order to swallow him; so he clutches at the twig of a wild bush growing in the cleft of the well and holds on to it. Then he sees some drops of honey hanging on the leaves of the bush, and so licks the leaves with his tongue. This story illustrates Tolstoy's own experience. Other things being equal, we would like the two drops of honey. But to Tolstoy, the two drops of honey are no longer pleasant as he contemplates death (Tolstoy 1882: 11–12). Tolstoy concludes, very persuasively, that the search for pleasure does not yield the meaning of life.[14]

We should note, however, that this is not Epicurus' view of pleasure, and that there is an area where he thinks he has much to teach us. Thus where pleasure itself is concerned, Epicurus thinks that, 'No pleasure is bad *per se*: but the causes of some pleasures produce stresses many times greater than the pleasures' (21D). And further, that 'the complete absence of pain is the highest pleasure' (21A). Furthermore, while Epicurus holds that physical pleasures are good (21L), he holds also that

> what produces the pleasant life is not continuous drinking and parties or pederasty or womanizing or enjoyment of fish and the other dishes of an expensive table, but sober reasoning which tracks down the causes of every choice and avoidance, and which banishes the opinions that beset souls with the greatest confusion. (21B(5))

Epicurus distinguishes between 'static' and 'kinetic' pleasures. Long and Sedley say that 'active stimulation of enjoyable bodily feelings or states of mind' (Long and Sedley 1987: 123) give rise to 'kinetic' pleasures; all we need for happiness, however, is 'static' pleasure – that is, freedom from bodily and mental pain. Other important distinctions are drawn by Epicurus between natural desires and empty desires, and natural desires and necessary desires (21B). A large part of philosophy has to do with deciding which desires fall into which category; and a large part of therapy has to do with eliminating mistakes we ordinarily make in this area.

Epicurus is fertile with new ideas, and his ideas speak to us directly across the centuries. He discusses questions that have considerable intrinsic interest: how far can we push the authority of the senses?; how seriously can philosophy be seen as medicine of the soul?; what are the attractions of non-reductive atomism? In general, however, we will not want to accept Epicurus' own views about these questions. Those attracted by his ideas on therapy will probably feel happier practising therapy outside of philosophy. Those attracted by atomism will probably prefer a reductionist form of atomism. And few will be persuaded to take the senses, or the newborn infant, as their guides to what is valuable in life. We may feel that there is something of value in the child's outlook on life; but that as we grow up, this outlook needs rather more by way of supplement than a knowledge of physics, or the application of reason to our desires.

THE STOICS

The Stoics are the great system-builders of the Hellenistic period. Cicero speaks of the 'remarkable coherence of the system and the extraordinary orderliness of the subject-matter' (*Fin*.iii. 74). He points to the problem with such coherence when he goes on to ask rhetorically, 'What is there which is not so linked to something else that all would collapse if you moved a single letter?' His Stoic speaker confidently responds, 'But there is nothing at all which can be moved'. Today, we may not share that confidence. In fact, in many areas of philosophy (in philosophy of mind, in logic, in metaphysics), Stoic views can seem surprisingly modern. But in other areas – notably in their view of the physical world – their views now seem archaic. The philosophical system of the Stoics can no longer be accepted in its entirety. None the less, the stoic account of the ideal (philosophical) life as lived by the Stoic sage remains very attractive. The Stoic sage is, in an important sense, detached from the passions and from his passions; but his life is not emotionally barren; he knows his place in the natural world, and identifies with the larger workings of the providential universe in which he lives. This universe is completely determined; but the sage exercises choice. His spontaneous desires and reasons will simply harmonise with fate, or the will of god, as reflected in nature as a whole. Unlike the Epicurean, he has matured emotionally as well as cognitively since his childhood. Unlike the Sceptic (the subject of our next section), there is no danger that he will become a mere spectator of his own life; he is very much in touch with himself and with the world as a whole.

In this section, I shall examine first the Stoic view of the general structure of philosophy; and then the question of the contribution that they think philosophy can make to the good life, as lived by the Stoic sage.

The Stoics divided philosophy into three parts: logic, physics and ethics. Various images are used to indicate the relation between the parts. Thus according to one account,

> They compare philosophy to a living being, likening logic to bone and sinews, ethics to the fleshier parts, and physics to the soul. They make a further comparison to an egg: logic is the outside, ethics what comes next, and physics the innermost parts; or to a fertile field: the surrounding wall corresponds to logic, its fruit to ethics, and its land or trees to physics; or to a city which is well fortified and governed according to reason. (26B)

Clearly the three elements of philosophy are to be seen as interlocking components of the whole. Thus, to continue the quotation: 'On the statements of some of them, no part is given preference over another but they are mixed together; and they [these Stoics] used to transmit them in mixed form'. But for most Stoics, there was none the less an order of priority, at least in exposition. Long and Sedley conclude, having surveyed the evidence, that most Stoics seem to have expounded the system in the order logic-physics-ethics, though Chrysippus favoured logic-ethics-physics.

Philosophy students will learn logic first, because it is through logic that we learn how to reason correctly and how to achieve philosophical results. We are part of nature, and Stoic physics tells us about nature. But ultimately we want to know how we should live, and how to be happy, and that is the subject of Stoic ethics, which teaches how to orient ourselves in relation to nature. This would suggest that ethics, although not first in order of exposition, is none the less central to the stoic conception of the nature and value of philosophy.

'Logic' comprises both rhetoric and dialectic. Long (1978) suggests that dialectic is a branch of Stoic philosophy that may have developed over the years; that the original concept of dialectic may have been quite narrow; for Zeno, dialectic may have been 'largely restricted to knowing how to acquit oneself creditably in debates about logical puzzles' (Long 1978: 105); but that with

Chrysippus a broader conception emerges both of dialectic and of logic as a whole. The following report on dialectic may give the view of Chrysippus:

> They take dialectic itself to be necessary, and a virtue which incorporates specific virtues. Non-precipitancy is the science of when one should and should not assent. Uncarelessness is a strong rational principle against the plausible, so as not to give in to it. Irrefutability is strength in argument, so as not to be carried away by argument into the contradictory [of one's own thesis]. Non-randomness is a tenor in the reception of impressions which is unchangeable by reason. (31B)

More generally, Long suggests, dialectic, for Chrysippus has a positive role in the discovery of truth; but also a negative role, in rebutting the arguments of the sceptical Academy. For such purposes, it may, for example, be good training to argue both sides of a question (that is how you learn how to undermine the opposition).[15] But what ultimately matters in Stoicism is not the everday cultivation of the virtues of the dialectician, but the truths that we arrive at, by means of dialectic, in physics and ethics, and the action appropriate to those truths.

The Stoics, like the Epicureans, say that, in the words of Long and Sedley, to be is to be a body: everything is a form of *pneuma*, 'breath'. Unlike the Epicureans, however, the Stoics do not face problems of reductionism, in consequence. Rather, they hold that *pneuma* comes in various degrees of tension, and exists at various levels of organisation. But it pervades the world throughout. A continuum links lifeless things like logs and stones to plants, animals, and the human soul (47P). All are part of nature; and nature, seen as a whole, is God. These Stoic doctrines immediately yield an answer to the question 'what is our place in nature?'. The answer is that all nature is one, and that we should live in accordance with nature. Thus Stoic physics has a very direct bearing on Stoic ethics. Cicero writes as follows:

> Nor again can anyone judge truly of things good and evil, save by a knowledge of the whole plan of nature, and also of the life of the gods, and of the answer to the question whether the nature of man is or is not in harmony with that of the universe. (*Fin* 3.73)

Cicero goes on to say that physics shows us the significance of ancient ethical maxims such as 'know thyself'. So physics helps us see where we belong in the cosmos; and it helps us understand better general ethics.[16]

The basic stance of Stoic ethics is naturalistic (see Long and Sedley 1987, section 57). Human beings, for the Stoics, are very much part of the natural world. Furthermore, in philosophy, we observe part of the natural world in order to find out about ethics. In fact, we study the behaviour of children to see what is natural – and we can conclude that the Epicureans are wrong in claiming that children and young animals simply pursue the pleasant. Thus 'they strive for their natural motion even against the pressure of pain' (57A). It emerges that our basic task in life, which we perform more or less successfully, is to orient ourselves in relation to nature.

The standard objection to all naturalistic theories of ethics is that they commit the naturalistic fallacy. Thus Long and Sedley ask 'how can it be consistent to derive "the good", a term exclusively limited to moral value, from natural impulses which justify the appropriateness of other values?' (Long and Sedley, 1987: 353). For Inwood, however, 'the problem of the "is" and the "ought" does not arise in the Stoic version of naturalism': ethical facts and psychological facts are alike derived from the Stoic concept of nature (Inwood, 1985: 199).[17] And maybe it is true that the Stoics can derive an 'ought' here without too much difficulty; the process of *oikeosis*, whereby we orient ourselves in relation to nature, is, for the Stoics, both natural and desirable – we do orient ourselves in relation to nature and we ought to orient ourselves in relation to nature. But the question remains whether the 'ought' we have derived here is a moral 'ought'.

Stoic ethics has a bearing on the everday conduct of human life. But Long and Sedley, in an interesting summary, suggest that what is required of us, as we become Stoics, is not so much that we change our circumstances, but that we change our outlook on our circumstances. We can continue to be family men, and to pursue our careers. What we must stop doing is finding in these activities the meaning of life (Long and Sedley, 1987: 345). This answer is based, of course, on a comparison of the everyday view of life with the view that the Stoics ascribe to the Stoic sage. So let us now examine further some of the leading characteristics of the sage.

The first point to note is that Stoic sages are few and far between. And yet the Stoic sage alone is truly virtuous and truly happy. So one can't hope to become truly virtuous and truly happy. And yet this is an all-or-nothing state (61I: a stick is either straight or crooked; 61T: In the sea a man at arm's length from the surface is drowning no less than one who has sunk five hundred fathoms). This seems problematic. But perhaps here Stoic physics can help us set the question in perspective. The Stoic sage achieves the goal of living perfectly in accordance with nature, and living in accordance with nature does admit of degrees. But the absolute degree is important because there is a whole, coherent, plan of the world, and either one goes along with this or one kicks against the pricks (compare the image of the dog on the lead, which is discussed below). Here, then, the Stoic conception of nature supports the Stoic view of ethics. The sage is the rare individual who has perfectly appropriated the God's-eye view of the world.

The second point to note concerns the Stoic sage's treatment of the passions.[18] For the Stoics, 'passion is an impulse which is excessive and disobedient to the dictates of reason, or a movement of the soul which is irrational and contrary to nature' (65A). Passion and impulse are terms of art; and this definition is not so helpful or informative as it may appear. The Stoics recognise the existence of 'normal, healthy, impulses' (Long and Sedley, 1987: 420). Passions are related to normal, healthy, impulses, as walking is related to uncontrolled running (see 65J). Passions are also said to be false judgements. This again, is unsurprising in the context of the Stoic system. Passions are false judgements (or are related to false judgements) in the sense that all impulses are judgements (or are related to judgements); but passions are false judgements that are rather harder to correct than are some other false judgements To return to 65A:

> when people have been deceived, for instance over atoms being first principles, they give up the judgement, once they have been taught that it is not true. But when people are in states of passions, even if they realize or are taught to realize that one should not feel distress or fear or have their soul, quite generally, in states of passions, they still do not give these up, but are brought by them to a position of being controlled by their tyranny.

The Stoics, then, are distrustful of passions and they think passions are to be avoided. And whereas the passions control the man in the street, the sage controls his passions. There are two aspects to this control. First there is his attitude towards 'affective reactions which are radically involuntary' (Inwood, 1985: 176) and which we would ordinarily see as passions. The sage may indeed suffer such reactions; but he will refuse to own them as passions. Thus,

> if anyone thinks that pallor, floods of tears, sexual arousal, heavy breathing or a sudden brightening of the eyes and the like, are evidence of passion and a mark of the mind, he is mistaken, and fails to realise that these are bodily drives. (65X)

The point is, I can detach myself from these sensations in the sense that I can refrain from acting upon them (whilst acknowledging the reality of the physical sensations).

What about cases where the sage does act, however? Inwood has recently argued that it is important here to accord due weight to the conception of impulse 'with reservation'. Inwood suggests that it is the mark of a sage that his impulses without reservation are directed at the good and bad; but that his impulses directed at the indifferents are impulses 'with reservation'. If the sage runs for political office and is defeated,

> he feels no pain. Nothing bad has happened and no contraction of the soul is called for. Did he not want the magistracy? Yes, but only with the reservation "if it is fated for me to win it; otherwise not". He never forgets that his desire was only for something truly good, an impulse of the correct sort to win office. Therefore the sage is never disappointed and is utterly free from the passions and regret. Nothing he wants, in the special sense in which a sage may be said to want things, is beyond attainment
>
> (Inwood, 1985: 167)

But 'reserving' the impulses he directs at indifferents will not, by itself, preserve the sage from the passions. He must also be able to avoid the passions in his responses to the turns of fortune that lie outside the sphere of his own agency. To this end, he must cultivate a sort of affective equivalent to the impulse with reservation, which is a state of emotional detachment from the world.

The Stoic sage is not emotionally concerned that his goals in life be realised. And he is not emotionally concerned at whatever befalls him.

As Rist has noted, an important part of the Stoic worldview is that nothing we value is to be seen as unique and irreplaceable (Rist, 1978: 263). Thus in discussing cases of loss and bereavement, Epictetus moves (without any sense that this is inappropriate) from the example of a favourite jug breaking, to the example of a wife or child dying (*Enchiridion* 3). It is also important to remember that human beings are mortal and that they may or may not be important *sub specie aeternitatis*. If your son dies, you should say, with Anaxagoras, 'well, I knew when I begot him that he was mortal'.[19] One must fit in with the divine plan, like the foot which would not intrinsically want to get muddy (58J), but which might have the impulse to get muddy if it had intelligence. One is a part of God, after all (God being seen here as a dispersed particular). Thus the sage is immune from the vagaries of chance. He will know that the world is providentially organised, even if the circumstances of his life are so extreme as to call for suicide.

We should pause at this point to consider an alternative interpretation, according to which the Stoic sage would not need to 'reserve' his impulses or remain detached from his family. If the Stoic sage were omniscient, he need never suffer a reverse at the hands of Zeus, or Fate. We know that Stoic sages are thin on the ground; and also, that know they know a lot more than the man in the street. If Stoic sages were common, it would be wildly implausible to claim that they were omniscient. As they are most uncommon, perhaps this line of interpretation is viable. Perhaps the Stoic sage, if he existed, would never entertain an impulse that was out of accord with the divine plan. Against this line of interpretation, however, Kerferd (1978) argues persuasively that the Stoic sage does not, in fact appear to be omniscient – that he is not 'the ultimate computer memory bank' (Kerferd, 1978: 127). Rather he knows not just what to do, but how to do it. (Compare Inwood 1985: 213–15: the Stoic sage goes home for Thanksgiving because he takes this to be in accordance with the divine plan. A lesser mortal just goes home for Thanksgiving.) It remains, however, a possibility that the world will not disappoint the Stoic sage, not because he is omniscient, but because that is the sort of world he lives in. Fate will play ball with the projects of the sage.[20]

Of course, we are mostly not sages and never will be. For us too, the Stoics have the occasional word of advice about the passions. Thus on the treatment of pain, Inwood notes Cicero's suggestion that

> the safest initial treatment for a bout of, say, regret over one's poverty (an example of *lupe*) is not to argue that poverty is not bad, but rather to say that one ought not to bear it badly . . . The direct assault on the error about the badness of poverty is said to be correct, but less usesful (*Tusculan Disputations*. 4.60). The first task is to relieve the contraction in the soul.
>
> (Inwood, 1985: 152–3)

Here we see a case where Stoic therapy for human suffering does not consist in conveying to the sufferer all the truth about his condition immediately. As we have seen (cf. 65A quoted above), full intellectual enlightenment about their state may not be that helpful to humans in the grip of the passions.

It is not just in their treatment of the passions that the Stoics are happy to run counter to the *endoxa*. This is equally the case in their treatment of the related topic of determinism. Long and Sedley say that determinism arises both from Stoic logic and from Stoic physics (Long and Sedley, 1987: 392). In the case of physics, the problem is that all events are caused, and that the causal chains that lead to action originate in causes external to the agent. In the case of logic, the problem concerns the definition of the possible. The Stoics want, in the phrase of Dennett, to prevent the possible from 'shrinking tightly around the actual' (Dennett, 1984: 145).

The Stoic solution of the logical difficulty is perhaps not all that successful. According to Long and Sedley, it leaves future contingents 'possible', 'only in a very restricted sense. It is possible *for* them to come about, we might say, but there is no possibility *that* they will come about' (Long and Sedley, 1987: 235). The solution is perhaps acceptable on the hypothesis of determinism, however. This hypothesis seems to call for some change in our beliefs; the question is simply how radical such a change must be.

In fact, the hypothesis of determinism does not have that radical an impact on the Stoic worldview. The Stoics are not just the first determinists; they are also the first compatibilists; and they argue strongly that we can hold adult human beings reponsible for their actions. For the Stoics, the real question we face is whether or not we achieve a smooth flow of life; and not whether, at a given moment, we could have done otherwise.[21] The Stoics take adult human responsible action to be characterised by the phenomenon of rational 'assent'. This is the respect in which adult human actions differ from the actions of children and animals, who do not assent, but merely 'yield' when they act purposively (Inwood 1985: 77–9). A related point is a distinction between different sorts of cause: there are 'internal' causes of human action ('complete and primary', 62C, Cicero *On Fate*) as well as 'external' causes ('auxiliary and proximate', Cicero).

The overall picture is that the wise man simply goes along with his own nature and divine nature, like the dog who realises that he is on a lead (62A: its voluntary action coincides with necessity).[22] If everything is reflected in everything else anyhow, we carry the entire fate of the world within ourselves, and it is part of our nature. And who would think it problematic that during my life, we play out our natures? In fact, we would all like to achieve self-fulfilment; and would much prefer to be the dog on a lead than a recalcitrant foot that tries in vain to avoid the mud.

There is no doubt that the life of a Stoic sage in a Stoic world would be very satisfying. The Stoic vision of the unity of the world allows the sage understanding, self-awareness, and gives him the strength to cope with life's reverses. It is all the more tragic that the world is not composed of *pneuma* in various degrees of tension with reference to which we can hope to orient ourselves. The wrongness of Stoic physics makes their worldview untenable. We may want to save their compatibilism and their treatment of the passions. But in that case, we must argue for them afresh, and fit them into a new worldview. In the Stoic conception of philosophy it is the results, and not the philosophising itself, that ultimately matters.

THE SCEPTICS

The ancient sceptic believes that he is happier than other men, and happier because of his philosophy. According to Sextus Empiricus, there are those in philosophy who claim to have discovered the truth (dogmatists such as Aristotle, Epicurus and the Stoics); those who claim that the truth is inapprehensible (such as the members of the sceptical Academy), and those – the sceptical Pyrrhonists – who continue their search (*PH* I.1). Sceptics continue their search because in their experience so far, they have found that there are equally persuasive arguments on both sides of every question.

Why does one search for the truth? The answer is that one's initial tranquillity is disturbed by the contradictions in things (their *anomalia*), and one hopes to regain one's tranquillity by discovering the truth (*PH* I.12). What does one gain out of continuing one's search for the truth? The sceptics argue that this turns out to be the way to regain one's tranquillity. This is something of a happy accident, in their view. Sextus tells us the story of Apelles who threw his paintbrush at the canvas in frustration at not being able to paint the foam at a horse's mouth, and achieved the result he wanted by happy accident. The sceptic too achieves his goal in life in this fashion (*PH* I.28–9).

The route that leads to scepticism, then, is circular: we return to our initial state of tranquillity. But the journey is worthwhile in so far as (a) once we are disturbed by the anomaly in things, there is no turning back and (b) the journey enables us to regain tranquillity (though not to discover the truth about things). The trouble for most of us (and certainly for all who grapple with philosophy) is that we stand somewhere in between the starting-point and the goal.

Let us follow the sceptics on their journey, asking first about the life of tranquillity from which one sets off, and to which one hopes to return. It is a common complaint that the life of scepticism is unlivable. But we should remember that we live this life *before* we are first struck by the contradiction in things, and set out on our journey. The life we must now try to describe, then, is a pre-philosophical life as much as a post-philosophical life.[23]

Sextus tells us that the sceptical way of life is fourfold, and is lived by the guidance of nature, in the constraint of the passions, in the tradition of laws and customs, and in the instruction of the arts (*PH* I.23–4). That tells us the content of the life. But the important thing is the way in which one views the life. In giving up the quest for certainty, one lives one's life, undogmatically, in accordance with appearances.

But what is it to live undogmatically, in accordance with appearances? A first answer might be that this is a life in which one stands back from oneself and lets one's instincts rule the day. The crucial point about such a life is that, in the phrase of Long and Sedley, it involves 'no intervention of assent' (Long and Sedley, 1987: 471) between an impulse and its realisation in action. But what is it like for assent to intervene, or fail to intervene, between an instinct and its realisation in action? Here we might think first about some of the lives described in Sacks' book *Awakenings*. The drug L-dopa gave rise in his patients to nervous tics. Some tried to integrate the tics into their life – to 'utilise, rationalise, mannerise or ritualise' them (Sacks, 1982: 100). They would endow them with a purpose and a meaning. Others did not see their tics as part of themselves, but adopted towards them, rather, the attitude of a spectator. They endowed the tics with no meaning, just let them happen, and were untroubled by them. (Sacks talks about not being 'possessed', 'dispossessed' or 'taken over' by them, Sacks, 1982: 100.) This might be the attitude of the sceptic towards his natural impulses.

But at this point we might ask, does the sceptic have natural impulses? After all, in the passage we have just looked at, Sextus himself says that 'we live in accordance with the normal rules of life, undogmatically, seeing that we cannot remain wholly inactive' (I.23). Why can't the sceptic remain wholly inactive? Or rather, why doesn't he remain wholly inactive? According to Hume, we would expect a Pyrrhonian sceptic to remain totally inactive:

> a Pyrrhonist . . . must acknowledge . . . that all human life must perish, were his principles universally and steadily to prevail. All discourse, all action, must immediately cease; and men remain in a total lethargy, till the necessities of nature, unsatisfied, put an end to their miserable existence.
> (Hume, 1748:160)

And Burnyeat paints a picture that is only slightly less bleak.[24] Burnyeat describes the sceptic as aiming for a state of 'detachment from oneself' (Burnyeat, 1980b: 129), characterised by 'a marked passivity in the face of both his sensations and his own thought processes' (Burnyeat, 1980b: 131). Emotions that depend on reason and thought will disappear (Burnyeat, 1980: 132), leaving him just physical responses to his environment. The sceptic can only assent to an appearance when his assent is constrained (Burnyeat, 1980b 131).[25]

The positions of Hume and Burnyeat are attractive. But we can offer a reply to them, on behalf of the sceptic – and a reply along

Humean lines, strangely enough. Animals do not remain wholly inactive, and they live the sort of life to which the sceptic hopes to return, a life in accordance with the appearances. And the sceptics' view of human development is that initially, we too live innocently, and unreflectively, a life in accordance with our natural impulses. However, one then grows to question these impulses, and wonders whether or not one should endorse them. Finally, casting aside reflection, one returns to the instinctual life. We might call to mind here Aristotle's view of children and animals: they don't make choices (*NE* 1111b) – that is, their actions may be voluntary, but they are not purposive; they have no conception of the overall good in life, and they can't, therefore, be called *eudaimon* (1100a1: this point applies only to children); nor can they display weakness of will (1147b4–5 – this point applies only to animals). On this view, animals and children are completely untroubled by the problems of philosophy. And the Stoic view of animals and children, is, of course, very similar. So we might have natural impulses, towards at least our basic physical needs, after the manner of children, and other animals, and still lead a tranquil, and reasonably full, life.

In their search for a life of 'pure' behaviour, ancient sceptics embark on a theme often explored in recent philosophical speculation about the meaning of life.[26] Thus Camus, in *The Myth of Sisyphus*, reminds us that 'we get into the habit of living before acquiring the habit of thinking' (Camus, 1942: 72). And Tolstoy's first solution to the problem of the meaning of life as reported by Edwards (Edwards, 1967: 123) is the way of ignorance, chiefly adopted by women, the very young and the very dull, who have not yet faced the problem of the meaning of life. Some authors compare the lives of animals and plants. Thus Baier writes that 'we do not disparage a dog when we say it has no purpose, is not a sheep dog or a watch dog or a rabbiting dog, but just a dog that hangs around the house and is fed by us' (Baier, 1957: 104). And Swenson notes that 'The lilies of the field cannot hear the voice of duty and obey its call; hence they cannot bring their will into harmony with the divine will' (Swenson, 1949: 28).

Nagel, in his paper on 'The Absurd', explicitly discusses the idea that 'philosophical perception of the absurd resembles epistemological scepticism' (Nagel 1979: 18). Nagel has in mind scepticism of the Cartesian variety. But there is much to be learnt from his discussion – especially as the position he sketches out seems much closer to scepticism of the ancient variety. Nagel writes

> In viewing ourselves from a broader perspective than we can occupy in the flesh, we become spectators of our own lives. We cannot do very much as pure spectators of our own lives, so we continue to lead them, and devote ourselves to what we are able at the same time to view as no more than a curiosity, like the ritual of an alien religion
>
> (Nagel, 1979: 20–1)

He goes on immediately to consider the life of animals (arguing that a mouse life could not be absurd), and also the life of impulse. In this case too, there is no room for standing back, and no scope for absurdity. In the case of the absurd, as elsewhere in philosophy, Nagel thinks problems arise in so far as we try to occupy two opposed viewpoints, the subjective view, the view from where we are, and the objective view, the view from nowhere. Our subjective concerns look absurd when viewed from nowhere.

Now ancient sceptics do not exactly adopt this position. The great realisation that overcomes the sceptic as he completes his journey is not that life is meaningless, or absurd. He suspends judgement on this question, as on all others, no doubt. But we can express their position in Nagel's terminology. Ancient sceptics hold that we cannot attain the objective viewpoint, but that this is the goal in philosophy, and that we should live, undogmatically, in accordance with the subjective viewpoint. They are the first (but not the last) philosophers to hold that too much philosophy (or perhaps any philosophy at all) is bad for you.

Now let us suppose we set out on the route to scepticism, and begin enquiring. Why is one worse off, when one is engaged in enquiry, but has not as yet become a sceptic? Sextus has an answer to this: one is going to get a lot more worked up about things. Thus Sextus writes that:

> the man who opines that anything is good or bad is for ever being disquieted: when he is without the things which he deems good he believes himself to be tormented by things naturally bad and he pursues after the things which are, as he thinks, good; which when he has obtained he keeps falling into still more perturbations because of his irrational and immoderate elation, and in his dread of a change of fortune

> he uses every endeavour to avoid losing the things which he deems good. (*PH* I.27)

We can adapt an example of Annas and Barnes (1985: 167) to illustrate what Sextus has in mind: I might decide that a decent salary is important for a good life. I will then worry about acquiring and holding on to a decent salary. But the sceptic will not worry about such questions. This is not, however, to say that the sceptic is completely untroubled: 'We grant that he is cold at times and thirsty' (*PH* I.29). But he is less troubled by this than other people because he does not additionally believe that it is a bad thing to be cold and thirsty. Another example comes from III.236, where Sextus notes that bystanders at an operation may suffer more than the patient: they think that the operation is a bad thing, whereas the patient just has the pain from the operation to contend with. Non-sceptics suffer a lot of avoidable pain. The only cares that trouble a sceptic are cares he cannot avoid. We cannot say, of course, what his overall level of happiness will be: the sceptic (like any child; unlike the Stoic) will be highly vulnerable to fortune. All we can say is that he will maximise his chances of an untroubled life.[27]

So sceptics think we are worse off when we are launched into philosophical enquiry. The goal of philosophical enquiry, finding the truth, is all right, the problem with it is that it cannot be attained. In fact, whatever question we address, we will find that we come up with equipollent arguments, and that we must suspend judgement on the issue.

Now the claim that we always just happen to encounter equipollent arguments in relation to every question we ask in philosophy seems very implausible (so implausible indeed, that Sedley (1983: 21) suggests that sceptics must in most cases have gone out in search of equipollent arguments).[28] But sceptics claim that it just so happens that there are arguments of equal strength on both sides of every question, and that there is no criterion by which to reject some of the arguments. Ancient sceptical arguments, such as the so-called 10 Modes of Aenesidemus (reported by Sextus in *PH* I) will take us some way towards this conclusion, but are not, I believe, ultimately persuasive.[29]

The transition from encountering equipollent arguments to suspension of judgement, however, is less problematic. It is helpfully discussed by Annas and Barnes (1985: 49), who point out that

Sextus says on occasion (I.34) that one 'ought' to suspend judgement when there is equipollence, but also that that one 'shall' or that one is 'compelled' to do so. His overall view, as expressed in I.7 is simply that sceptical arguments are like drugs: they are in fact efficacious in bringing about suspension of judgement, and that is all there is to it.

Suspension of judgement then leads the philosopher to tranquillity of mind. Sextus says, as we have seen, that this is a happy accident (*PH* I.26). Burnyeat, followed by Annas and Barnes, questions whether suspension of judgement will lead to tranquillity. Some of the crucial ideas in this area were first aired by Naess. Does the sceptic doubt or does he suspend judgement? (Naess, 1968: 27–8). Is the end-state 'ad hoc, provisional, transient, or even spasmodic?' (Naess, 1968: 29) Does the sceptic, if impelled by argument, necessarily have beliefs, or can he be like those who practise religious observances without full belief? (Naess, 1968: 43).

Burnyeat argues that if the sceptic emerges in a state of bafflement rather than belief, he will be prey to acute anxiety (Burnyeat, 1980b: 139). But if he emerges in a state of equilibrium, he will emerge in a state of belief. Philosophical arguments aren't like perceptual appearances. One cannot detach oneself from one's assent to philosophical arguments.

This is an interesting idea, but it may depend on an over-simple view of the nature of suspension of judgement. Stough (1987) distinguishes between 'active' and 'passive' suspension of judgement; passive suspension of judgement occurs when, for example, I am altogether unimpressed by the claims of a used car salesman; active suspension of judgement is the rational conclusion or attitude I adopt when I have weighed the arguments on both sides of a question very carefully, and found them to balance. In the 'passive' case, my faculty of judgement is never stirred into life; in the 'active' case, it is operative, but ineffectual, and must 'actively' be suspended. 'Passive' suspension characterises the prephilosophical life; 'active' suspension is the reward of sceptical philosophy.

It may also be helpful in this context to reflect on the famous phrase of Coleridge, 'suspension of disbelief'. In this state, one suspends one's faculty of belief – one neither believes nor disbelieves, though if one were either to believe or disbelieve in this particular case, one would disbelieve. Now I think suspension of judgement is supposed to be rather like suspension of disbelief. Sextus says that 'suspense is a state of mental rest' (*PH* I.10).[30] The idea is not that I am baffled, nor that my beliefs stand in equilibrium (though it may, in this case, appear to me that my beliefs stand in equilibrium), but that my faculty of belief is switched off. I am getting on with my life. It is perhaps not all that important whether I reach this state passively or actively. All that matters is that I am not judging for the time being.

Annas and Barnes are also unhappy about tranquillity as a goal in life: 'we may well find such tranquillity a strange, or even a repellent, conception of what it is for a human being to be happy' (Annas and Barnes, 1985: 170). It is 'boring' and 'ignoble', and undervalues intensity and engagement in life. In short, perhaps (though Annas and Barnes don't actually say this) sceptics think that we cannot discover a meaning in life – and this is an uncomfortable thought to live with.

We are approaching here an area where ancient scepticism is at its most powerful, and also its most disquieting. After all, there is no agreement as to the meaning of life. Several alternative ideas, religious and non-religious, are on offer, but none seems compelling, and all are hard to reject out of hand. It's also quite possible to doubt whether there is a meaningful question here in the first place (maybe that's why we can't answer it).

The closest Sextus comes to tackling the question of the meaning of life, is his discussion of the question of whether there is an art of living, at *PH* III.239ff. His discussion is rather diappointing. It consists in a little gentle anti-Stoic propaganda, together with some misgivings about whether teaching is possible in general. But there is a sense in which the whole sceptic position is a discussion of the question of the meaning of life. For the realisation that we cannot discover the meaning of life can be founded on a series of smaller realisations. If there is no case, in the field of conduct, where I can make up my mind that there is a right answer, then I shall not be able to accept any overall conception of the good life.

We can best appreciate the power of the sceptical position in relation to practical questions, if we look at a few examples. Sextus has, as it were, a master argument that deals with all practical questions. As he explains when introducing the Tenth Mode, we encounter a great deal of *anomalia* when we examine diverse rules of conduct, habits, laws, legendary beliefs, and dogmatic conceptions that guide the conduct of dogmatists (*PH* I.145). Furthermore there are disagreements among the dogmatists concerning the good the bad and the indifferent (*PH* III. 169–87). We cannot, then, hope to reach conclusions in this area. Sextus' arguments remain powerful. But we might ourselves now mount a rather more complex set of arguments in favour of scepticism in ethics (thus Mackie (1977), in arguing the case for moral scepticism, supplements the argument from relativity with what he calls the argument from queerness, which is a version of the argument that contrasts ethics with science). And we would certainly have a greater variety of dogmatic ethical philosophies to counteract. So let us look at a number of cases in which we face practical dilemmas, from our own perspective. I shall look, first, at a case where it may be difficult to weigh up our moral, as against our non-moral desires; then at a case where different moral arguments seem to pull in different directions; and finally at a case where abstract considerations of metaphysics might be thought to have some bearing on everyday life.

Suppose first, then, that I think that there are powerful arguments against committing adultery, but also that, in a particular case, I think there is something to be said in favour of it.[31] Pre-scepticism, I worry about doing the right thing; and I try to decide which of my impulses to endorse. Post-scepticism, I suspend judgement: I do whatever I do, and I have no additional belief that this is right or this is wrong, I simply act. Must I have a belief here? And if I don't have a belief, must I be anxious? Perhaps I once judged that there were equipollent reasons for and against this adultery. But now I simply act or refrain from action. (For Sextus' view of adultery, see *PH* I.152 and III.209.)

Second, let us consider a situation where different moral considerations conflict. For example, let us consider Sartre's example of a young man in wartime occupied France who must decide whether to join the Free French or to stay 'near his mother and help her to live' (Sartre, 1946: 223). Sartre argues that neither the Christian nor the Kantian ethic can resolve this moral dilemma and that 'nothing remains but to trust in our instincts' (Sartre, 1946: 224). Bambrough discusses this case in the course of his 'proof' of the objectivity of ethics (Bambrough, 1979: 95–6). He argues that if this is a case of moral conflict where the considerations are finely balanced, and at the end of the day one must simply act, not all cases are like this case. Sartre really needs to add, to be more like the ancient sceptic, that all cases are like this one, and that in ethics one must always trust in one's instincts.

Finally, let us think about the question of religion. Suppose I think there is an answer to the question whether or not there is a God, but I don't seem to be able to settle the question to my satisfaction: I can argue either side of the case with equal facility. Perhaps I think it may or may not be theoretically important, even. My philosophical accounts balance out: they are practically impotent. In such a case, I will detach myself, not from my assents to philosophical arguments, but from the philosophical question (for Sextus' view of religion, see *PH* III.218–19).

So it may be that in the case of many practical questions, and also in the case of the meaning of life, the sceptic can argue a powerful case. This need not lead the sceptic to suicide or to abandoned *actes gratuits*. It may mean we just lead a simpler kind of life, in the manner of children and animals. For Camus, Sisyphus is the absurd hero (Camus, 1942: 78) and one must imagine Sisyphus happy (Camus, 1942: 80) (though he also says 'It would be a mistake to think that happiness necessarily springs from the absurd discovery. It happens as well that the feeling of the absurd springs from happiness', Camus, 1942: 79).

So much, then, for the transition from equipollent arguments to suspension of judgement and tranquillity of mind. But there are other questions we must ask about ancient scepticism. Is it self-refuting? Is it possible to live a life wholly free from belief? For we might think that the sceptic manifests beliefs, and thus refutes himself pragmatically, either through his actions, or when he speaks or thinks, or when he argues for scepticism.

Let us ask first about the relation between action and belief. We might perhaps think that in explaining any action, we must ascribe both beliefs and desires to an agent.[32] If this is indeed so, then perhaps simply by acting, the sceptic is convicted of holding beliefs. In response to this charge, however, the sceptic can perhaps revert to the idea we have discussed above, and claim that he acts on his natural instincts or impulses, in the manner of children and animals, and that his actions do not necessarily display beliefs.[33]

But perhaps speech and thought, if not behaviour, bring problems for the sceptic. Thus Barnes suggests that in the Tropes themselves, the sceptic is committed, when he says or thinks that a tower seems round, to beliefs such as that he exists himself, that (the present) time exists, that external objects exist; and finally, that he reports in his utterances or thoughts, his own beliefs (Barnes, 1982: 4). Barnes suggests a partial solution to these problems. Perhaps sceptical *apaggeleiai*, 'announcements' or 'reports', are like Wittgensteinian 'avowals' – that is, they are more like behaviour than assertions, or reports about the sceptic's belief. At the same time, he thinks there are problems in interpreting Sextus' remarks about recollective sign-inference in *PH* II along these lines (Barnes, 1982: 16–17). However, reverting to the medical metaphor, he concludes that perhaps this is an area of life where we are never troubled by anomaly, and live in philosophical innocence.

There remains, finally, the possibility that the sceptic refutes himself by expressing beliefs when he argues for scepticism. Ancient sceptics were aware of the potential problem in this case. Sextus emphasises that the sceptic does not dogmatise (*PH* I.13–15). He tells us about the sceptic expressions or formulae that they are self-applicable, and that 'we make no positive assertion regarding their absolute truth' (PH I.206). Sextus employs several images in *Adversus Mathematicos* 480–1 to illustrate the self-referential nature of sceptical arguments: they are like fire that destroys itself when it consumes its fuel, like purgatives that expel themselves along with noxious fluids from the body, or like a ladder that we can kick away after we have climbed it. In one area, they seem to be vulnerable to self-refutation – in their arguments against proof. Burnyeat points out that arguing against proof is pragmatically self-refuting, but that supporting the sceptic position by bare assertion won't do either: bare assertion can be met with bare assertion, and the case against proof will not outweigh the case for the defence of proof (Burnyeat, 1976: 53–4). We may compare here the more robust attitude of Fogelin who says that 'sceptical arguments are self-refuting, but they saw no embarrassment in this since they never claimed to establish anything by reasoning' (Fogelin, 1987: 228). Sextus certainly, at II.188, takes the same attitude towards arguments against proof as to all other sceptical arguments. Sceptics can shrug off the charge of self-refutation, even if they cannot escape from it.

There are, however, major weaknesses in the sceptical conception of philosophy. As we have seen, one problem is that the claim that there are equally powerful arguments to hand on all sides of every question does not seem very convincing. (Only in the special case of arguments about the meaning of life does this claim have any plausibility. And even in this case, not just any view will be defensible.)

Furthermore, scepticism is highly reliant on a particular conception of human nature. Sceptics think it so happens that human beings are constituted such that tranquillity is the upshot of equipollent arguments. If human beings were differently constituted, the result would be different. And it may well be that the ancient sceptics' conception of human nature is seriously awry: their conception of how man responds to equipollence of argument, and of how man is at his happiest, are both, at least, open to question.

Finally, there seems to be an internal tension in the sceptical position, as commentators have suspected. We have seen that Sextus says that sceptics continue their enquiries; also, however, that they live in a state of tranquillity. And there may ultimately be a certain tension between these two claims. Naess claims that suspension of judgement 'slowly develops into a firmly based state of mind' (Naess, 1968: 5).[34] It seems, however that the tranquil life of the sceptic must rather be *ad hoc* and provisional. For he will always have to look at new arguments. He will have two modes of being, a philosophical mode, which he will always be prepared to enter, and a practical mode, in which he suspends judgement. If he is to continue his enquiries, he cannot switch off his faculty of judgement permanently, as perhaps he could if he had solved the problems of philosophy. But perhaps he must do this, if he is really to return to a simpler way of life. Otherwise, what happens to his faculty of judgement when it is not in play? It would seem that the sceptic becomes fragmented here, into an acting part and a philosophical part. The charge that he becomes dissociated from himself, and becomes a spectator of his own conduct, may ultimately hold good. There is some attraction in the idea that I should become a spectator of my desires and beliefs. If I do, I need no longer concern myself about the problems to which they may give rise. But ultimately, this does lead to a disintegration of the self; it is hard to see the sceptical way of life as satisfactory. Much less is it the ideal form of life for human beings.

CONCLUSION: THE NATURE OF PHILOSOPHY

In the introduction to this book, I asked how ancient philosophy differs from modern philosophy, and outlined three possible answers to this question: ancient philosophy seems more practically oriented than its modern counterpart; the scope of philosophy in antiquity seems wider than it is today; and the life of the professional philosopher was very different in antiquity, when philosophers were typically members of philosophical schools and were not academics employed by universities. I believe that as a result of our survey of ancient conceptions of philosophy, we are now better placed to understand the nature of the contrast between ancient and modern philosophy.

We have seen that some philosophers define philosophy in terms of a set of questions that need answering; others characterise it in terms of philosophical method; while a third group may see philosophy in terms of a set of philosophical results, which may be shared by the adherents of a philosophical school. We have also seen there is a tendency, in antiquity, for philosophers to hold that the philosopher leads a highly distinctive and uniquely happy style of life.

Let us first ask about the nature of philosophical questions. As we have seen (in the introduction), it has sometimes been argued that philosophy tends to contract, and that the questions asked by ancient philosophers are not purely philosophical in character, but have become at least in part the concern of psychologists, cosmologists, theologists, economists and anthropologists.

We are now, I believe, in a position to dismiss this view. Philosophy does not contract. As we survey the development of philosophy in antiquity, the main impression to emerge is that the philosophical vision of the world has grown in depth, scope and complexity; there is a gradual increase in the number of philosophical questions that seem to need answering.[1]

Nor would it seem that the boundaries between philosophy and other disciplines were very differently drawn in antiquity. Certainly Plato was interested in mathematics and Aristotle was interested in biology; but such interests, external to philosophy as it is practised today, were not seen by the ancients as part of philosophy. Plato sees mathematics, not as part of philosophy, but as a discipline that is useful in leading the intellect on towards being, and towards philosophy. And Aristotle sees the sciences as autonomous and independent of each other, but interconnected and organised by metaphysics or 'first philosophy'.

Moreover, it would not seem that many of the views adopted by ancient philosophers have been rendered archaic through progress in what we now see as neighbouring disciplines. Some Presocratic views about what there is may be scientific rather than philosophical in character; some of Aristotle's reflections on the Prime Mover rely on an outmoded physics; so too does the stoic notion of *oikeiosis*. But it is not clear that ancient philosophy differs from modern philosophy on this score. Philosophical reflection is always carried out in the context of contemporary scientific beliefs; and some modern philosophical views (views about determinism, for example) may yet come to seem very narrowly tied to the particular scientific beliefs now current. The difference between ourselves and the ancients is a difference in our actual scientific beliefs and not a difference in our conceptions of philosophy. In general, if we do not feel inclined to accept most of the views of ancient philosophers, that is as a result of progress within philosophy, and not because of progress in economics, cosmology, theology, and so on. Most of the questions asked by ancient philosophers are genuinely philosophical in character.

There are certain very general abiding questions that underlie most philosophical activity, and that most philosophers, ancient and modern, have hoped to answer – questions about what the world is like, about how we can come to know what the world is like, and about where we human beings fit into the grand scheme of things. We ask such questions if we want to find the meaning of life, or some meaning in life, and philosophy is one of a number of routes we might explore to this end. Most ancient philosophers see these questions as central to their concept of philosophy; and almost all ancient philosophers take a stand on these issues. That is one reason, though not the only or the most important reason, why their philosophical work bears very directly on the everyday conduct of life.

Of course it is not just philosophers who aspire to answer such questions, but also religious leaders, creative writers – and perhaps in primitive societies the local magician. But only philosophers offer philosophical answers to these questions, in the sense that they are arrived at, communicated, or assessed by a philosophical method.[2] We have seen that Plato criticises the poets for trying to deal with these questions non-philosophically. Not that there is a single method of enquiry which is the philosophical method of enquiry. We find a great variety of philosophical methods in play among the ancient philosophers, and a great variety of conceptions of philosophical method. Among the Presocratics, the Milesians formulate bold conjectures about the physical world, Heraclitus offers philosophical reminders, Parmenides argues deductively from first principles, Zeno sets out sceptical paradoxes and Anaxagoras and the atomists draw us philosophical pictures. Socrates introduces the method of *elenchos*. Plato develops the notion of 'dialectic', with his image of the ascent from the cave, and the elaborate educational system sketched out in the *Republic*. Aristotle employs a historical method in philosophy, and tries to preserve the *endoxa*. The Stoics believe we discover the truth about physics and ethics through Stoic logic, while the Epicureans and the sceptics give the impression that they will try any technique of argument or persuasion so long as it brings results. Most of these philosophical methods have their modern counterparts; and perhaps they all involve the use of reason and argument in a way that literature, religion and magic do not. Certainly, philosophy proceeds partly through criticism of the work of other philosophers.

The role of reason and argument in philosophy remains puzzling, however. Reason and argument may help us discover new truths, or reject mistaken theories; but we have seen that many ancient philosophers (and some moderns too) hold that understanding, rather than truth, is the goal in philosophy. And such philosophical understanding (unlike philosophical doctrines or even philosophical arguments) must be acquired first-hand: it cannot be taken on trust from a teacher. The significance of arguments (such as the ontological argument for the existence of

God) is not that they yield up new philosophical truths for the most part, but that they provide an important set of orientation points for the philosopher. They yield the data we later hope to mould into a theory that will help us understand the world.

The extent to which philosophy can, and must be, learnt, also remains puzzling. Simone de Beauvoir (1958) relates an autobiographical incident concerning a discussion she had in her adolescence with her parents and some friends about the existence of God. De Beauvoir floated the name of Kant – without response; but someone said to her afterwards that of course one cannot discuss such questions sensibly without taking Kant into consideration. It is possible to sympathise both with Simone de Beauvoir and with her parents. On the one hand, one cannot hope to contribute to a philosophical debate from a standpoint of ignorance. And yet the idea that it is not possible to discuss such a question without philosophical learning and expertise seems wrong. Is it really necessary for the man in the street to decide whether existence is a predicate before he can think sensibly about the existence of God?

Yet technical and abstruse questions form an ineliminable part of philosophical enquiries. If, for example, we want to decide whether or not to practise *melete thanatou*, we had better know what we think about the theory of Forms; for Aristotle, this involved formulating his highly technical theory of being. Ancient philosophy seems, and indeed perhaps is, a natural extension of human life. But the study of philosophy leads on to specialisation and technicality. We might say, using Craig's terms (Craig 1987), that philosophy (the technical discipline) is related to philosophies (the world-views discussed by philosophers) and philosophies interest us all, but philosophy need not do so.[3]

We have seen that philosophy may also be defined in terms of the acceptance of certain philosophical doctrines. For Heraclitus, a philosopher (not that Heraclitus uses this word) will be one who understands the *logos*. For Plato, a philosopher is one who knows and loves the Forms. For Aristotle, a philosopher is one who knows how the various departments of knowledge are to be interrelated. For Epicurus, a philosopher is one who trusts to the intuitions of the child and who believes in the the authority of the senses. In general, as we have seen, it is when philosophy is seen in terms of the acceptance of philosophical doctrines that we can expect philosophical schools to develop. The problem with defining philosophy in terms of the acceptance of particular philosophical doctrines has also become clear: there is a tension between the acceptance of certain philosophical doctrines as the goal in philosophy and the free play of reason and argument – which may be our best means, in philosophy, of deciding whether or not to accept a philosophical doctrine as true.

Coming to believe in the truth of a certain philosophical world-view will often have implications for the conduct of our lives. We might think of Kleist's reaction to the philosophy of Kant. The Penguin translators of Kleist's short stories quote a letter of Kleist's in which he writes that 'The thought that here on earth we know nothing of the truth, absolutely nothing . . . has shaken me in the very sanctuary of my soul – my only purpose, my supreme purpose, has collapsed, I have none left' (Luke and Reeves, 1978: 10). They comment that 'it was the Kantian epistemological theory that seems above all to have disturbed him' (Luke and Reeves, 1978: 9). Kleist gave up a commission in the Prussian army, became a writer, and eventually killed himself.

Kleist's reaction to Kant may seem largely incidental to Kant's philosophy.[4] But there are also cases where there is a closer connection between reaching a conclusion in philosophy through argument and being influenced in our everyday conduct of life. Thus Parfit claims that as a result of accepting certain philosophical arguments, he has come to fear death less. Thus he writes:

> Thinking hard about these *arguments* [my italics] removes the glass wall between me and others. And, as I have said, I care less about my death. This is merely the fact that, after a certain time, none of the experiences that occur will be related, in certain ways, to my present experiences. Can that matter all that much?
>
> (Parfit, 1984: 282)

Similarly, other modern philosophers may have hoped to influence the lives of their readers and students by persuading them of certain philosophical truths. If we come to believe Anselm's 'proof' of the existence of God, this may affect the conduct of our lives.[5] Or if we come to believe Kant's account of ethics, we may start asking ourselves questions about the categorical imperative before we act. But the idea in all these cases is that we embrace the truths revealed by philosophy, not that we necessarily become philosophers ourselves, or adopt a distinctively philosophical lifestyle.[6]

But for ancient philosophers it is not just the questions that we study, nor the methods we employ in studying them, nor the conclusions that we reach, that characterise philosophy and explain its value. Rather, the philosopher leads a particular, distinctive and valuable, lifestyle. Socrates devoted his life to the practice of *elenchos*. The Platonic philosopher cultivates death, contemplates the Form of Beauty, and practises politics (applied philosophy) in the ideal state. The Aristotelian philosopher aims either to lead the life of practical wisdom in a *polis* with his friends, or, perhaps, to spend his life in theoretical contemplation. All the Hellenistic schools of philosophy promise the philosopher personal happiness, and believe that happiness arises from the correct orientation towards the world; the Stoics believe the process of orientation is largely natural; the sceptics think we must learn the impotence of reason and argument; only for Epicurus does the correct orientation have to do with learning certain truths – those truths, however, point us away from reason and towards the authority of the child and the senses. For ancient philosophers, then, the value of philosophy lies as much in a particular lifestyle and in the practice of philosophy as in the particular conclusions we reach through our skills in argument. And here indeed ancient philosophy does differ from its modern counterpart.

Philosophers today hope for less from philosophy than their ancient forebears, and place less trust in the philosophical results that they achieve. Philosophical questions are simple, meaningful, important, and straightforwardly related to issues in everyday life. But answers to philosophical questions are hard to come by. Discussion of philosophical questions soon becomes abstract, abstruse and highly technical. Progress in philosophy is non-cumulative; new perplexities arise as old perplexities are resolved, and new arguments and observations may cause us to revise the best entrenched philosophical theories. And yet the work of past philosophers cannot be bypassed by those who wish to understand the subject. Philosophers share a public inheritance and tradition which is appropriated in the course of a philosophical training.

Those today who seek understanding of themselves and their relation to the world may turn to other disciplines – to the naturalistic study of man undertaken by psychologists, and to the experience of various forms of psychotherapy. It is not that as these disciplines have emerged, so our conception of philosophy has been purified. Our conception of philosophy remains pretty well unchanged by these developments – Davidson feels as much at liberty to discuss such irrational behaviours as weakness of will and self-deceit as any psychologist or psychoanalyst. He follows in the tradition of Plato, and we can learn much from the work of both philosophers. But philosophy is not now our only source of insight into ourselves and into the world.

In these circumstances, it is unsurprising that the study of philosophy no longer seems the key to a happy and fulfilled human life, as it did to the ancients.[7]

NOTES

INTRODUCTION: PHILOSOPHY, ANCIENT AND MODERN

1 There is also, however, a letter in which Wittgenstein says:

> What is the use of studying philosophy if all it does for you is to enable you to talk with some plausibility about some abstruse questions of logic etc. and if it does not improve your thinking about the important questions of everyday life?
>
> (Malcolm, 1958: 39)

2 Continental philosophers, to take the most obvious example, differ radically from analytic philosophers in their approach to the subject.

3 Another optimist is Parfit, who explains the lack of progress in ethics to date by referring to the scarcity of atheists who have made ethics their life's work (Parfit, 1984: 453).

4 See Craig (1987). Though Craig describes philosophy as 'logical embroidery upon a given design' (1987: 6), he thinks, none the less, that one of the designs may be the right one (Craig, 1987: 8). 'Descriptive metaphysics' as practised by Strawson (1959), would also seem to consist in mere articulation of our worldview.

5 An interesting variant on this view is expressed by Mothersill (1984), who holds that 'the line between perplexities and problems can be drawn within philosophy itself' (Mothersill, 1984: 24). A perplexity in her view is an intractable problem. She gives an example: Russell's theory of descriptions transmutes a perplexity, first formulated by Parmenides, into a problem. This, in her view, is a case of progess in philosophy.

6 For a recent statement of this view, see Berlin, 1978: 8–9. See also the view of Schlick, quoted in Chapter 4 below.

7 See Chapter 3 for a discussion of Plato's attempts to distinguish between philosophy and its images – art, rhetoric and eristic.

8 See Chapter 5 below; Popper's ideas about schools and philosophy will also be discussed there. Cohen refers to 'the school of fawning disciples that sometimes collects around a powerful philosophical mind' that 'does little to advance the subject' (Cohen, 1986: 116)

9 'According to Wittgenstein, both in his earlier and in his later phases

[establishing truths] is *not* the object of philosophy . . . Philosophy is concerned . . . to rectify certain kinds of misunderstanding' (Dummett, 1978: 438).

10 Compare the assessment of Grayling: 'The Wittgensteinians accordingly make a distinctive, although relatively small group in contemporary philosophy' (Grayling, 1988: 115)

11 As we will see, one of the questions raised by ancient philosophy concerns the relation between practice and contemplation. See the discussions of Plato and Aristotle in Chapters 3 and 4. It is worth asking, in response to Craig's view, how many world-views there are for philosophers to elaborate and articulate.

12 Another approach is that of Cohen (1986). Cohen thinks we can define analytic philosophy with reference to the problems that it treats, or its subject matter – analytic philosophy is 'the normative study of reasoning' (Cohen, 1986: 63). Cohen suggests that there are no fewer than eight sorts of normative problems about reasons and reasoning that analytic philosophers must tackle (Cohen, 1986: 50–3). We may perhaps feel that almost any philosophical problem can be construed as a problem about reasoning (about what is a good reason for what at an appropriate level of generality, Cohen, 1986: 50); but this does not tell us much about the nature of philosophy or analytic philosophy.

1 THE PRESOCRATIC PHILOSOPHERS: THE FIRST PHILOSOPHICAL ARGUMENTS

1 In *Magic, Reason and Experience*, Lloyd points also to the Greek interest in foundational questions and generalised forms of scepticism as unique features of Greek speculative thought (Lloyd, 1979: 233).

2 With Lloyd's argument from politics, compare Cohen's claim that philosophy is 'a cultural movement that makes for tolerance, universal suffrage, ethical pluralism, non-violent resolution of disputes, and a freedom of intellectual enterprise, and is provoked by them' (Cohen, 1986: 62).

3 Lloyd refers to the 'limited' nature of sixth-century speculative thought (Lloyd, 1979: 262). He has in mind a point about the limited scope of philosophical enquiry in the sixth century (see further, Lloyd, 1979: 226–267, esp. pp.235–240).

4 Williams thinks the question 'why were the Milesians rational?' is more fruitful that the question 'why were they philosophical?' (Williams, 1981: 218). The only answer he gives to the question 'why were they rational?' is that they knew what questions needed answering; and this seems rather disappointing.

5 Matthews suggests that as children grow older their interest in philosophy becomes less obvious and less intense (Matthews, 1980: 106).

6 I thus think Dummett is mistaken is suggesting that 'the belief in a unique common-sense view . . . postulates a theory that is not a theory' (Dummett, 1981: 19). The quotations from Moore and Russell

show that they think common sense offers a theory which is in competition with philosophical (and possibly scientific) theories.

7 We should note that if Thales claimed, not that everything is water, but that everything originated from water, this idea also looks like a scientific conjecture.

8 Popper refers variously to their 'cosmological interest' (Popper, 1958: 141) and to 'the general problem of change' (Popper, 1958: 142) – a problem that he sees as philosophical rather than scientific.

9 Lloyd notes that early Greek speculative thinkers tend to be incautious and dogmatic, rather than self-critical (Lloyd, 1979: 234).

10 Compare also Frischer: 'Thales propounds a new ideology that supports the tyrant's new dominant class of nonaristocratic hoplites by debunking the aristocratic myth of descent from the gods who created the world' (Frischer, 1982: 18–19).

11 This may not be a genuine fragment. For a recent defence of its authenticity, see Barnes (1979a).

12 This is the interpretation of Popper (see Popper, 1945: 14).

13 I owe this turn of phrase to Malcolm Schofield. See also Hussey (1982).

14 'Song of Myself' section 51. This passage is quoted by Barnes (1979a: 79).

15 See Guthrie 1978: Chapter 7.

16 Though fr. 79, 'the name of the bow is life, its work is death' is tied to the Greek language.

17 See Burnyeat (1987) and Nehamas (1985a).

18 Rorty (1987) suggests that seeing a platypus might affect us in the same kind of way as hearing a metaphor. Bumps on the head are recommended by Furth (1968: 269) as a way of conveying the central message of Parmenides.

19 Indeed, he offers so many examples of the unity of opposites that KRS talk of 'different kinds of instance of the essential unity of opposites' (1983: 188–9).

20 Another philosopher who resembles Heraclitus closely in terms of style is Nietzsche. A Heraclitean reading of Nietzsche has recently been offered by Nehamas (1985b). For Nehamas' Nietzsche, the self is to be created after the manner of a literary text; the world is construed as a text of which our lives are interpretations; his own philosophical texts 'show his perspectivism without saying anything about it' (Nehamas 1985b: 40).

21 Thus Kripke (1982) sees Wittgenstein as setting up a sceptical paradox to which he then proposes a sceptical solution. Cavell (1979) holds that Wittgenstein stresses, in a manner that is important for ethics and aesthetics, as well as for traditional epistemology, the signficance of our shared forms of life.

22 The only parallel that comes to mind is the speech of Diotima in the *Symposium* – though Diotima is a priestess and not a goddess.

23 See for example Rorty (1982).

24 Contrast the view of Burnyeat (1982a).

25 It remains hard to assess the effectiveness of Parmenides' argument.

It does seem persuasive to say that, if a term is meaningful, there must be something there for it to refer to. But today we might think that it seems more plausible in the case of proper names than in the case of descriptions.

26 This was Owen's verbal expansion of 'Eleatic Questions' as offered in lectures. Barnes says that by indicating the flaws of the Way of Opinion, the goddess 'will ensure that Parmenides does not succumb to meretricious temptation' (Barnes, 1979a; 157). The Way of Truth might already seem to ensure this, however.

27 Parmenides also remarks that his argument goes round in a circle: 'It is all the same to me where I start off from, because I'll get back there again' (fr. 5, tr. Austin).

28 If we ask what form of madness is in question, we might perhaps compare the construction of the world of the autistic child offered by Josephine Klein (1987). Such constructions are of course highly conjectural by nature; and for all I know, Klein could, in presenting the following construction, be relying on knowledge of Parmenides. Still, for what it is worth, the autistic child, on this story, tends to see the world as himself, and as 'complete, perfect, unending, boundless, timeless' (Klein, 1987: 90). His idea is that he should be 'absolutely everything everywhere'. What he does not want to realise is that he is 'bounded on all sides by a skin' (Klein 1987: 91). What happens as reality impinges is that 'the seamless robe of perfection is rent with holes' (Klein, 1987: 95).

29 For a recent defence of this passage as accurate historical evidence concerning the views of Zeno, see Makin, 1982, Note 1.

30 After all Barnes (1979a) has ascribed problems with the notion of contradiction to both Heraclitus and Parmenides; and though Barnes may have rather overstated his case here, it is at least possible that Zeno too is not completely clear about this topic.

31 Hussey remarks that not all the arguments may be supposed to be equally cogent (Hussey, 1972: 101).

32 For a fuller account of Plato's thinking about opposition, see Jordan (1984); Austin (1986).

33 But perhaps a rigorous presentation can be a form of defence. Compare Cohen's book *Karl Marx's Theory Of History*, which is subtitled 'A Defence', but which is, in fact, as Cohen points out, a rigorous presentation of that theory (Cohen, 1978: ix).

34 It may be that Kripke incorrectly attributes this notion of a 'sceptical' solution to a sceptical paradox to Hume. See G. Strawson (1989).

35 Barnes disagrees with Lear: 'Zeno's argument is valid; but it relies on a false premiss' (Barnes, 1979a: 284), namely that 'if 'a' occupies at 't' a space equal to its own volume, then 'a' rests at 't' ' (Barnes, 1979a: 279).

36 Barnes tells us that he *believes* that nothing can perform infinitely many tasks (Barnes, 1979a: 273), but he cannot show this to be false. Some ideas which he does feel happy about are that: 'sequences with no last task cannot be completed' (Barnes, 1979a: 268); 'to complete a set of tasks is to perform all the tasks and not the last task' (Barnes,

1979a: 268); 'there is a first point of b's having completed the tasks in s – viz. the point at which he touches B. Hence there is no last point at which he completes the task in S' (Barnes, 1979a: 271).

37 But cf.: 'the Atomists cut the Gordian knot of the Eleatic elenchos' (KRS, 1983: 433).

38 Cf. Schofield, (1980: 78).

39 Barnes takes this as an attempt to formulate a self-evident truth (Barnes, 1979b: 31).

40 Though, as Guthrie points out, for Anaxagoras, there was, there, also 'an infinite number of seeds in no way resembling each other' (fr. 4,) (Guthrie, 1965: 297).

41 This is also the view of Barnes, (1979b: 23–4).

42 Kripke claims in his work on names that unlike other philosophers who have given an account of names, he is advancing a picture and is abstaining from formulating a theory (Kripke, 1980: 94).

43 Owen is persuasive in finding indirect reference to Parmenides (Owen 1966a: 323).

44 This is, of course, provided by Plato in his *Sophist*.

45 See KRS (1983: 416, note 3 with references).

46 The atomists also feel free to simply disagree with Zeno on the question of divisibility, claiming that atoms are indivisible, though they come in a variety of shapes and sizes.

47 KRS (1983: 415 n.1) are cautious. Barnes discusses the question at length (1979b: 44–50).

48 See Barnes for a discussion that takes a rather different line from that followed here (Barnes, 1979b: 69ff.)

49 I here follow the view of Williams (1978). Barnes takes a rather different view of the distinction (Barnes, 1979b: 69–70).

2 SOCRATES: A METHOD OF DOUBT

1 Arguably, when Plato does just become interested in philosophical conclusions, the dialogue form ceases to interest him.

2 Vlastos also reflects on the strength of character that must have been necessary for Socrates to overcome his personal ugliness (Vlastos, 1958: 17).

3 The irony here is what Vlastos (1987: 86) calls a 'simple' irony. In an alternative terminology that I have heard employed in lectures by Christopher Ricks, it is a mere sarcasm, and not a true irony.

4 Robinson also mentions particularity and accidentalness (Robinson, 1953: 16).

5 Vlastos is confident that Socrates does lay claim to knowledge, pointing to *Apology* 29b6–7, and *Gorgias* 479e (Vlastos, 1983: 46). Irwin works with a distinction between knowledge and true belief rather than with a distinction between knowledge in the strong sense and knowledge in the weak sense (Irwin, 1977: 40, 62, 69).

6 In fact, Vlastos (1983: 43 n.41) holds that you need contra-endoxic premisses to get to contra-endoxic conclusions. Kraut (1983: 63) sees the point.

7 For the concept of 'high redefinition' and this example of it, see Edwards (1949: 31).
8 Burnyeat suggests adopting different attitudes towards the status of examples in ethics as compared with epistemology (Burnyeat, 1977a: 382, 394).
9 In contemporary epistemology, traditional analyses of knowledge in terms of justified true belief have given way to causal accounts, causal theories in their turn have been supplanted by conditional theories, and conditional theories are now in trouble. The problems for each and every new theory advanced have arisen from recalcitrant counter-examples. In this area, examples seem to function like experimental data in science, and our philosophical theories must accommodate our pre-philosophical intuitions. In this domain of philosophy, there really are outmoded and unassertible theories (even perhaps falsified theories). Maybe Moore and not Socrates or Plato, was right about the significance of examples in epistemology.
10 See, for example, *Laches* 192. 'Courage is wise endurance' is a candidate definition. Socrates claims it is refuted if we agree that courage is not wise endurance in spending money.
11 Compare also Barnes (1969).
12 We might also ask how seriously the example in the *Laches* is really intended – the name of Prodicus is mentioned in connection with this distinction at 197d, and this may be a hint to the reader to be on his guard. Plato may not intend us to endorse Prodicus' hair-splitting about words.
13 For continuing scepticism about the existence of *akrasia*, see Robinson (1954: 85).
14 The question is sometimes raised whether Socrates is a precursor of 'linguistic' philosophy as practised by J.L. Austin. Irwin has suggested that Socrates does not ask us for our linguistic intuitions but for our moral intuitions (Irwin, 1977: 63–4). It may be that when he asks 'Is this act courageous?', he seems to be asking for our linguistic intuitions but that if he were to ask 'Is this act right?', he would be asking for our moral intuitions. (I don't understand Irwin's actual example.) Perhaps the two questions are not unconnected. Learning what we call an X may be learning what an X is (cf. Cavell, 1979: 176–7). Furthermore, learning what we call courageous may be part of learning what is right.
15. Burnyeat (1977b) cites *Theatetus* 210, *Charmides* 164dff., *Apology* 21b-23b, and *Sophist* 203be in support of this claim.
16 I owe this observation to Galen Strawson, who has drawn my attention to the lives of primitive hunter-gatherers in favourable conditions.

3 PLATO: THE LIFE OF PHILOSOPHY

1 See, for discussion of the fallacy Brown (1986).
2 Many of my comments on the *Euthydemus* derive from a seminar on the dialogue organised by Myles Burnyeat in 1983.
3 Another problem is that the projects of the assassin are highly vulner-

able to chance. Compare Malraux's *La condition humaine* for an account of suicide attack by an assassin on an armoured car, which turns out to be empty.

4 See Mackenzie, (1981: Appendix 2).

5 Cf. B. Williams on harm of the body in Socratic ethics: if the soul is what matters, why should we refrain from harming other people's bodies? (Williams, 1985: 34).

6 Here we might want to think about Melanie Klein's idea that reparation is the best way to cope with the guilt subsequent on wrongdoing. cf. G. Taylor, 1985: 93.

7 Malcolm Schofield points out to me that we are worried by the oratory of Le Pen.

8 These remarks constitute a summary of Halliwell (1984).

9 Proust advances a rather different theory about the relation of literature to life. The narrator remarks, discussing his adolescent readin-g,that 'Souvent j'avais envie pendant quelques heures d'agir dans la vie comme ces personnages'. He describes the problem with this as follows:

> Ce n'est pas que les romans soient faux, ni que la vie ait moins de possibilités romanesques qu'autrefois. C'est que ce qui, dans la vie pratique aussi bien qu'en médecine, en politique, en art, trouve ce qu'on doit faire, c'est l'instinct, ce n'est pas la théorie.
> (Proust 1913: 792–3)

10 There may be problems with all representational theories of art. See Sheppard (1987) Chapter 2.

11 For contemporary discussions of the appropriate attitude towards death, see Williams (1973), Parfit (1984) and Nagel (1986).

12 Note that there are arguments for the immortality of the soul from the dualism of mind and body and also arguments for this dualism and that the former depend upon the latter.

13 The argument from *palingenesis*: opposites come to be from opposites; so living people come to be from dead people and vice versa. The argument from recollection: to explain the reflection that sometimes occurs to us on seeing equal sticks and stones, that these equal sticks and stones are not the equal itself, we must refer to Forms. This implies that the soul exists before its union with the body. The argument from *homoiosis*: there are sensible things subject to generation and decay, and Forms which are immutable; and the soul is like Forms and is immutable.

14 For such a survey of the arguments, see Gallop (1975).

15 Compare Gibb (1986) on the importance of a life balanced between bodily and mental pleasures.

16 Santas (1988) also notes the relevance of *Phaedrus* 233a: 'lovers' judgements are obscured by their passion'.

17 The view of Freud on this question is like that of Aristophanes in being focused on our internal life histories.

18 Santas also compares the *Phaedrus* (Santas, 1988: 162).

19 This account is based on that of Santas (1988).

20 One further point may be worth adding – namely that neither Plato nor Freud may have hit the nail on the head in this area. If love is not sexual in the first instance (and it could well not be), then no theory of aim-inhibited, or sublimated libido is called for. But if love is originally directed towards the parents (as seems very likely), then the idea that in adulthood, we are engaged, if we are fortunate, on the ascent of desire, also seems to miss the mark. We may perhaps be seeking to recreate an original mother-child dyad we once shared in.

21 Both Nussbaum (1986a) and Vlastos (1988) are very impressed by the speech of Alcibiades.

22 See Chapter 3 of my *Plato's Arguments for Forms* (Jordan, 1983). Irwin calls the conclusion that philosophers alone have knowledge 'a bizarre result' (Irwin, 1977: 283).

23 Thus Erich Fromm, in *Psychoanalysis and Zen Buddhism*, asserts in the course of his exposition of Zen Buddhism that

> The average person is like the man in Plato's Cave, seeing only shadows and mistaking them for substance. Once he has recognized this error, he knows only that the shadows are not the substance. But when he becomes enlightened . . . he sees the substance and not the shadows. He is awake . . . Zen is aimed at knowledge of one's own nature . . .
>
> (From. 1960:75–6)

24 Recollection as practised in the *Meno* and *Phaedo* can also reveal to us that the sensible world is not all there is. So too can reflection on the coincidence of big and small in my second finger, as recommended in *Republic* VII.

25 I am grateful to Myles Burnyeat for drawing this passage to my attention.

26 The notion of 'quasi-recollection' is developed by Irwin (1977).

27 In the case of ethics, for example, as Irwin has argued, if there are Forms, then there will be experts in ethics, and ethics will be objective, rational and learnable (Irwin, 1977: 217).

28 See, on moral reasoning, the findings of Kohlberg (1981). We might also think of the low standard of moral understanding manifested at the time of the Falklands War.

4 ARISTOTLE: PHILOSOPHY, METHOD, BEING AND THE GOOD LIFE

1 In this paragraph, I draw on the work of Owen, outlined in section 2 below.

2 For *gnorizo*, *A Greek English Lexicon* gives 'gain knowledge of', 'become acquainted with', for *gnorimon*, 'familiar', and for adverb *gnorimos*, 'intelligibly' (Liddle, Scott and Jones, 1968).

3 But in the case of logic, Aristotle says that he has done the work himself, from scratch (De Sophisticis Elenchis 183b).

4 There is a further question in this case, raised by Hocutt (1974), of

how this all relates to the account in the *Posterior Analytics*, which ties the theory of the four causes to the theory of the syllogism.

5 Rawls says he believes his view 'in all essentials' goes back to Aristotle's procedure in the *NE* (Rawls, 1972: 51, n.26).

6 In fact, as we will see on pp. 129–38, there is some evidence that Aristotle saw systematic understanding of the world as the goal in philosophy. But this is still not to present a theory of philosophical error, of course.

7 See also Barnes (1980), who says that Aristotle's method in ethics will deliver an ethics of common sense that is 'parochial, descriptive and morally conservative' (Barnes, 1980: 496); that the method is 'philosophically enervating' (Barnes, 1980: 497) and 'vicious' (Barnes, 1980: 510).

8 This fear is voiced by Barnes, who consoles himself with the thought that the method 'has, in the last analysis, very little content and restricts very little the propositions Aristotle surveys' and that his 'actual philosophising was not greatly affected by his reflection on how philosophy ought to be conducted' (Barnes, 1980a: 510).

9 Similar difficulties in relating Aristotle's theory of philosophy to his practice are found in Aristotle's account of *akrasia*. As Burnyeat has argued, Aristotle is here, in general, responding to Socratic intellectualism in ethics, by emphasising the importance of developmental psychology for the study of ethics (Burnyeat, 1980a: 70). In the discussion of *akrasia* itself, though, this general outlook leads to a change in Aristotle's perception of the nature of the problem. According to Burnyeat, 'what needs explanation is not so much why some people succumb to temptation as why others do not' (Burnyeat, 1980a: 85). So one should not look for Aristotle to provide too much by way of explanation of akratic action in 'the immediate circumstances of the conflicted decision' (Burnyeat, 1980a: 85). The nature of the presenting *aporia* has been transformed for Aristotle, because his general view of ethics is so different from that of Socrates.

10 For the claim about Greek ethics, see Williams (1981: 251). There are three respects in which he thinks it is in 'much better shape' than modern ethics – it has no God; it takes as central questions of character; it makes no use of 'blank categorical moral imperative'. The view about Aristotelian philosophy of mind is one I have heard expressed by Myles Burnyeat.

11 Part of a section entitled 'Implications for Modern Philosophical Problems'.

12 Compare too: 'hermeneutics is an expression of the hope that the cultural space left by the demise of epistemology will not be filled' (Rorty, 1978: 315). Is Rorty here fair to Quine? In Quine's discussion with Magee (Quine, 1978), Quine says 'I think of philosophy as continuous with science, even as part of science . . . Philosophy lies at the abstract and theoretical end of science . . . Philosophy seeks the broad outlines of the whole system of the world' (Quine, 1978: 143–4). See also *Word And Object*: 'The quest for a simplest, clearest overall pattern of canonical notation is not to be distinguished from

a quest of ultimate categories, a limning of the most general traits of reality' (Quine, 1960: 161). See also *Ontological Relativity* for the view that 'epistemology, or something like it, simply falls into place as a chapter of psychology and hence of natural science. It studies a natural phenomenon, viz. a physical human subject' (Quine, 1969: 82).

13 The paradox of misuse is that a craft can be used for good or for ill – a good doctor will make a good poisoner; but justice can only give rise to good. MacIntyre himself discusses the relation between Aristotle's account of *akrasia* and R.M. Hare's discussion of 'backsliding' in his *Freedom and Reason* (Hare, 1963). MacIntyre thinks that Socrates' point is misrepresented by Hare, who tries to discuss it within an alien paradigm of thought, ignoring important differences in cultural and moral context.

14 Nozick himself does not discuss history of philosophy; what follows is an extrapolation (I hope a reasonable one) from his views on the nature of philosophical questions and arguments.

15 But see Fine (1982) for powerful criticisms of some aspects of Owen's position. Owen suggests that Aristotale's distinction between 'strong' and 'weak' prediction derives from reflection on the so-called Third Man Regress Argument against the theory of Forms, which is set out in Plato's *Parmenides* (132–3). We should note that when Aristotle discusses the Third Man Regress Argument he remarks that we can block the regress by distinguishing between 'this' (*tode it*) and 'such' (*toionde*) (*De Sophisticis Elenchis* 178b36–9). He does not talk of the need to distinguish 'weak' and 'strong' prediction in reponse to the Regress.

16 To generalise: for any predicate F, particular F's will both be and not be F. An alternative view is that for any predicate F, where F is 'incomplete', any sensible thing that is F will also not be F.

17 I wrote this paragraph as a result of a very helpful conversation with Jorge Secada.

18 Of course, substances are each non-identical with one another, just as Platonic Forms are each non-identical with one another. For Plato this leads, given that the range of Forms is such that it includes one and many, identical, non-identical, being and notbeing, to the problems discussed in the *Sophist* and the *Parmenides*. In those dialogues, Plato modifies his earlier views. Aristotle, however, with his doctrine of substance and theory that 'one' and 'being' are homonymous, presents an entirely distinct resolution of the problems that arise from Plato's middle period metaphysics.

19 Aristotle also holds that only substances are 'separable'. We really face a choice between dealing with substantial being and coincidental being.

20 Thus Kripke says about Nixon 'supposing Nixon is in fact a human being, it would seem we cannot think of a possible counterfactual situation in which he was, say, an inanimate object; perhaps it is not even possible for him not to have been a human being' (Kripke, 1980: 46).

21 Vlastos defines 'real' as 'cognitively dependable' in one of its uses (Vlastos, 1965: 63).

22 We might compare Anscombe's discussion of the unquantified 'man is pale and dark'. Propositions of this form certainly interest Aristotle; it is hard now to see why. Anscombe writes that '"man is white" and "man is not white" can both be true together: it is only when we introduce quantifiers (as we should say) that we form contradictions of this kind that cannot both be true' (Anscombe, 1961: 40). In 'Aristotle And The Sea Battle' she adds, 'I believe that we (nowadays) are not interested in these propositions' (Anscombe, 1956: 44).

23 We may also, of course, have a different view of the *aporiai*. For Aristotle's view of the *aporiai*, see *Metaphysics* B1.

24 Nussbaum (1986a: 377) points to stylistic oddities like the opening of X.6 in support of her case.

25 This case is discussed first by Williams (1976).

26 Irwin (1985a) says the virtues are 'causally responsible' for happiness (*kyriai*). This is no doubt the right interpretation of a troublesome passage; but the essential point is that small or medium sized reverses will not affect the inner world, or the harmony between the inner and the outer.

27 Nussbaum mentions *MM* 1207a4–6: 'where there is most insight and reason, there is least luck' (Nussbaum 1986a: 318). Nussbaum comments that torture can affect the inner world (Nussbaum, 1986a: 326). She points out that external pressures can affect us internally. She also quotes a remarkable passage in the *Rhetoric* which suggests that people are typically worn down by the experience of life, and that virtues connected with trust in the world are more easily available to the young (Nussbaum, 1986a: 336).

28 Compare Cooper (1977); Nussbaum, (1986a: 356).

29 Lear describes Aristotle as an 'objective idealist' (Lear 1988: 308). For Aristotle, objects conform to a mind (in this sense Aristotle is an idealist); but they do not conform to the human mind (as for Kant) or to the absolute (as for Hegel) or to the practices of a tribe (as for the later Wittgenstein), but to the active, divine, mind (in this sense Aristotle is an objective idealist). Contrast Nussbaum's view that Aristotle is a realist (Nussbaum, 1986a: 257).

30 Urmson suggests, very persuasively, that Aristotle should say that the acratic pursues pleasant sensations, rather than that he pursues the pleasures of touch. The same is presumably true for children. (See Urmson, 1988: Chapter 8.)

31 Although in Book I, Aristotle seems to think otherwise: 'The many, the most vulgar . . . like the life of gratification . . . the life they decide on is fit for grazing animals' (1095b17–20).

32 Another Aristotelian account of ethics is that of MacIntyre (1981). MacIntyre rejects Aristotle's *ergon* argument, and focuses instead on man's social nature. From this he presents a transcendental deduction of the virtues, which is allied to a Wittgensteinian conception of moral education as an initiation into a number of moral practices (a form of life), through the telling of stories. A satisfactory human life has

narrative unity. He holds that his account is Aristotelian in three important respects – in its account of the virtues, in its account of pleasure, and in its linking of evaluation with explanation (MacIntyre 1981: 184–5).

33 We might also note Nagel's point that man might have a 'conjunctive' *ergon* (Nagel, 1972).

34 We may contrast Parfit's conception of ethics, which is based on person-stages, or Nagel's, which is based on the existence of impersonal, objective, reasons for action.

5 THE HELLENISTIC PHILOSOPHERS: PHILOSOPHY, NATURE AND THERAPY

1 I owe this observation to Malcolm Schofield.

2 On Aristotle and the medical analogy, Nussbaum cites *EE* 1.5, 1215–16; and *NE* VI 13.

3 On glorification of the child, Nussbaum quotes Diogenes Laertius X.137; Cic. *Fin.* 1.30ff; 71ff.; 171.

4 Socrates, for example, had held that virtue is knowledge, and that knowledge is knowledge of crafts; and he certainly sometimes thought in this context of therapeutic crafts as well as of productive crafts.

5 We should, however, note the notion of 'cognitive psychotherapy', that of exposing our preferences in life to scrutiny in the light of logic and the facts, espoused by Hare (1981: 101 and 108).

6 Thus one might compare here the view of Hanna Segal that Kleinians 'follow the classical Freudian technique with the greatest exactitude', but that Klein 'saw aspects of the material not seen before . . . which dictated new interpretations' (Segal, 1967: 4). Thus Klein is able to follow the Freudian technique, but offer new views about the the early development of the mind, and new intepretations to patients.

7 Compare Freud: 'We avoid telling him at once things we have often discovered at an early stage, and we avoid telling him the whole of what we think we have discovered' (Freud, 1938: 411). Or Winnicott: 'If only we can wait, the patient arrives at understanding creatively and with immense joy, and I now enjoy this joy more than I used to enjoy the sense of having been clever' (Winnicott, 1971: 102).

8 Long suggests that 'empiricism provides the clearest internal connection between [Epicurus'] different ideas' (Long, 1974: 21), by which he has in mind Epicurus' emphasis on 'the evidence of immediate sensation and feeling' (Long, 1974: 19). For the second view, see Nussbaum, 1986b: 40).

9 There are, of course, more convincing attacks on the emotion of love, such as Proust's view that love involves a largely illusory projection of qualities from the imagination of the lover onto the loved, or Parfit's view that we do not love another person 'timelessly considered, but another person during a period in this person's life' (Parfit, 1984: 305).

10 Let us note what Long and Sedley say about the positive role of the gods in Epicurus' system: the gods are like an idealised self-image to

which we aspire to match our own behaviour. Long and Sedley admit that their view is conjectural. But it is supported by for example 23J, where Epicurus claims that he who puts into practice Epicurean moral teaching 'will live like a god among men'. For Manolidis (1987) too, the gods are paradigms of the happy life; and Frischer (1982) likens the gods to the Epicurean disciples in the garden, who can proseletyse by example, as their images are dispersed about the world.

11 See Manolidis (1987). On this view, his argument is a sort of precursor to G.E. Moore's refutation of scepticism.

12 Long and Sedley ascribe to Epicurus a prima facie identity theory of mind together with an 'interactionist dualism' (Long and Sedley, 1987: 110).

13 Epicurus does, sometimes, take note of the views of his predecessors on pleasure. Thus in 21X (Lucretius 6), we are told that when Epicurus saw that we have all we need, materially, to be content, but that we are none the less always wrecking our lives, he saw that the 'flaw was . . . caused by the vessel itself' and that 'the cause was partly leaks and holes'. (This is a clear echo of the *Gorgias*.)

14 Note how, in this story, Tolstoy reduces the 'active' pleasure of authorship to the 'passive' pleasure of licking honey (for these terms, see Chapter 3 above).

15 Long suggests that dialectic helps us know we are living in accordance with nature – through grasping what is true (Long, 1978: 116). But this is how I live in accordance with nature, not how I know I live in accordance with nature. Long also suggests that dialectic promotes self-knowledge (Long, 1978: 117); in particular he suggests that Epictetus makes this claim (Long, 1978: 120).

16 Thus Inwood, who cites Cic *Fin*. 2.34 as well as 3.73 (Inwood, 1985: 3).

17 Striker thinks it is a problem for Aristotle to 'justify the conclusion that *moral* virtue is perfection of natural capacities' (Striker,1983: 150). In the Stoic system, she detects a shift from self-preservation via self-perfection to observing and following nature (Striker, 1983: 156).

18 In the case of the passions, Long and Sedley suggest that 'the Stoics treated passion in several novel ways which are among the best guides to their view of the good and happy life' (Long and Sedley, 1987: 419).

19 See further, Rist (1978). Rist suggests that this may be why all we can do in relation to other people is to 'appropriate' them (Rist, 1978: 265).

20 Compare G. Strawson's concept of the 'Natural Epictetan': Natural Epictetans are 'never failing, never disappointed in their congenial world, always able to do what they want to do because always wanting to do only what they are able to do' (G. Strawson, 1986: 249–50). There is a natural fit between their desires and the way the world is.

21 Thus Inwood analyses the Stoic conception of freedom in terms of the absence of constraint to obey the divine will (Inwood, 1985: 110).

22 I take it we can ignore the 'naïve' fatalism of the conclusion of this report, which tells us that we will be compelled in any case to follow

what is destined, like a dog tied to a cart that it does not want to follow. G. Strawson uses the term 'naïve' fatalism to refer to the view that what we do makes no difference to what happens. 'Sophisticated' fatalism consists in coming to terms with the fact that one is wholly determined. See G. Strawson, (1986: 281 n.22).

23 Cf. Barnes: 'some may never light on the anomaly in things' (Barnes, 1982: 18).

24 Burnyeat does not believe Hume's charge (Burnyeat, 1980: 132).

25 The view of Long and Sedley, above, that assent is bypassed, seems preferable. The main passage that seems to support Burnyeat's line that assent is involved is *PH* 1.193, which talks about our being driven to *sugkatathesis* (other passages cited by Burnyeat simply talk of *pathe* being forced upon us). Being driven to assent here, is, indeed, contrasted with the usual sceptical state of nonassertion, which we apply to 'dogmatic assertions about what is non-apparent'. It is still unclear, however, whether it is really like a saying 'yes' to a proposition. See further the discussion on p. 168.

26 I would like to thank Alice Keen for drawing to my attention the relevance of the question of the meaning of life here, and in particular, the significance of Nagel's paper on 'The Absurd'.

27 At this point, Annas and Barnes retort that scepticism may in fact increase my cares: 'if I do not know whether a decent salary is good or bad, may not that very ignorance cause me worry?' (Annas and Barnes, 1985: 167). We shall deal with this objection when we look at the transition from equipollence of arguments to suspension of belief.

28 Contrast Naess, who takes Sextus at his word (Naess, 1968: 21). M. Williams writes about Descartes in relation to equipollence that

> 'the time was fast approaching when no-one could seriously claim to be able to argue as convincingly for Aristotle's physics as for Newton's. The classical route to scepticism through the balancing of conflicting opinions was being closed off, at least for large areas of enquiry. (M. Williams, 1986: 137)

But contrast Annas and Barnes: 'In our day [scepticism] is still the rational position on many philosophical points, and in large areas of science where dispute remains endemic' (Annas and Barnes, 1985: 63).

29 We may contrast Descartes' argument for scepticism, which does not exploit the notion of equipollence, and just urges the possibility of error. Another difference between Sextus and Descartes is that Descartes actively summons up doubts; doubts just assail the ancient sceptic.

30 For Burnyeat on *epechein*, see Burnyeat, (1980: 131).

31 This may not be an uncommon state of affairs. Compare Davidson:

> 'If we were to guess at the frequency with which people perform actions for which they have reasons [of one sort or another], I think it would be vanishingly small. To aid your imagination:

what is the ratio of actual adulteries to adulteries which the Bible says are committed in the heart?' (Davidson, 1976: 264)

32 This I take to be the standard Aristotle/Davidson analysis of action. Compare Gewirth (1978), who holds that if an agent does something, this indicates that he thinks it good.

33 Naess tries out two lines of defence for the sceptic – that the sceptic acts as an experimenter (Naess, 1968: 41–2), and that he acts unconsciously (Naess, 1968: 44–6). We might also take note of Anscombe (1957), who argues that 'I did it for no particular reason' or 'I did it on impulse' will sometimes, but not always, make sense when we're explaining action (§§17–18). She later (§37) discusses, and dismisses, the idea of 'just wanting' something that is not seen as desirable. It certainly is hard to make sense of this idea. (Gewirth's discussion of the former idea, 1978: 49, is unsatisfactory.) We might further note, however, that some philosophers doubt whether animals have beliefs; and that this has to do with the fact that animals do not speak.

34 Naess cites I.8, 10, 196, 205 in support of this claim. He says that doubting may not be the main ingredient in suspension of belief (Naess, 1968: 28).

CONCLUSION: THE NATURE OF PHILOSOPHY

1 This is demonstrated by the most casual comparison between KRS (1983) and Long and Sedley (1987).

2 On the relation between philosophy and literature in the Greek context, see Nussbaum (1986a). In the modern context, we might wonder how the novels of Sartre and Camus relate to their philosophical writings. Camus remarks, reviewing Sartre's *La nausée*, 'Un roman n'est jamais qu'une philosophie mise en images' (Camus, 1938: 1417).

3 Perhaps one could compare the motivation to study history and the practice of the study of history. It may be that we are motivated to study history because we want to tell a coherent story about how we have arrived where we now find ourselves. But what we find, when we actually study history, is that, for the most part, one little event follows another; and grand theory is easier to refute than to construct. Compare Plumb (1972).

4 Kleist is not quite alone in reacting this way to works of metaphysics and epistemology: one of my students reported a similar reaction to reading Quine's 'Two Dogmas Of Empiricism' (Quine, 1951).

5 But of course Anselm directs his argument at the *insipiens* (fool). He himself believes in God from faith.

6 An exception here is Nietzsche, whose goal in philosophy seems closer to the ancients': if we believe Nietzsche, this will affect our lives, not simply because he persuades us of certain philosophical truths, but because we come to realise that we should embark on a certain form of life – a life of self-creation. I would like to thank Nick Tyrrell and Jorge Secada for helpful discussions of these ideas.

7 I would like to thank Catherine Barlen, Alice Keen, John Sutton,

Nick Tyrrell and Henry Wickham for participating in a discussion in December 1987, from which this conclusion has grown.

BIBLIOGRAPHY

Annas J. and Barnes J. (1985), *The Modes of Scepticism*, Cambridge: Cambridge University Press.

Anscombe, G.E.M. and Geach, P.T. (1961), *Three Philosophers*, Oxford: Blackwell.

Anscombe, G.E.M. (1956), 'Aristotle and the Sea-Battle', in *Mind* 65, 1–15, reprinted in her *From Parmenides to Wittgenstein* (1981), Oxford: Blackwell.

Anscombe, G.E.M. (1957), *Intention*, Oxford: Blackwell.

Anscombe, G.E.M. (1961), 'Aristotle', in Anscombe and Geach (1961).

Austin, S. (1986), *Parmenides: Being Bounds Limits*, New Haven: Yale University Press.

Baier, K. (1957), 'The Meaning of Life', Inaugural Lecture delivered at Canberra University College, 1957, reprinted in Klemke (ed.) (1981).

Bambrough, J.R. (1979), *Moral Scepticism and Moral Knowledge*, London: Routledge & Kegan Paul.

Bambrough, J.R. (1986), 'Question Time', in Shanker (ed.) (1986).

Barnes, J. (1969), 'Aristotle's Theory of Demonstration', *Phronesis* 14, 123–52.

Barnes, J. (1979a), *The Presocratic Philosophers* Vol.I, London: Routledge & Kegan Paul.

Barnes, J. (1979b), *The Presocratic Philosophers* Vol.II, London: Routledge & Kegan Paul.

Barnes, J. (1980), 'Aristotle and the Methods of Ethics', *Revue internationale de philosophie*, 34, 490–511.

Barnes, J. (1982), 'The Beliefs of a Pyrrhonist', in *Proceedings Of the Cambridge Philological Society* 28, 1–29.

de Beauvoir, S. (1958), *Memoires d'une jeune fille rangée*, Paris: Gallimard.

Belfiore, E. (1983), 'Plato's Greatest Accusation against Poetry', in F.J. Pelletier and J. King-Farlow (eds), *New Essays On Plato*, *Canadian Journal of Philosophy*, Supplementary Volume IX, 39–62:

Berlin, I. (1950), 'Logical Translation', in *Proceedings of the Aristotelian Society* 50, 157–88; reprinted in *Concepts and Categories* (1978), 56–80.

Berlin, I. (1978), 'An Introduction To Philosophy', in B. Magee (ed.), *Men Of Ideas*, Oxford: Oxford University Press (1982).

Brown, L. (1986), 'Being in the *Sophist*: A Syntactical Enquiry', in *Oxford Studies In Ancient Philosophy* iv, 49–70.

Burnyeat, M.F. (1976), 'Protagoras and Self-Refutation in Later Greek Philosophy', *Philosopical Review* 85, 44–69.

Burnyeat, M.F. (1977a), 'Examples In Epistemology', *Philosophy* 52, 381–97.

Burnyeat, M.F. (1977b), 'Platonic Inspiration, Socratic Midwifery', *Bulletin Of the Institute Of Classical Studies*, 24, 7–13.

Burnyeat, M.F. (1980a), 'Aristotle on Learning to be Good', in A. O. Rorty (ed.) *Essays on Aristotle's Ethics*, Berkeley: University of California Press.

Burnyeat, M.F. (1980b), 'Can the Sceptic Live his Scepticism', in M. Schofield *et al, Doubt and Dogmatism*, Oxford: Clarendon Press.

Burnyeat, M.F. (1982a), 'Idealism and Greek Philosophy: What Descartes saw and Berkeley Missed', *Philosophical Review* 91, 3–40.

Burnyeat, M.F. (1982b), 'Review of C.H. Kahn, *The Art and Thought of Heraclitus*', *New York Review of Books*, May 13, 1982, 44–7.

Burnyeat, M.F. (1984), 'The Sceptic In his Time and Place,' in R. Rorty *et al.* (eds), *Philosophy In History*, Cambridge: Cambridge University Press, 225–54

Burnyeat, M. F. (1987), 'Wittgenstein and Augustine De Magistro', *Proceedings of the Aristotelian Society Supplementary Volume* 611–24.

Bury, R. G. (1933), *Sextus Empiricus*, trans R. G. Bury, Vol I, Cambridge, Mass.: Harvard University Press and London: Heinemann.

Camus, A. (1938), review of Sartre, *La nausée, Alger Républicain*, 20, October, 1938, reprinted in *Essais* ed. by R. Quillot and J. Faucon, Paris: Gallimard, 1965.

Camus, A. (1942), 'The Absurdity of Human Existence', excerpts from *Le Mythe de Sisyphe*, Paris: Gallimard, reprinted in Klemke (ed.) (1981).

Cavell, S. (1962), 'The Availability of Wittgenstein's Later Philosophy', in *Must We Mean What We Say?*, Cambridge: Cambridge University Press, 1973.

Cavell, S. (1964), 'Existentialism and Analytic Philosophy', *Daedalus* xciii, 946–74, reprinted with introductory comments in his *Themes Out of School* (1984), San Francisco: North Point Press.

Cavell, S. (1979), *The Claim of Reason*, Oxford: Clarendon Press.

Cohen, G. (1978), *Karl Marx's Theory Of History: A Defence*, Oxford: Clarendon Press.

Cohen, L.J. (1986), *The Dialogue Of Reason*, Oxford: Clarendon Press.

Cooper, J. (1977), 'Aristotle on Friendship', in Rorty (ed.) (1980).

Cornford, F.M. (1930), 'Anaxagoras' Theory of Matter', *Classical Quarterly* 24, 14–30 and 83–95, reprinted in Furley and Allen (1971).

Craig, E. (1987), *The Mind of God and the Works Of Man*, Oxford: Clarendon Press.

Davidson, D. (1970), 'How is Weakness of the Will Possible?', in J. Feinberg (ed.), *Moral Concepts*, Oxford: Oxford University Press, reprinted in *Essays on Actions and Events*, Oxford: Oxford University Press, 1980.

Davidson, D. (1976), 'Hempel on Explaining Actions', in *Erkenntnis* 10, 239–53, reprinted in *Essays on Actions and Events*, Oxford: Oxford University Press, 1980.

Davidson, D. (1978), 'What Metaphors Mean', *Critical Enquiry* 5, 31–47, reprinted in *Inquiries into Truth and Interpretation*, Oxford: Oxford University Press, 1984.

Davidson, D. (1982), 'Paradoxes Of Irrationality', in R. Wollheim and J. Hopkins (eds), *Philosophical Essays On Freud*, Cambridge: Cambridge University Press.

Davidson, D. (1985), Introduction to E. Lepore and E. McLaughlin (eds) *Actions And Events*, Oxford:, Blackwell.

Dennett, D. (1984), *Elbow Room*, Oxford: Clarendon Press

Diels, H. and Kranz, W. (1960), *Die Fragmente der Vorsokratiker*, 3 vols, 10th edition, Berlin:Weidmann.

Dover, K.J. (1968), 'Socrates in the *Clouds*', Oxford: Clarendon Press, reprinted in G. Vlastos (ed.), *Socrates*, New York: Doubleday, 1971.

Dummett, M. (1978), 'Can Analytic Philosophy be Systematic and Ought it to Be', in *Truth And Other Enigmas*, London: Duckworth.

Dummett. M. (1981) 'Common Sense and Physics, in G. Macdonald (ed.), *Perception and Identity*, London: Macmillan.

Edwards, P. (1949), 'Russell's Doubts about Induction', *Mind* 68, 141–63, reprinted in R. Swinburne (ed.), *The Justification of Induction*, Oxford: Oxford University Press.

Edwards, P. (1967), 'The Meaning and Value of Life', *Encyclopaedia Britannica*, volume 4, 467–77, reprinted in Klemke (ed.) (1981).

Falconer, W. A. (1932), *Cicero*, vol. xx *De Senectute*, *De Amicitia*, *De Divinatione*, trans. W. A. Falconer, Cambridge, Mass.: Harvard University Press and London: Heineman.

Fine, G., (1982), 'Owen, Aristotle and the Third Man Regress', *Phronesis* 27, 13–33.

Fogelin, R.J. (1987), *Wittgenstein*, 2nd edition, London: Routledge & Kegan Paul.

Freud, S., (1938), 'An Outline of Psychoanalysis', in *Penguin Freud Library*, vol. 15, Harmondsworth: Penguin, 1986.

Frischer, B. (1982), *The Sculpted Word*, Berkeley/Los Angeles: University of California Press.

Fromm, E. (1960), *Psychoanalysis and Zen Buddhism*, London: Unwin Paperbacks, 1986.

Furley, D.J. and Allen, R.E., (1971, 1975), *Studies in Presocratic Philosophy*, 2 vols, London: Routledge & Kegan Paul.

Furley, D. (1973), 'Notes on Parmenides', in E.N. Lee *et al.* (eds), *Exegesis And Argument*, Phronesis, supplementary Volume I.

Furley, D. (1976), 'Anaxagoras in Response to Parmenides', *Canadian Journal Of Philosophy*, supplementary volume ii, 61–85, reprinted in J.P. Anton and A. Preus (eds), *Essays In Ancient Greek Philosophy* Vol II. Albany: State University of New York Press.

Furth M. (1968), 'Elements of Eleatic Ontology', *Journal of the History of Philosophy,* 111–32, reprinted in Mourelatos (ed.) (1974).

Gallop, D. (1975), *Plato: Phaedo*, Oxford: Clarendon Press.

Geach, P.T. (1966), 'Plato's *Euthyphro*: Analysis and Commentary', *The Monist* 50, 369–82.

Gewirth, A. (1978), *Reasons and Morality*, Chicago: University of Chicago Press.

Gibb, B. (1986), 'Higher and Lower Pleasures', *Philosophy* 61, 31–59.

Grayling, A.C. (1988), *Wittgenstein*, Oxford: Oxford University Press.

Guthrie, W.K.C. (1962), *History of Greek Philosophy*, Vol.I, Cambridge: Cambridge University Press.

Guthrie, W.K.C. (1965), *History of Greek Philosophy*, Vol.II, Cambridge: Cambridge University Press.

Guthrie, W.K.C. (1975), *History of Greek Philosophy*, Vol.IV, Cambridge: Cambridge University Press.

Guthrie, W.K.C. (1978), *History of Greek Philosophy*, Vol.V, Cambridge: Cambridge University Press.

Guthrie, W.K.C. (1981), *History of Greek Philosophy*, Vol.VI, Cambridge: Cambridge University Press.

Halliwell, S. (1984), 'Tragedy and Philosophy', paper delivered at New Hall Classics Colloquium, 1984.

Hare, R.M. (1963), *Freedom And Reason*, Oxford: Oxford University Press.

Hare, R.M. (1981), *Moral Thinking*, Oxford: Clarendon Press.

Hocutt, M. (1974), 'Aristotle's Four Becauses', *Philosophy* 49, 385–99.

Holmes, R. (1980), *Shelley on Love*, an anthology. London: Anvil Press Poetry.

Horton, R. (1967), 'African Traditional Thought and Western Science', *Africa*, 37.

Horton, J. (1982), 'Tradition and Modernity Revisited', in S. Lukes and M. Hollis (eds), *Rationality and Relativism*, Oxford: Blackwell.

Hume, D. (1748), *Enquiries Concerning Human Understanding and concerning the Principles of Morals*, ed. by L.A. Selby-Bigge, 3rd edition, Oxford: Clarendon Press, 1975.

Hussey, E. (1972), *The Presocratics*, London: Duckworth.

Hussey, E. (1982), 'Epistemology and Meaning in Heraclitus', in M. Schofield and M. Nussbaum (eds), *Language and Logos*, Cambridge: Cambridge University Press.

Inwood, B. (1985), *Ethics and Human Action in Early Stoicism*, Oxford: Clarendon Press.

Irwin, T.H. (1977), *Plato's Moral Theory*, Cambridge: Cambridge University Press.

Irwin, T.H. (1979), *Plato: Gorgias*, Oxford: Clarendon Press.

Irwin, T.H. (1985a), 'Permanent Happiness: Aristotle and Solon', *Oxford Studies in Ancient Philosophy* III, 89–124.

Irwin, T. H. (1985b), *Aristotle Nichomachean Ethics*, trans. Indianapolis: Hackett Publishing Co.

Jordan, R.W. (1983), *Plato's Arguments for Forms, Proceedings of the Cambridge Philological Society*, supplementary Volume IX.

Jordan, R.W. (1984), 'Plato's Task in the *Sophist*', *Classical Quarterly* n.s. 34, 113–29.

Kahn, C. (1973), *The Greek Verb 'To Be' in Ancient Greek*, Foundations of Language Supp Ser.16, The verb 'be' and its synonyms, 6, Dordrecht.

Kahn, C. (1981), *The Art and Thought of Heraclitus*, Cambridge: Cambridge University Press.

Kenny, A. (1966), 'Aristotle On Happiness', *Proceedings of the Aristotelian Society* 66, 93–102; reprinted in J. Barnes *et al.* (eds), *Articles on Aristotle* Vol.II, London: Duckworth.

Kenny, A. (1986), 'Aristotle on Moral Luck', in *The Heritage of Wisdom*, Oxford: Blackwell.

Kerferd. G. (1969), 'Anaxagoras and the Concept of Matter Before Aristotle', *Bulletin of the John Rylands Library* 52, 129–143, reprinted in Mourelatos (ed.) (1974).

Kerferd, G. (1978), 'What Does the Wise Man Know?', in Rist (ed.) (1978).

Kirk. G.S., Raven. J. and Schofield, M. (1983), *The Presocratic Philosophers*, 2nd edition, Cambridge: Cambridge University Press.

Klein, J. (1987), *Our Need for Others*, London: Tavistock Publications.

Klemke, E.D. (ed.) (1981), *The Meaning of Life*, Oxford: Oxford University Press.

Kohlberg, L. (1981), *The Philosophy of Moral Development*, Essays on Moral Development, Vol.I., San Francisco: Harper & Row.

Kraut, R. (1983), 'Comments on Vlastos', *Oxford Studies in Ancient Philosophy* i, 59–70.

Kripke, S. (1980), *Naming and Necessity*, Oxford: Blackwell.

Kripke, S. (1982), *Wittgenstein on Rules and Private Language*, Oxford: Blackwell.

Kuhn, T.S. (1962), *The Structure of Scientific Revolutions*, Chicago: University of Chicago Press.

Lear, J. (1980), *Aristotle and Logical Theory*, Cambridge: Cambridge University Press.

Lear, J. (1981), 'A Note On Zeno's Arrow', *Phronesis*, 26, 91–104.

Lear, J. (1988), *Aristotle: The Desire to Understand*, Cambridge: Cambridge University Press.

Lewis, D (1986), *Philosophical Papers* Vol II, New York: Oxford University Press.

Liddle, H. C. Scott, R. and Jones H. S. (1968), *A Greek-English Lexicon*, revised H. S. Jones, with supplement. Oxford: Clarendon Press.

Lloyd, G.E.R. (1979), *Magic, Reason and Experience*, Cambridge: Cambridge University Press.

Lloyd, G.E.R. (1988), *The Revolutions of Wisdom*, Berkeley: University of California Press.

Long, A. (1974), *Hellenistic Philosophy*, London, Duckworth.

Long, A. (1978), 'Dialectic and the Stoic Sage', in Rist (ed.) (1978).

Long, A. and Sedley, D. (1987), *The Hellenistic Philosophers*, Vol. I, Cambridge: Cambridge University Press.

Luke, D. and Reeves, N. (1978), *The Marquise von O* and other stories by J. Kleist, Harmondsworth: Penguin.

MacIntyre, A. (1981), *After Virtue*, London: Duckworth.

MacIntyre, A. (1984), 'The Relationship of Philosophy to its Past', in R. Rorty (ed.), *Philosophy In History*, Cambridge: Cambridge University Press.

Mackenzie, M.M. (1981), *Plato on Punishment*, Berkeley: University of California Press.

Mackie, J. (1977), *Ethics: Inventing Right and Wrong*, Harmondsworth: Penguin.

Makin, S. (1982), 'Zeno On Plurality', *Phronesis* 27, 223–38.

Malcolm. N. (1958), *Ludwig Wittgenstein: A Memoir*, Oxford: Oxford University Press.

Manolidis, G. (1987), *Die Rolle der Physiologie in der Philosophie Epikurs*, Frankfurt: Athenaeum.

Matthews, G. (1980), *Philosophy and the Young Child*, Cambridge, Mass.: Harvard University Press.

McKeon, R. (1941), *The Basic Works of Aristotle*, New York: Random House.

Moore, G.E. (1953), *Some Main Problems of Philosophy*, Cambridge: Cambridge University Press.

Mothersill, M. (1984), *Beauty Restored*, Oxford: Oxford University Press.

Mourelatos. A. (ed.) (1974), *The Presocratics*, New York: Anchor Books.

Naess, A. (1968), *Scepticism*, London: Routledge & Kegan Paul.

Nagel, T. (1970), 'Death', *Nous* iv, reprinted in *Mortal Questions*, Cambridge: Cambridge University Press, 1979.

Nagel, T. (1972), 'Aristotle On *eudaimonia*', *Phronesis*, 252–9.

Nagel, T. (1979), 'The Absurd', in *Mortal Questions*, Cambridge: Cambridge University Press.

Nagel, T. (1986), *The View from Nowhere*, New York : Oxford University Press.

Nagel, T. (1987), *What Does it All Mean?*, New York: Oxford University Press.

Nehamas, A. (1985a), 'Meno's Paradox and Socrates as Teacher', *Oxford Studies in Ancient Philosophy* iii, 1–30.

Nehamas, A. (1985b), *Nietzsche: Life as Literature*, Cambridge, Mass.: Harvard University Press.

Nozick, R. (1981), *Philosophical Explanations*, Oxford: Clarendon Press.

Nussbaum, M. (1986a), *The Fragility of Goodness*, Cambridge: Cambridge University Press.

Nussbaum, M. (1986b), 'Therapeutic Arguments: Epicurus and Aristotle', in M. Schofield and G. Striker (eds), *The Norms Of Nature*, Cambridge: Cambridge University Press.

Owen, G.E.L. (1957), 'Logic And Metaphysics in some Earlier Works Of Aristotle', in G.E.L. Owen and I. During (eds), *Aristotle And Plato in Mid-Fourth Century*, Goteborg: Elanders Boktryckeri Aktiebolag, 163–90 reprinted in Owen (1986).

Owen, G.E.L. (1957–8), 'Zeno And The Mathematicians', *Proceedings of the Aristotelian Society*, 199–222, reprinted in Owen (1986).

Owen, G.E.L. (1960), 'Eleatic Questions', *Classical Quarterly*, 84–102, reprinted in Owen (1986).

Owen, G.E.L. (1961), '*tithenai ta phainomena*', in S. Mansion (ed.) *Aristote et les problèmes de méthode*, Louvain: Publications Universitaires de Louvain, 83–103, reprinted in Owen (1986).

Owen, G.E.L. (1966a), 'Plato and Parmenides on the Timeless Present', *The Monist*, 317–40 reprinted in Owen (1986).

Owen, G.E.L. (1966b), 'The Platonism of Aristotle', in *Proceedings of the British Academy* 51, 125–50, reprinted in Owen (1986).

Owen, G.E.L. (1986), *Logic, Science and Dialectic*, ed. by M. Nussbaum, London: Duckworth.

Parfit, D. (1984), *Reasons and Persons*, Oxford: Clarendon Press.

Parkes, C.M. (1986), *Bereavement*, 2nd edition, Harmondsworth: Penguin.

Plumb, J.H. (1972), *The Death of the Past*, Harmondsworth: Penguin.

Popper, K.R. (1945), *The Open Society and its Enemies*, vol. I Plato, 5th edition, London: Routledge & Kegan Paul, 1966.

Popper, K.R. (1958), 'Back to the Presocratics', in *Conjectures And Refutations*, London: Routledge & Kegan Paul.

Popper, K.R. (1959), *The Logic of Scientific Discovery*, London: Hutchinson.

Popper, K.R. (1986), 'How I See Philosophy', in Shanker (ed.) (1986).

Proust, M. (1918), *A l'ombre des jeunes filles, en fleur*, in *Remembrance of Things Past*, vol I, tr. C.K. Scott Moncrieff, London: Chatto, 1981.

Proust, M. (1913), *Du côté de chez Swann*, in *A la recherche du temps perdu*, vol. I, ed. J-Y Tadié, Paris Gallimard, 1987.

Quine, W.V.O. (1951), 'Two Dogmas Of Empiricism', *Philosophical Review*, reprinted in *From A Logical Point Of View*, 2nd edition, . New York: Harper & Row 1961.

Quine, W.V.O. (1960), *Word And Object*, Cambridge, Mass.: MIT Press.

Quine, W.V.O. (1969), *Ontological Relativity and Other Essays*, New York and London: Columbia University Press.

Quine, W.V.O. (1978), 'The Ideas of Quine', in B. Magee (ed.), *Men Of Ideas*, Oxford: Oxford University Press, 1982.

Rawls, J. (1972), *A Theory of Justice*, Oxford: Oxford University Press.

Rist, J. (1978), 'The Stoic Concept of Detachment', in Rist (ed.) (1978), 259–72.

Rist, J. (1978), *The Stoics*, Berkeley: University of California Press.

Robinson, R. (1953), *Plato's Earlier Dialectic*, 2nd edition, Oxford: Clarendon Press.

Robinson, R. (1954), 'Aristotle on Akrasia', *Revue philosophique*, reprinted in J. Barnes *et al* (eds), Articles on Aristotle, Vol.II. London: Duckworth, 1977.

Rorty, R. (1978), *Philosophy and the Mirror of Nature*, Oxford: Blackwell.

Rorty, R. (1982), 'Is There a Problem about Fictional Discourse?', in *Consequences of Pragmatism*, Brighton: Harvester.

Rorty, R. (1984), 'The Historiography of Philosophy: Four Genres', in

R. Rorty, J.B. Schneewind and Q. Skinner (eds), *Philosophy in History*, Cambridge : Cambridge University Press.

Rorty, R. (1987), 'Hesse and Davidson on Metaphor', *Proceedings of the Aristotelian Society* Supplementary Volume 61 283–96.

Ross, W.D. (1949), *Aristotle*, 5th edition, London: Methuen.

Russell, B. (1912), *The Problems of Philosophy*, Oxford: Oxford University Press.

Sacks, O. (1982), *Awakenings*, 2nd edition, London: Pan Books.

Sartre, J.-P. (1946), excerpt from *Existentialism and Humanism*, reprinted in O. Hanfling (ed.), *Life And Meaning: A Reader*, Oxford: Basil Blackwell in association with the Open University, 1987.

Santas, G. (1988), *Plato and Freud*, Oxford: Blackwell.

Schlick, M. (1932), 'The Future of Philosophy', in R. Rorty (ed.), *The Linguistic Turn*, Chicago: University of Chicago Press, 1967.

Schofield, M. (1980), *An Essay on Anaxagoras*, Cambridge: Cambridge University Press.

Sedley, D. (1983), 'The Motivation of Greek Scepticism', in M. Burnyeat (ed.) *The Skeptical Tradition*, Berkeley: University of California Press.

Segal, H. (1967), 'Melanie Klein's Technique', in *The Work of Hanna Segal*, London: Free Association Books and Maresfield Library, 1986.

Shanker, S.E. (ed.) (1986), *Philosophy in Britain Today*, London: Croom Helm.

Sheppard, A, (1987), *Aesthetics: an Introduction To Philosophy of Art*, Oxford: Oxford University Press.

Shorey, P. (1935), *Plato's Republic*, trans. P. Shorey, Cambridge, Mass.: Harvard University Press and London: Heinemann.

Sisson, C. H. (1976), Lucretius, *De Perum Natura, The Poem on Nature*, trans. C. H. Sisson, Manchester: Carcanet New Press.

Sorabji, R.R.K. (1974), 'Body and Soul in Aristotle', *Philosophy* 49, 63–89, reprinted in J. Barnes, M. Schofield and R. Sorabji, *Articles on Aristotle*, Vol.4 Psychology and Aesthetics, London: Duckworth 1979.

Stough, C. (1987), 'Knowledge and Belief: A Discussion of Julia Annas and Jonathan Barnes, *The Modes of Scepticism, Ancient Texts and Modern Interpretations*, and Harrold Tarrant, *Scepticism or Platonism? The Philosophy of the fourth Academy*', *Oxford Studies in Ancient Philosophy* V, 217–34.

Strang, C. (1963), 'The Physical Theory of Anaxagoras', *Archiv für Geschichte der Philosophie*, 45, 101–18, reprinted in Furley and Allen (1975).

Strawson, G. (1986), *Freedom and Belief*, Oxford: Clarendon Press.

Strawson, G. (1989), *The Secret Connexion, Causation, Realism and David Hume*, Oxford : Clarendon Press.

Strawson, P.F. (1959), *Individuals*, London: Methuen.

Strawson, P.F. (1981), 'Perception and its Objects', in G.H. Macdonald (ed.), *Perception And Identity*, London: Macmillan.

Striker, G. (1983), 'The Role of Oikeosis in Stoic Ethics', in *Oxford Studies in Ancient Philosophy* i, 145–68.

Swenson, D.F. (1949), 'The Dignity of Human Life', in *Kierkegaardian Philosophy in the Faith of a Scholar*, reprinted in Klemke (eds.) (1981).

Taylor, G. (1985), *Pride, Shame and Guilt*, Oxford: Clarendon Press.

Tolstoy, L. (1882), excerpt from *My Confession*, reprinted in Klemke (ed.) (1981).

Trilling, L. (1972) *Sincerity and Authenticity*, Oxford: Oxford University Press.

Urmson, J.O. (1988), *Aristotle's Ethics*, Oxford: Oxford University Press.

Vlastos G. (1950), 'The Physical Theory Of Anaxagoras', *Philosophical Review* 59, 31–57, reprinted in Furley and Allen (1971).

Vlastos G. (1955), 'On Heraclitus', *American Journal of Philosophy* 76, 337–66, reprinted in Furley and Allen (1971).

Vlastos, G. (1958), 'The Paradox of Socrates', in G. Vlastos (ed.), *Socrates*, New York: Anchor Books, 1971.

Vlastos, G. (1959), 'A Note On Zeno B1', *Gnomon* 31, 195–9, reprinted in Furley and Allen (1975).

Vlastos, G. (1965), 'Degrees of Reality in Plato', in J.R. Bambrough (ed.), *New Essays On Plato and Aristotle*, London: Routledge & Kegan Paul, reprinted in Vlastos (1973).

Vlastos, G. (1966a), 'A Note On Zeno's Arrow', *Phronesis* 11, 3–18, reprinted in Furley and Allen (1975).

Vlastos, G. (1966b), 'Zeno's Race Course', *Journal of the History of Philosophy* 4, 95–108, reprinted in Furley and Allen (1975).

Vlastos, G. (1969), 'The Individual as Object of Love in Plato', in Vlastos (1973).

Vlastos, G. (1973), *Platonic Studies*, Princeton: Princeton University Press.

Vlastos, G. (1983), 'The Socratic Elenchos', *Oxford Studies in Ancient Philosophy* i, 27–58.

Vlastos, G. (1985), 'Socrates' Disavowal of Knowledge', *Philosophical Quarterly* 35, 1–31.

Vlastos, G. (1987), 'Socratic Irony', *Classical Quarterly* n.s. xxxvii, 79–96.

Williams, B. (1972), *Morality*, New York: Harper & Row, Harmondsworth: Penguin, 1973.

Williams, B. (1973), 'The Makropulos Case: Reflections on the Tedium of Immortality', in *Problems of the Self*, Cambridge: Cambridge University Press.

Williams, B. (1976), 'Moral Luck', *Proceedings of the Aristotelian Society* L, 115–35.

Williams, B. (1978), *Descartes*, Harmondsworth: Penguin.

Williams, B. (1980), 'Internal and External Reasons', in R. Harrison (ed.), *Rational Action*, Cambridge: Cambridge University Press.

Williams, B. (1981), 'Philosophy', in M.I. Finlay (ed.), *The Legacy of Greece*, Oxford: Clarendon Press.

Williams, B. (1985), *Ethics and The Limits of Philosophy*, London: Fontana/Collins.

Williams, B. (1988), 'What Does Intuitionism Imply?', in J. Dancy, J.M.E. Moravcsik and C.C.W. Taylor (eds) *Human Agency: Language, Duty, and Value*, Stanford: Stanford University Press.

Williams, M. (1986), 'Descartes and the Metaphysics of Doubt', in A.O. Rorty (ed.), *Essays On Descartes' Meditations*, Berkeley: University of California Press.

Winnicott, D.W. (1971), *Playing and Reality*, London: Tavistock Publications, reprinted Harmondsworth: Penguin, 1974.

Wittgenstein, L. (1921), *Tractatus Logico-Philosopicus*, tr. D.F. Pears and B.F. McGuinness, London: Routledge & Kegan Paul, 1961.

Wittgenstein, L. (1953), *Philosopical Investigations*, Oxford: Basil Blackwell, 2nd edn, 1958.

Wittgenstein, L. (1958), *The Blue and Brown Books*, Oxford: Blackwell.

Wittgenstein, L. (1979), *Wittgenstein's Lectures, Cambridge 1932–35* ed. by A. Ambrose, Oxford: Blackwell.

Woods, M. (1982), *Aristotle's Eudemian Ethics, Books I, II and VIII*, trans. with commentary M. Woods, Oxford: Clarendon Press.

von Wright, G.H. (1963), *The Varieties of Goodness*, London: Routledge & Kegan Paul.

INDEX